NELSON BLACK

MATHS IN ACTION
PLUS

AUTHORS

G. Brown	St Anne's RC High School, Stockport
G. Marra	Linlathen High School, Dundee
K. Methven	Jedburgh Grammar School
E. Mullan	Galashiels Academy
R. Murray	Hawick High School
J. Thomson	Galashiels Academy

STUDENTS' BOOK

Thomas Nelson and Sons Ltd
Nelson House Mayfield Road
Walton-on-Thames Surrey
KT12 5PL UK

Cover photograph courtesy of Darryl Williams/Steelcase Strafor plc

© G. Brown, G. Marra, K. Methven, E. Mullan, R. Murray and J. Thomson 1996

First published by Thomas Nelson and Sons Ltd 1996
I(T)P Thomas Nelson is an International Thomson Publishing Company
I(T)P is used under licence

ISBN 0-17-431447-7
NPN 9 8 7 6 5 4 3

All rights reserved. No paragraph of this publication may be reproduced, copied or transmitted save with written permission or in accordance with the provisions of the Copyright, Design and Patents Act 1988, or under the terms of any licence permitting limited copying issued by the Copyright Licensing Agency, 90 Tottenham Court Road, London W1P 9HE.

Any person who does any unauthorised act in relation to this publication may be liable to criminal prosecution and civil claims for damages.

Printed in China

CONTENTS

1	NUMBERS IN ACTION	1
2	ALL ABOUT ANGLES	15
3	LETTERS AND NUMBERS	25
4	MAKING SENSE OF STATISTICS	32
5	FRACTIONS, DECIMALS AND PERCENTAGES	40
6	DISTANCES AND DIRECTIONS	47
7	POSITIVE AND NEGATIVE NUMBERS: TEMPERATURE	59
8	ROUND IN CIRCLES	67
9	COORDINATES	77
10	MEASURES	86
11	TYPES OF TRIANGLES	99
12	PROPORTION	109
13	THREE DIMENSIONS	118
14	TIME	126
15	TILING AND SYMMETRY	133
16	FORMULAE	141
17	PROBABILITY	150

1 NUMBERS IN ACTION

Rulers and Scales

This ruler measures centimetres.

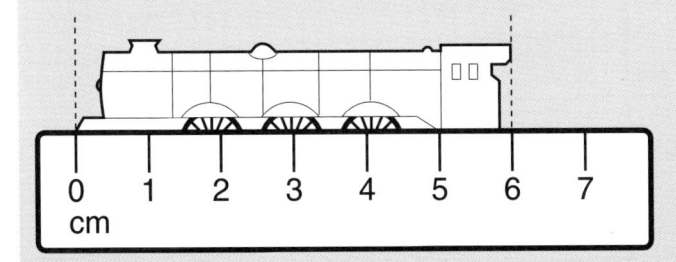

The toy engine is **6 cm** long.

This ruler measures **half** centimetres.

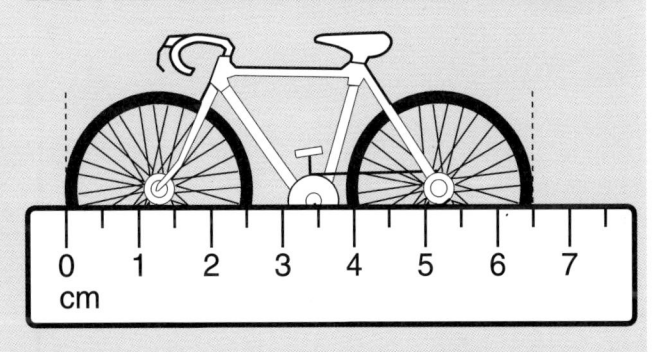

The toy bike is **6 and a half cm** long.
We write **6½ cm**.

This ruler measures **tenths** of centimetres.

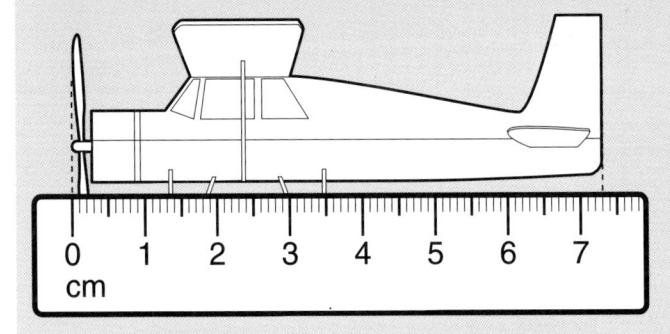

The model plane is 7 cm and 3 tenths long.
We write **7.3 cm**.

1 NUMBERS IN ACTION

EXERCISE 1

1 Give the length of each model below.

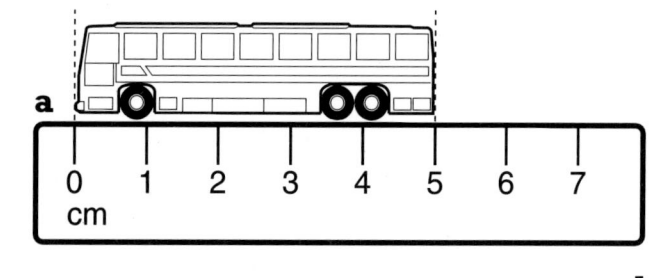

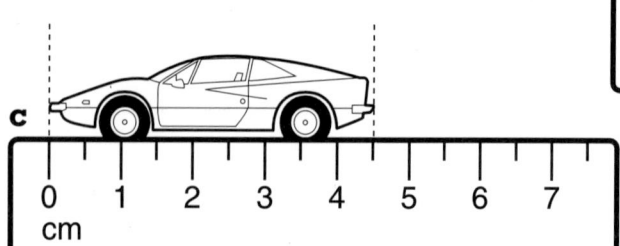

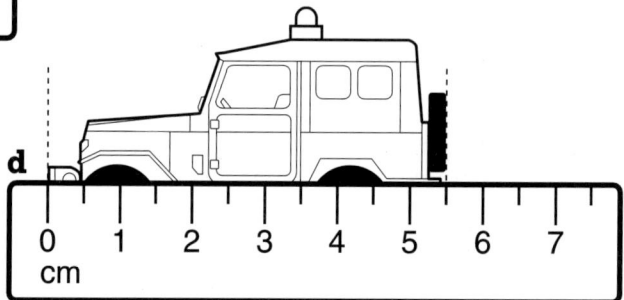

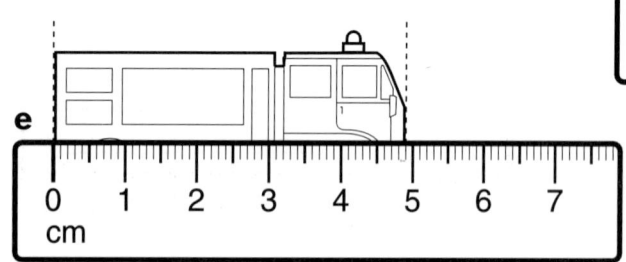

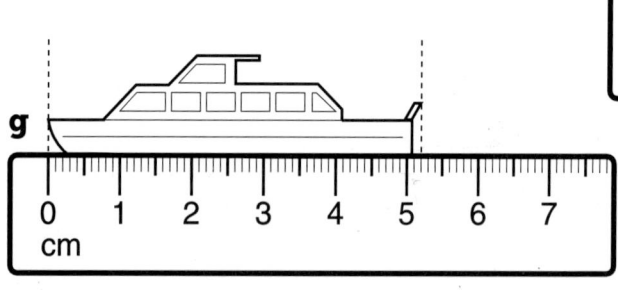

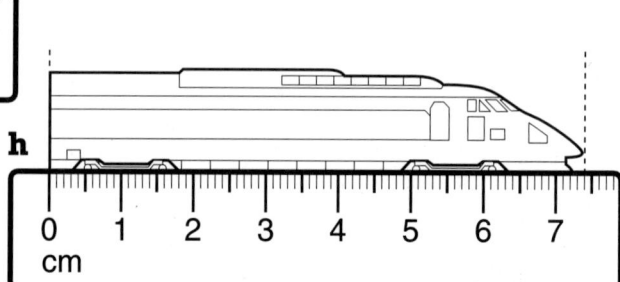

a 5 cm

b 3 cm

c 4 cm

d 5 cm

e 5 cm

f 4 cm

g 5 cm

h 7 cm

1 NUMBERS IN ACTION

2 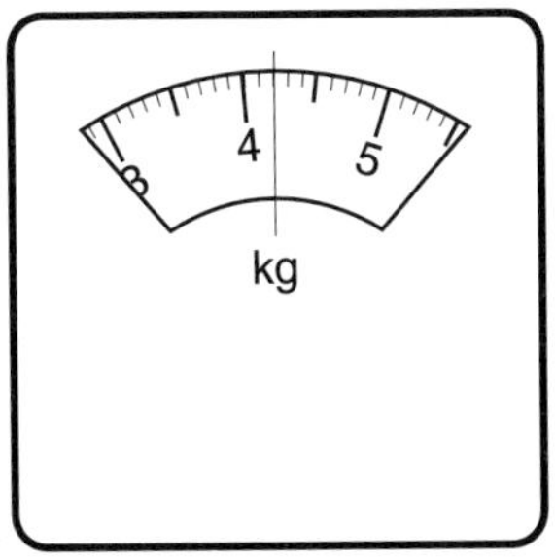 These scales can measure weight in **tenths** of kilograms.
Here it is reading 4 kg and 2 tenths.
We write **4.2 kg**.

Write down the following weights in the same way.

a   b 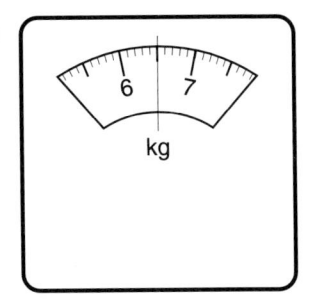   c

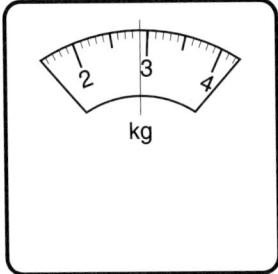

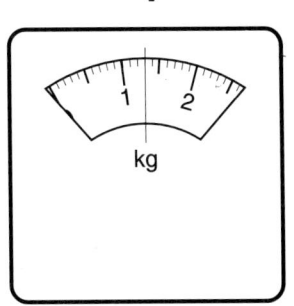

3 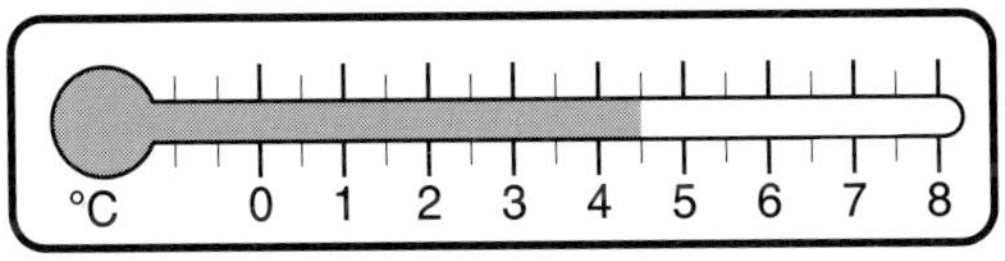 The thermometer is used to measure the temperature of the room.
It reads 4 and a half degrees.
We write **4.5 °C**.

What temperature is being shown by these thermometers?

a   b    c 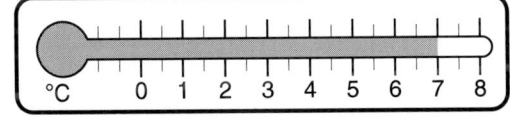   d

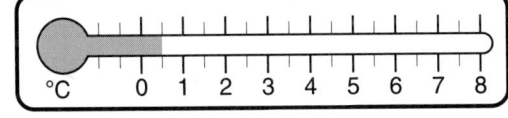

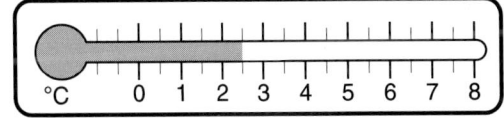

4 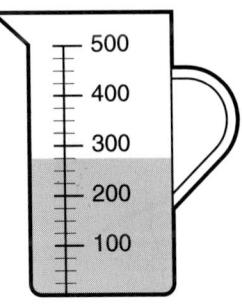 Each mark on the jug is worth 25 millilitres.
This jug is holding 200 plus 75 millilitres, which is 275 millilitres.

How much is in each jug here?

a   b    c 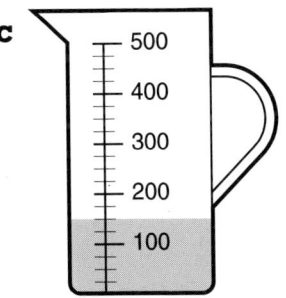   d

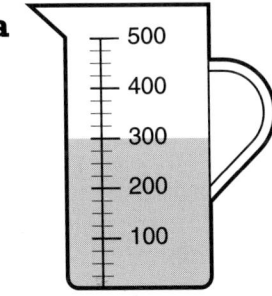

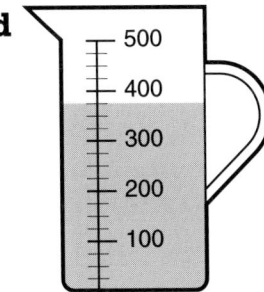

3

1 NUMBERS IN ACTION

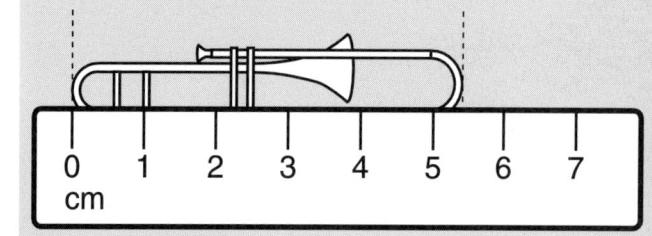

The Nearest Mark

Often the reading you want falls between two marks on the scale. When this happens read to the nearest mark.

The length of the model trombone is between 5 cm and 6 cm.

Using the top ruler we say its length is 5 cm **to the nearest centimetre**.

Using this ruler we say its length is 5.5 cm **to the nearest half centimetre**.

If you are exactly halfway between marks then **read the higher mark**.

EXERCISE 2

1 Read the points shown to the nearest **centimetre mark**.

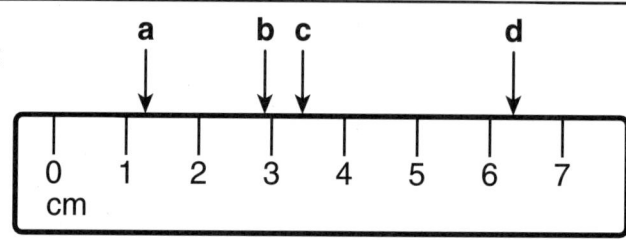

2 Read the points shown to the nearest **half centimetre mark**.

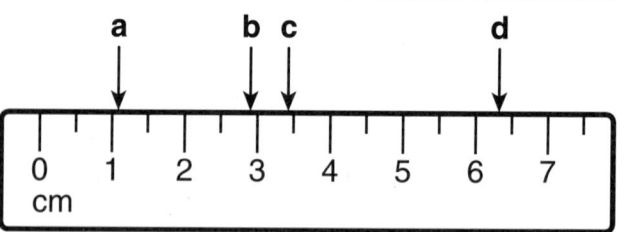

3 Give these weights to the nearest **kilogram mark**.

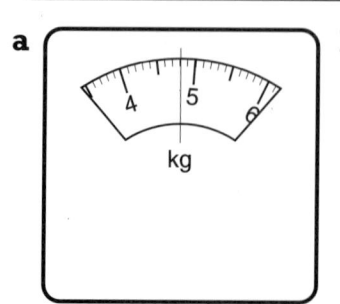

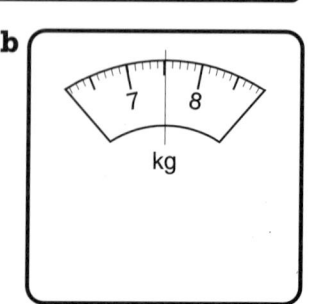

4 How many millilitres of liquid are in each jug to the nearest **100 mark**?

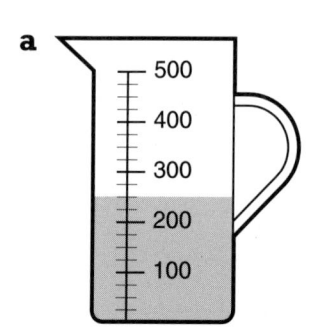

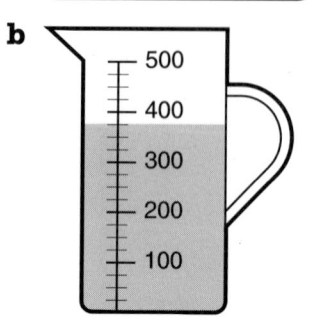

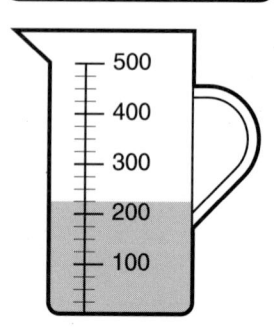

4

5 Give the temperature to the nearest **5 °C mark**.

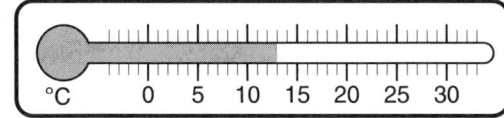

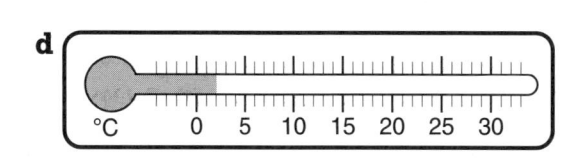

a
b
c
d

6 The class is collecting for a charity appeal. This chart shows what has been collected.

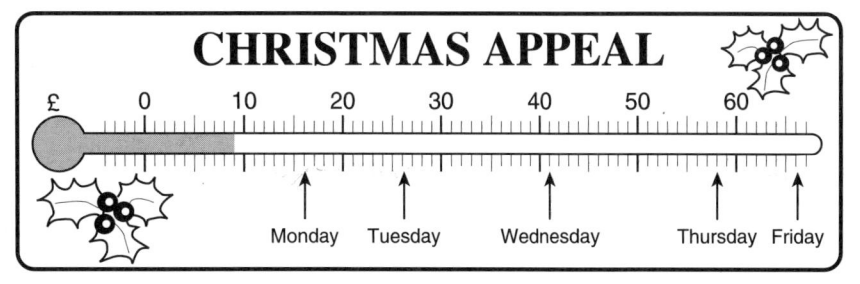

CHRISTMAS APPEAL

Monday Tuesday Wednesday Thursday Friday

a To the nearest **£1 mark**, how much was collected by:
(i) Monday (ii) Tuesday (iii) Friday?

b To the nearest **£10 mark**, how much was collected by:
(i) Tuesday (ii) Wednesday (iii) Thursday (iv) Friday?

Rounding Numbers

James has £27.
To the nearest **£10 mark** we call it £30.

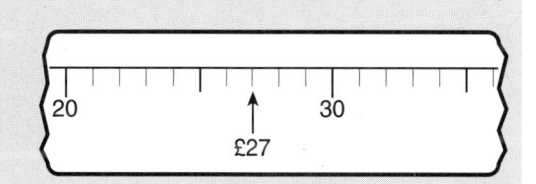

EXERCISE 2B

1 Find the following amounts on the number line above.
Say what is the nearest **£10 mark** to each.

a £22 **b** £33 **c** £35

The process of giving the nearest mark is called **rounding**.

2 Use the given number lines to help you **round** these amounts to the nearest £10.

a £76 **b** £89 **c** £91
d £99 **e** £71 **f** £80
g £231 **h** £256 **i** £245

1 NUMBERS IN ACTION

3 Use the given number lines to help you **round** these amounts to the nearest £100.

a £430 **b** £560 **c** £610
d £550 **e** £670 **f** £678
g £4340 **h** £4560 **i** £4528

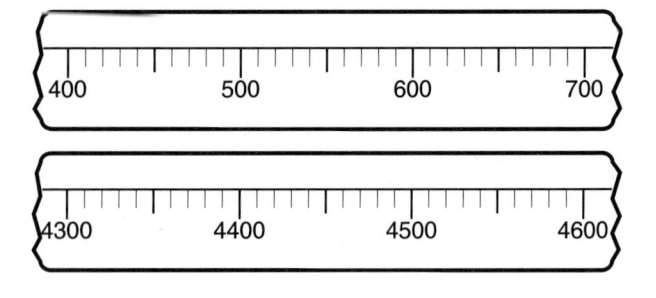

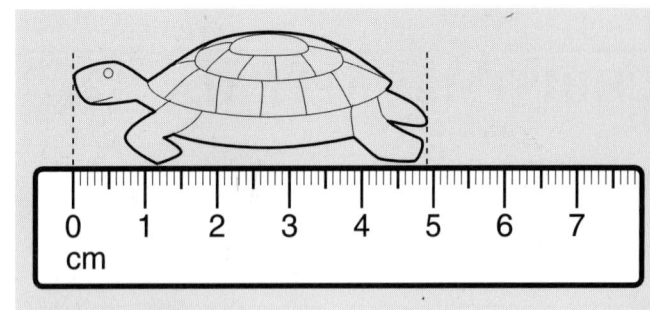

This toy tortoise is 4 cm and 9 tenths long.

We write **4.9 cm**.

To the **nearest cm** it **rounds** to 5 cm.

EXERCISE 3

1 **a** Find these numbers on the ruler above.
  b Round each number to the nearest centimetre.
   (i) 3.7   (ii) 5.2   (iii) 7.1   (iv) 2.3   (v) 0.7   (vi) 0.3

2 **a** Write down the length of each model.
  b Round each measurement to the nearest centimetre.
   (i)
   (ii)

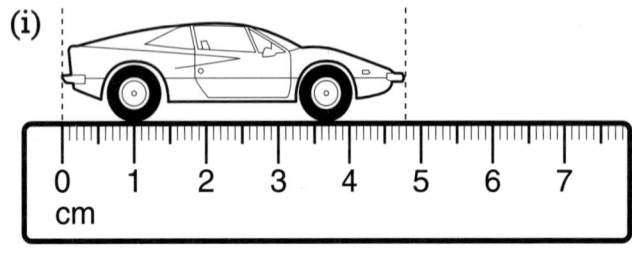

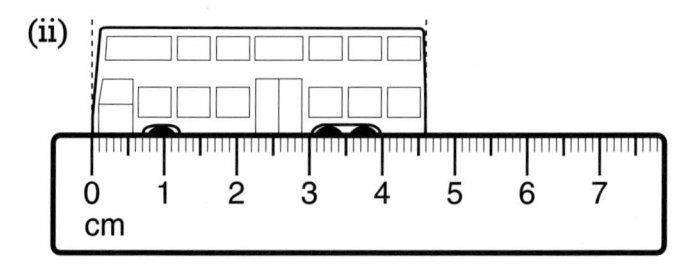

3 Round the following numbers to the nearest centimetre.
   a 3.6 cm   **b** 12.5 cm   **c** 79.4 cm   **d** 35.7 cm   **e** 98.8 cm

6

Adding and Subtracting Decimal Numbers

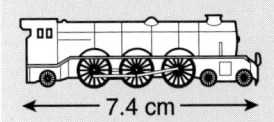

The model train measures 7 cm and 4 tenths.
We write 7.4 cm, using the point to mark the tenths.

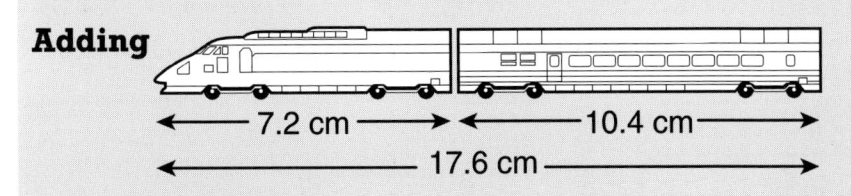

Adding

The engine is 7.2 cm long. The carriage is 10.4 cm.
Together they are 7.2 + 10.4 cm. The train is 17.6 cm long.

```
  7.2
+10.4
-----
 17.6
```
Keep the points in line

Subtracting

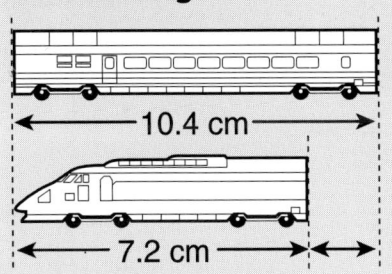

How much longer is the carriage?
10.4 − 7.2 cm.
The carriage is 3.2 cm longer.

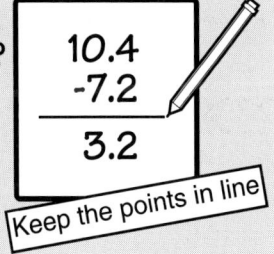

```
 10.4
 -7.2
-----
  3.2
```
Keep the points in line

EXERCISE 4

1 Add the following pairs of numbers:

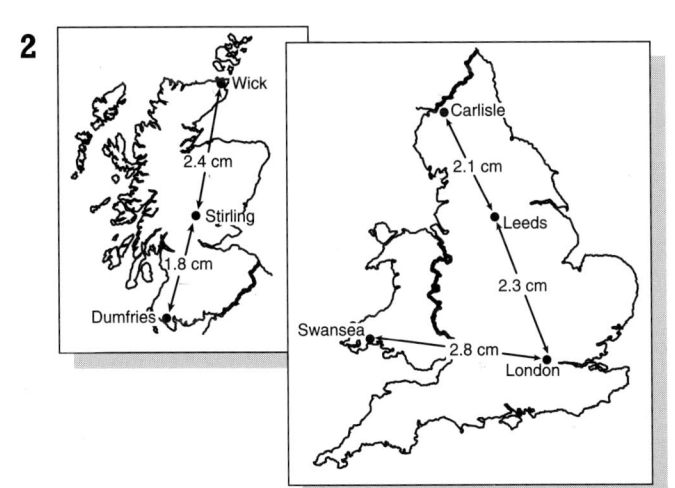

	a	b	c	d	e	f
	8.4	5.6	2.3	3.3	3.5	4.6
	+ 1.1	+ 3.2	+ 6.2	+ 4.1	+ 2.3	+ 7.2

	g	h	i	j	k	l
	7.4	6.5	5.7	7.8	13.5	24.6
	+ 1.7	+ 2.8	+ 6.9	+ 9.8	+ 12.3	+ 17.2

2 Kirsty measured the distance between towns on some maps.

Find the total distance by adding:

a from Wick to Dumfries
b from Carlisle to London
c from Carlisle to Swansea through London.

Map distances:
- Wick to Stirling: 2.4 cm
- Stirling to Dumfries: 1.8 cm
- Carlisle to Leeds: 2.1 cm
- Leeds to London: 2.3 cm
- Swansea to London: 2.8 cm

7

1 NUMBERS IN ACTION

3 Subtract:

a	8.6 − 1.4	**b**	7.9 − 3.5	**c**	6.8 − 5.7	**d**	8.8 − 6.8	**e**	10.6 − 6.5	**f**	76.1 − 21.0
g	18.7 − 11.5	**h**	36.9 − 22.4	**i**	24.3 − 24.2	**j**	27.8 − 0.8	**k**	34.5 − 14.4	**l**	94.5 − 12.4

4

Jim's weight

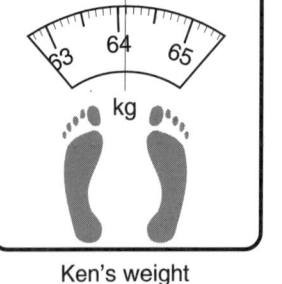

Ken's weight

Jim weighs 76.2 kg.

a How heavy is Ken?
b Subtract their weights to see how much heavier Jim is.

5 The model aeroplane is 6.8 cm long.

a What is the distance from the front to point A?
b By subtracting, find the distance from point A to the back.

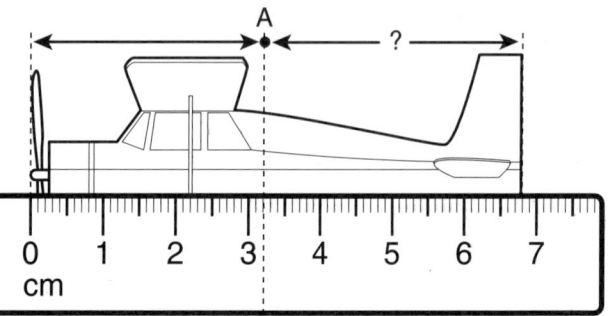

6

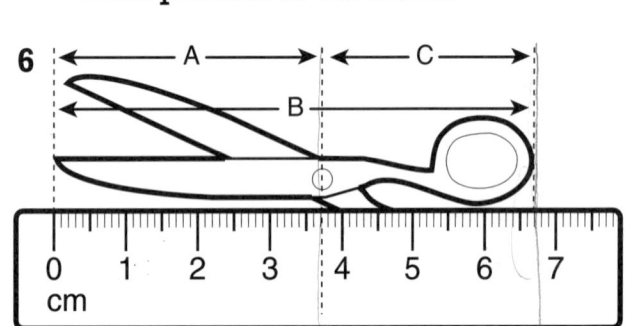

a Read the length from the ruler of:

   (i) A   (ii) B

b Find the length C by subtracting.

7 a Use the ruler to find the size of:

   (i) A   (ii) B

b Subtract your answers to find the size of the balloon itself, C.

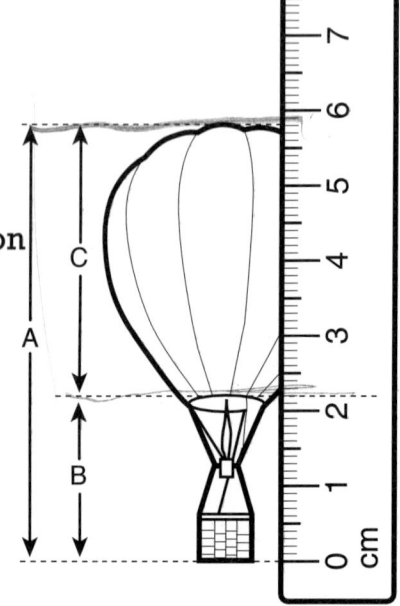

8

1 NUMBERS IN ACTION

Adding and Subtracting Money

The point separates the pounds and the pence, so keep the points in line.

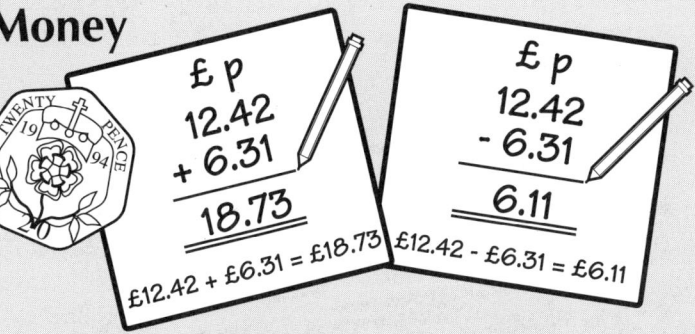

£ p
12.42
+ 6.31

18.73

£12.42 + £6.31 = £18.73

£ p
12.42
- 6.31

6.11

£12.42 - £6.31 = £6.11

EXERCISE 4B

1 Add the following pairs of prices.

	a £	b £	c £	d £	e £
	6.21	4.10	6.15	7.40	9.81
	+ 3.26	+ 2.15	+ 5.32	+ 1.67	+ 0.75

	f £	g £	h £	i £	j £
	14.23	26.25	27.25	7.82	0.07
	+ 13.41	+ 33.06	+ 4.26	+ 23.26	+ 9.96

2 Mark's mug of coffee costs £0.97.
His round of sandwiches costs £1.47.

Add these together to find the total cost of his lunch.

3 Fiona had a game of golf on holiday.
It cost £14.50 for the game.
Hire of clubs was £8.25.

How much did it cost her altogether?

4 Subtract the following pairs of prices.

	a £	b £	c £	d £	e £
	6.37	4.15	6.47	7.44	8.89
	− 3.21	− 2.10	− 5.24	− 2.33	− 0.75

	f £	g £	h £	i £	j £
	24.23	87.97	26.25	8.82	10.97
	− 13.12	− 42.40	− 3.04	− 1.01	− 9.96

1 NUMBERS IN ACTION

5 Meeta had £3.66. She spent £2.25 on a model dinosaur. Subtract to find how much money she had left.

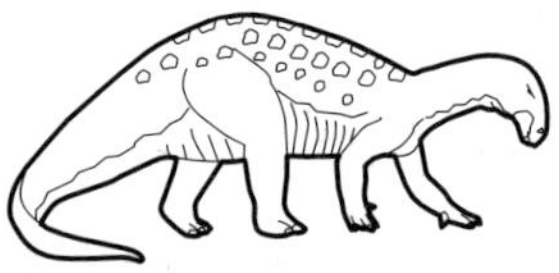

6 The toy helicopter is now on sale. Subtract to find out how much cheaper it is.

SALE
Was £18.77
Now only
£12.56

Multiplying and Dividing by 1, 10 and 100

Check these using your calculator. See what happens to the decimal points.

$3.26 \times 1 = 3.26$ $\qquad$ $5.48 \times 1 = 5.48$
$3.26 \times 10 = 32.6$ $\qquad$ $5.48 \times 10 = 54.8$
$3.26 \times 100 = 326$ $\qquad$ $5.48 \times 100 = 548$

EXERCISE 5

1 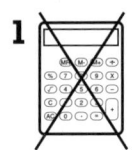
   a (i) 2.64×1 (ii) 2.64×10 (iii) 2.64×100
   b (i) 4.83×1 (ii) 4.83×10 (iii) 4.83×100
   c (i) 8.97×1 (ii) 8.97×10 (iii) 8.97×100
   d (i) 5.20×1 (ii) 5.20×10 (iii) 5.20×100
   e (i) 0.25×1 (ii) 0.25×10 (iii) 0.25×100
   f (i) 0.02×1 (ii) 0.02×10 (iii) 0.02×100

2 It cost £0.05 to call a friend for one minute. Multiply to find the cost of:

   a 10 minutes   **b** 100 minutes.

3 Use a calculator to do these:

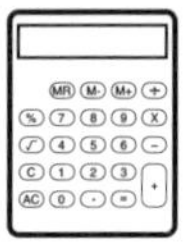

   a (i) $123 \div 1$ (ii) $123 \div 10$ (iii) $123 \div 100$
   b (i) $287 \div 1$ (ii) $287 \div 10$ (iii) $287 \div 100$
   c (i) $411 \div 1$ (ii) $411 \div 10$ (iii) $411 \div 100$
   d (i) $521 \div 1$ (ii) $521 \div 10$ (iii) $521 \div 100$

4 
   a (i) $279 \div 1$ (ii) $279 \div 10$ (iii) $279 \div 100$
   b (i) $497 \div 1$ (ii) $497 \div 10$ (iii) $497 \div 100$
   c (i) $760 \div 1$ (ii) $760 \div 10$ (iii) $760 \div 100$
   d (i) $500 \div 1$ (ii) $500 \div 10$ (iii) $500 \div 100$

5 a A party for 100 people at the café costs £245. Divide to find out what it costs for one person.

   b At the same café 10 hot dogs cost £16.30. What does one cost?

   c 10 portions of popcorn cost £5.20. What does one cost?

Multiplying and Dividing Decimal Numbers

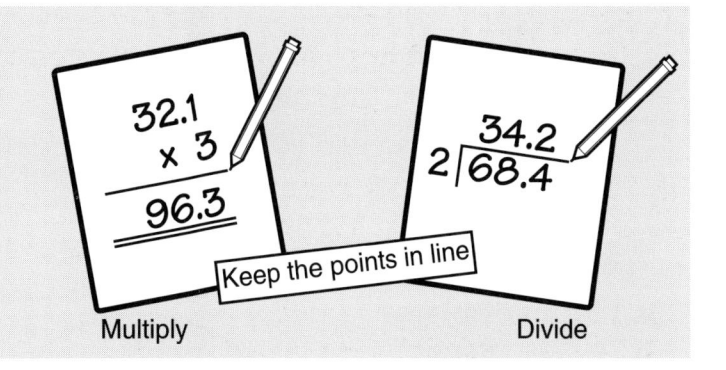

Multiply · Divide

Keep the points in line

EXERCISE 6

1 Multiply:

a 32.2 × 4

b 24.3 × 2

c 71.2 × 3

d 53.1 × 5

e 54.3 × 3

f 41.6 × 6

g 83.4 × 2

h 56.8 × 7

i 5.43 × 3

j 4.16 × 6

k 8.34 × 2

l 5.68 × 7

2 'Model Travel Shop' is on sale. Multiply to find the cost of:

a 3 ambulances
b 6 cars
c 7 planes
d 4 hovercrafts.

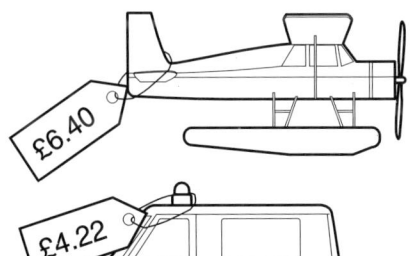

Plane £6.40, Car £2.45, Ambulance £4.22, Hovercraft £13.50

3 Divide:

a 24.6 ÷ 2
b 63.6 ÷ 3
c 88.48 ÷ 4
d 56.0 ÷ 5
e 24.66 ÷ 6
f 21.7 ÷ 7
g 8.08 ÷ 8
h 81.18 ÷ 9
i 48.6 ÷ 2
j 96.9 ÷ 3
k 48.04 ÷ 4
l 15.25 ÷ 5
m 36.60 ÷ 6
n 49.7 ÷ 7
o 72.88 ÷ 8
p 27.9 ÷ 9

4 Four people share a taxi. The bill comes to £16.80. Divide to find how much each person pays.

5 Three lengths of fence run for 3.69 metres. How long is one length of fence?

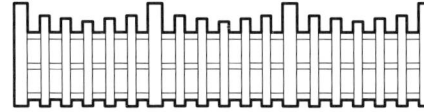

EXERCISE 7

Now you can use your calculator again.

1. Work out the cost of:

   a 12 dinner plates
   b 24 side plates
   c 17 saucers.

   Dinner plate £2.43 each
   Side plate £1.34 each
   Saucer £0.95 each

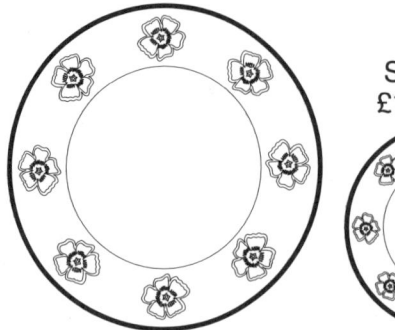

2. The coffee maker holds 1.02 litres of coffee.
   This is enough for 12 cups.
   How much does a cup hold?

3. Peter measured his windows for curtains.
   He needed 2.56 metres for one window.
   He had 8 windows all the same.
   What total length of curtain does he need?

4. A party of people went to the Italian restaurant for a meal. The total bill came to £94.64. They decided to share the cost. How much did each pay if there were:

   a 7 people
   b 8 people?

5. There are 24 bottles of cola.
   The total cost is £22.80.
   What is the cost of 1 bottle?

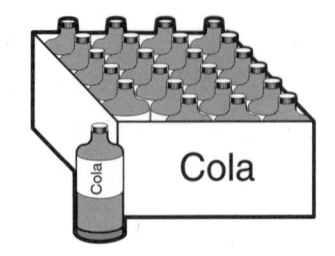

1 NUMBERS IN ACTION

CHECK-UP ON NUMBERS

1 What number is picked out on each scale?

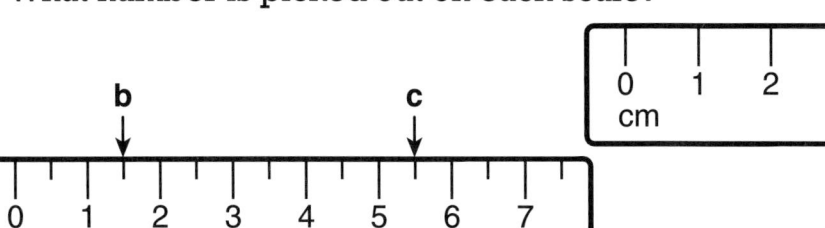

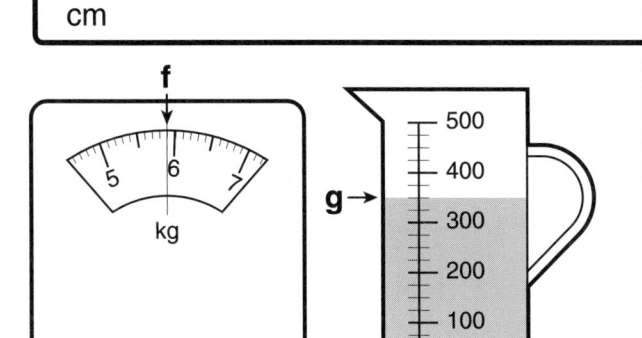

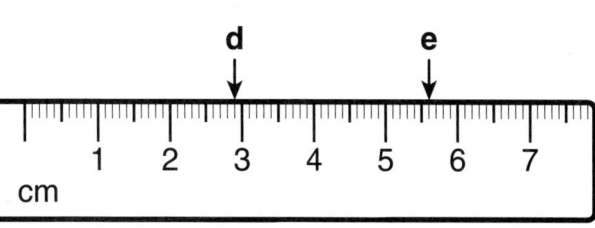

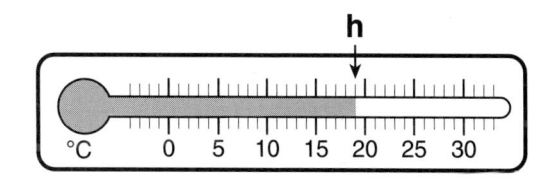

2 Read these:

 to the nearest centimetre mark

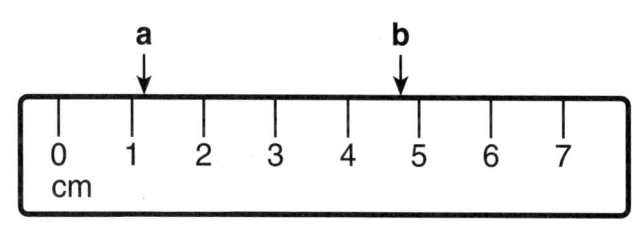

 to the nearest half centimetre mark

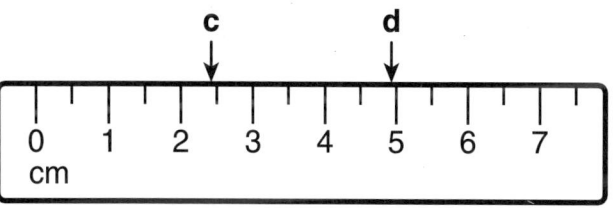

 to the nearest kilogram mark

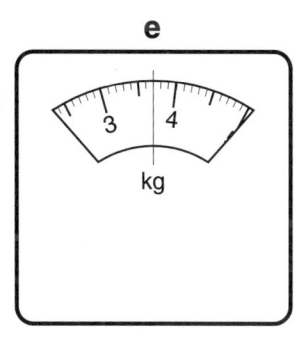

 to the nearest 100 mark.

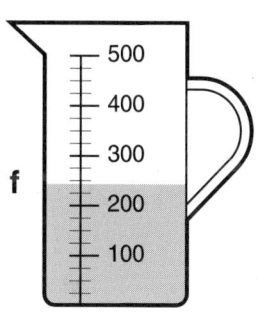

3 Round each amount to the nearest £10:
   a £63   **b** £75   **c** £26

4 Round each amount to the nearest £100:
   a £346   **b** £750   **c** £372

5 Round each length to the nearest centimetre:

   a 4.7 cm   **b** 2.3 cm   **c** 6.5 cm

6 Calculate:

   a   5.7 + 3.2   **b**   6.4 − 3.2   **c**   6.54 + 3.12   **d**   8.65 − 2.35

   e (i) 5.83 × 1   (ii) 5.83 × 10   (iii) 5.83 × 100

   f (i) 583 ÷ 1   (ii) 583 ÷ 10   (iii) 583 ÷ 100

   g 6.9 × 3   **h** 24.5 × 4   **i** 36.8 ÷ 4

7 Getting onto the ski slopes costs Mike £12.65 a day.
Hiring equipment costs him £25.75.
How much in total does a day's skiing cost?

8 The cruise was to be a distance of 98.4 km.
So far they had sailed 46.8 km.
How far had they still to go?

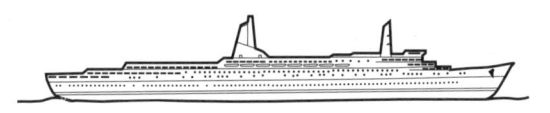

9 Each of the presents weighs 9.87 kg.
What is the total weight of all six?

10 In the bus there are 8 equally spaced rows of seats.
This takes up 10.8 metres.
How much space does each row of seats get?

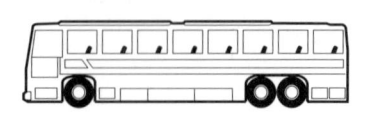

2 ALL ABOUT ANGLES

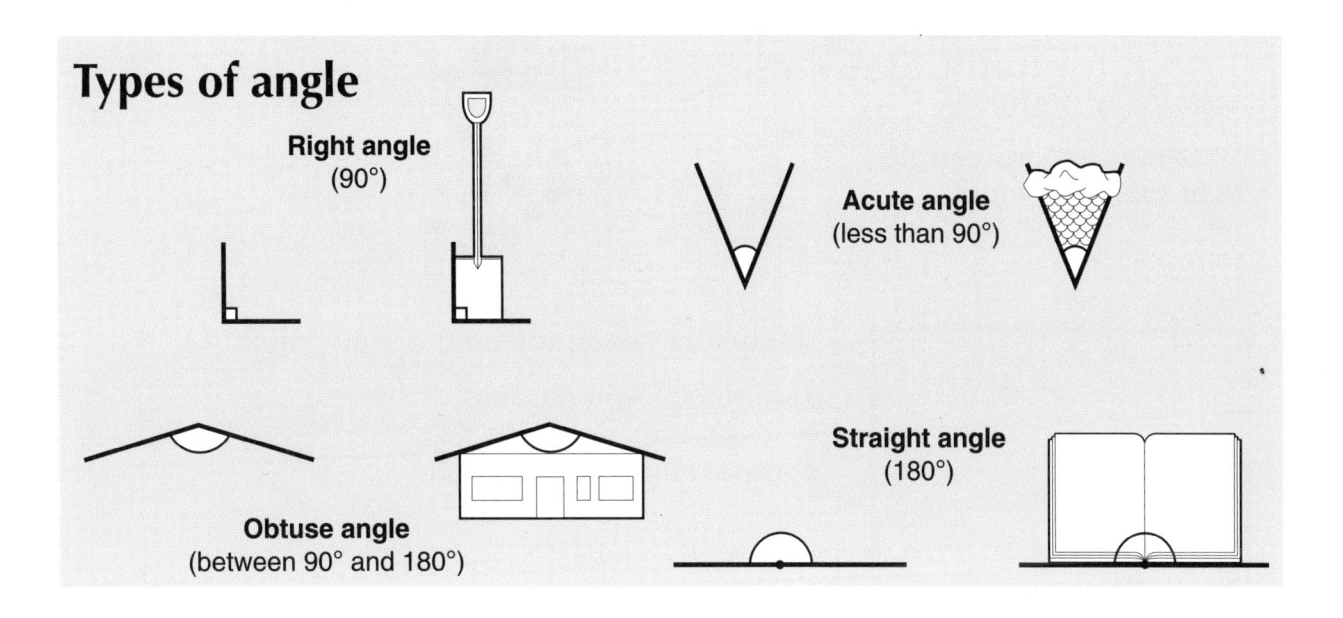

Types of angle

Right angle (90°)

Acute angle (less than 90°)

Obtuse angle (between 90° and 180°)

Straight angle (180°)

EXERCISE 1

1. What types of angle are the following?

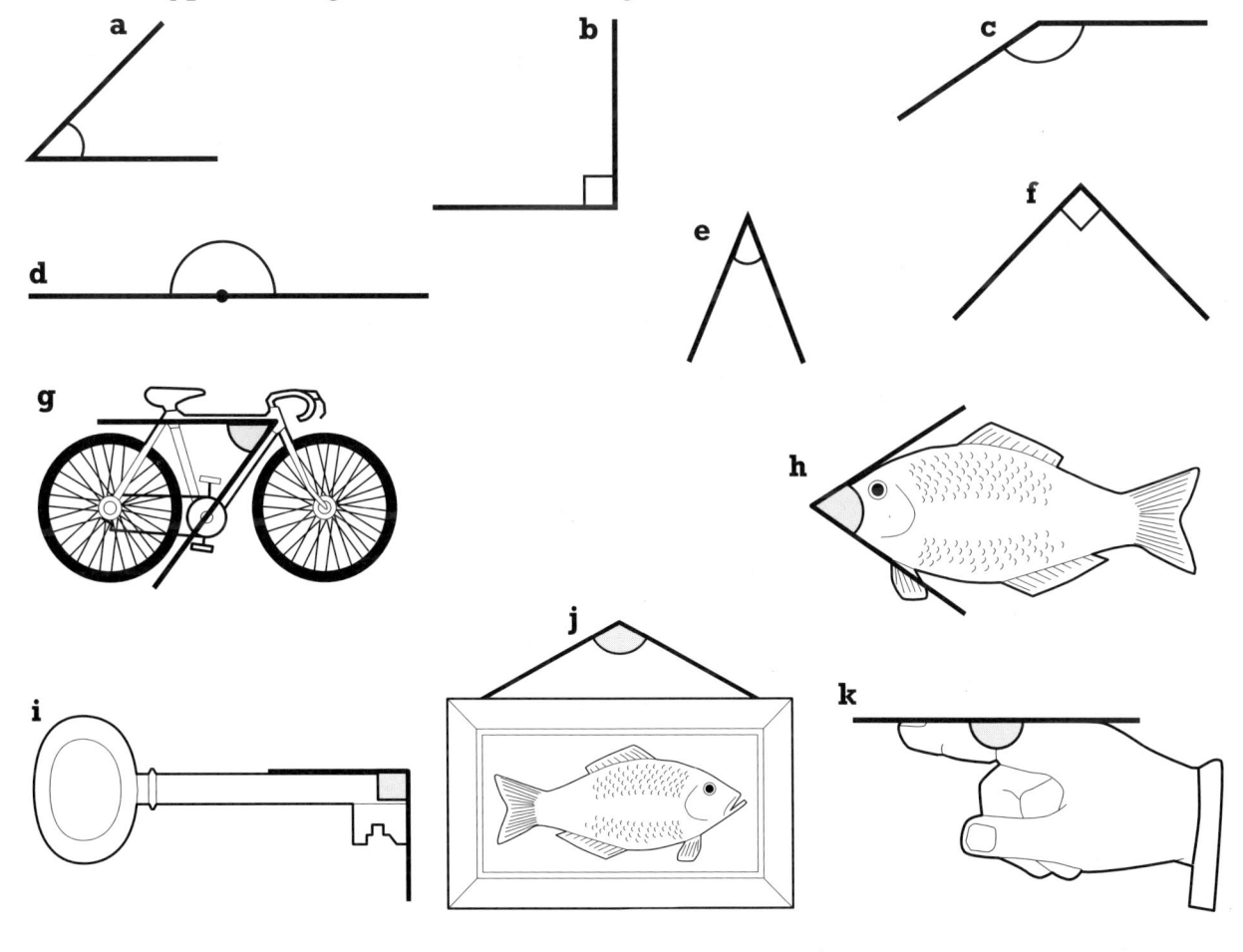

a, b, c, d, e, f, g, h, i, j, k

15

2 How many right angles:
  a make a straight line
  b fit round a point?

3 How many degrees:
  a are in a straight angle
  b fit round a point?

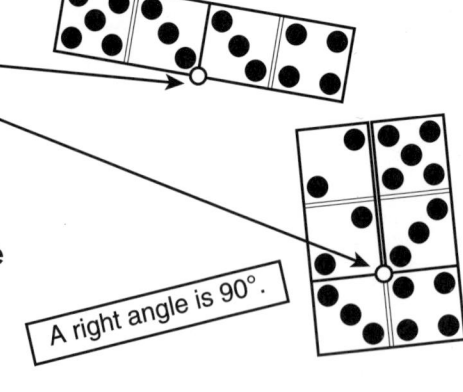

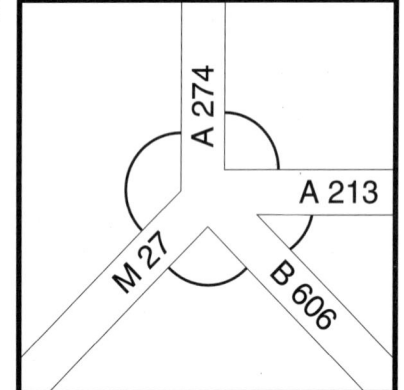

A right angle is 90°.

4 Name any two roads on the map which:
  a meet at right angles
  b meet at an acute angle
  c meet at an obtuse angle.

Naming and Drawing Angles

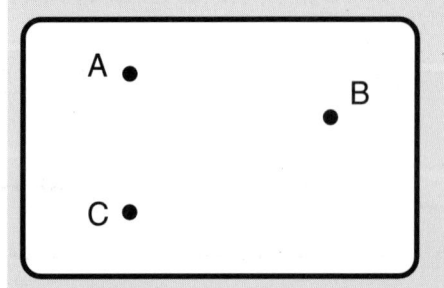

We name these points A, B and C.

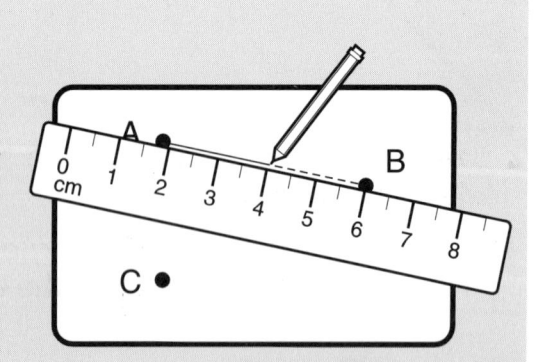

We name this line AB.

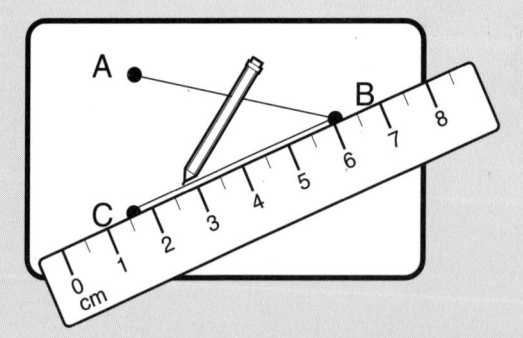

We name this angle ∠ABC.

To name an angle we use the letters in the order in which we draw the angle.

2 ALL ABOUT ANGLES

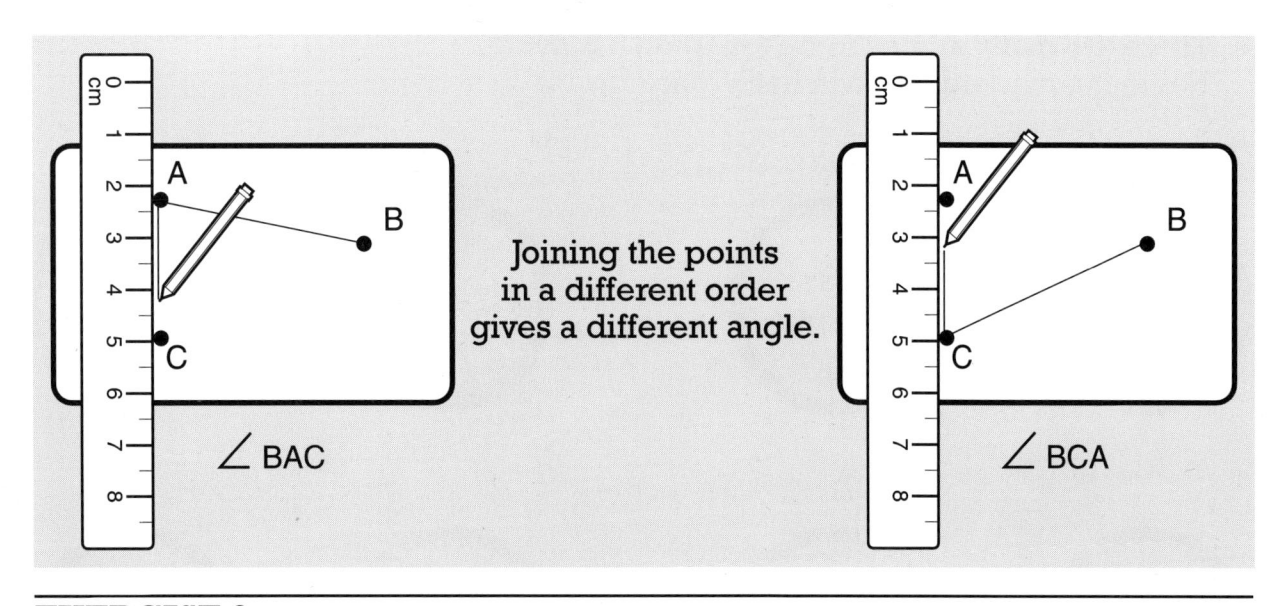

∠BAC   Joining the points in a different order gives a different angle.   ∠BCA

EXERCISE 2

1 Write down the names of these angles. (Remember to include the angle sign, ∠.)

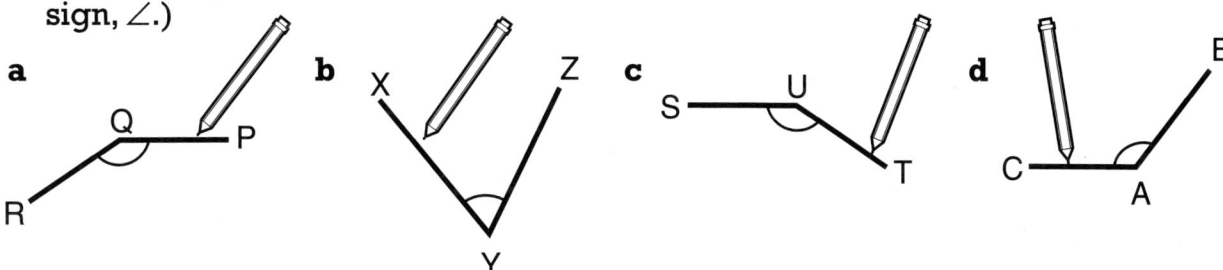

a, b, c, d

2 Trace the three points K, L and M into your jotter. Make **two** copies.

  a Join one set to form the angle ∠KLM.
  b Join the other set to form the angle ∠LKM.

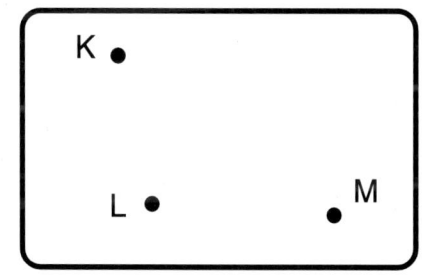

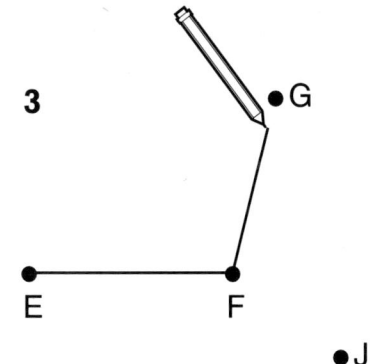

3 Adam drew ∠EFG.
Bill drew ∠GFE.
Is there any difference?

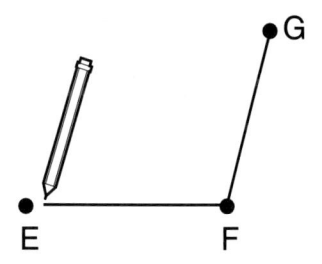

4
  a Name the obtuse angle.
  b Name the acute angle.
  c Name the straight angle.

17

2 ALL ABOUT ANGLES

5 There are many angles to be found on a bicycle.
Name the marked angle in each diagram.

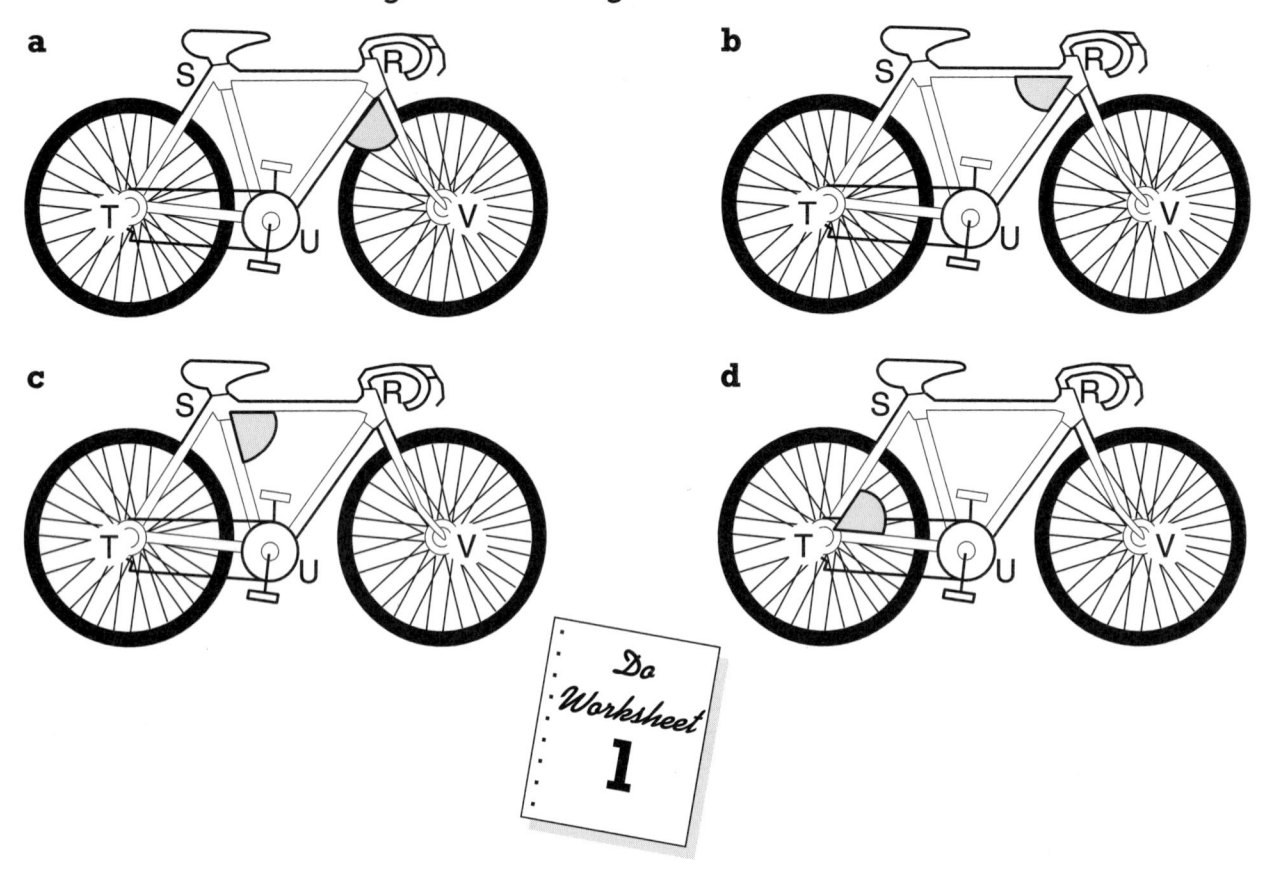

a

b

c

d

Do Worksheet 1

Measuring Angles

We measure length in centimetres using a ruler.

We measure time in seconds using a watch.

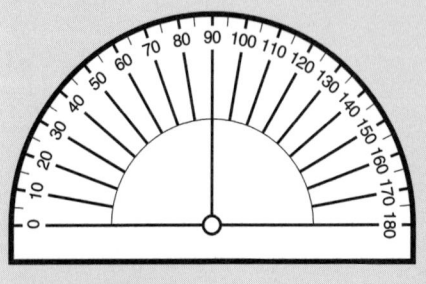

We measure angles in degrees using a protractor.

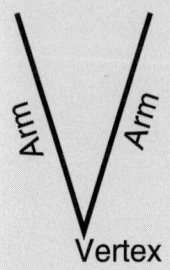

An angle is made of two lines called **arms** which meet at a point called a **vertex**.

2 ALL ABOUT ANGLES

To measure the size of this angle:
1. Put the centre of the protractor on the **vertex**.
2. Put the 0° line on one **arm**.
3. Read the size of the angle **from the other arm**.

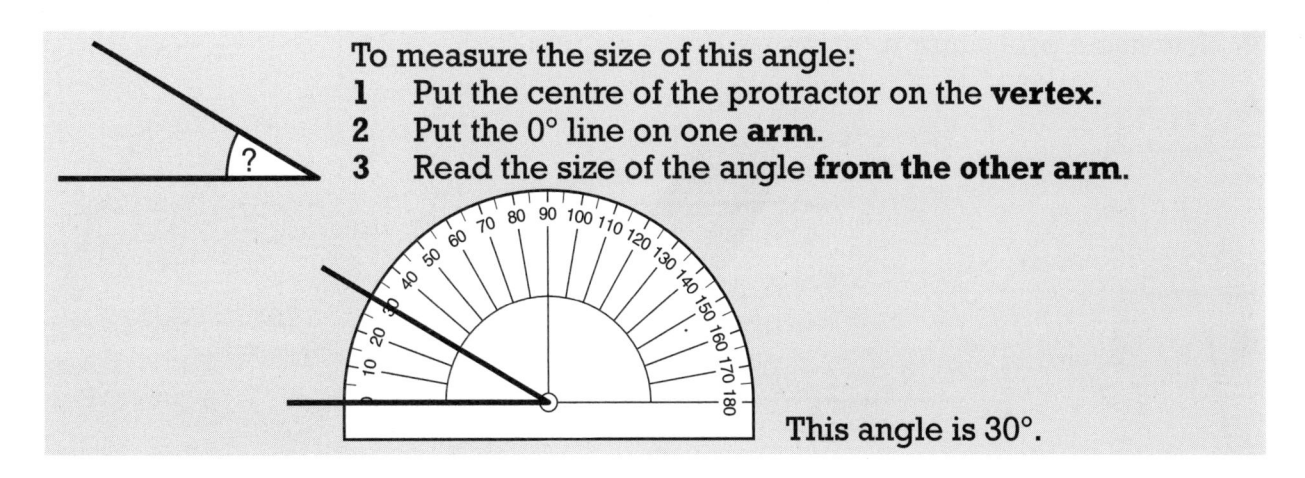

This angle is 30°.

EXERCISE 3

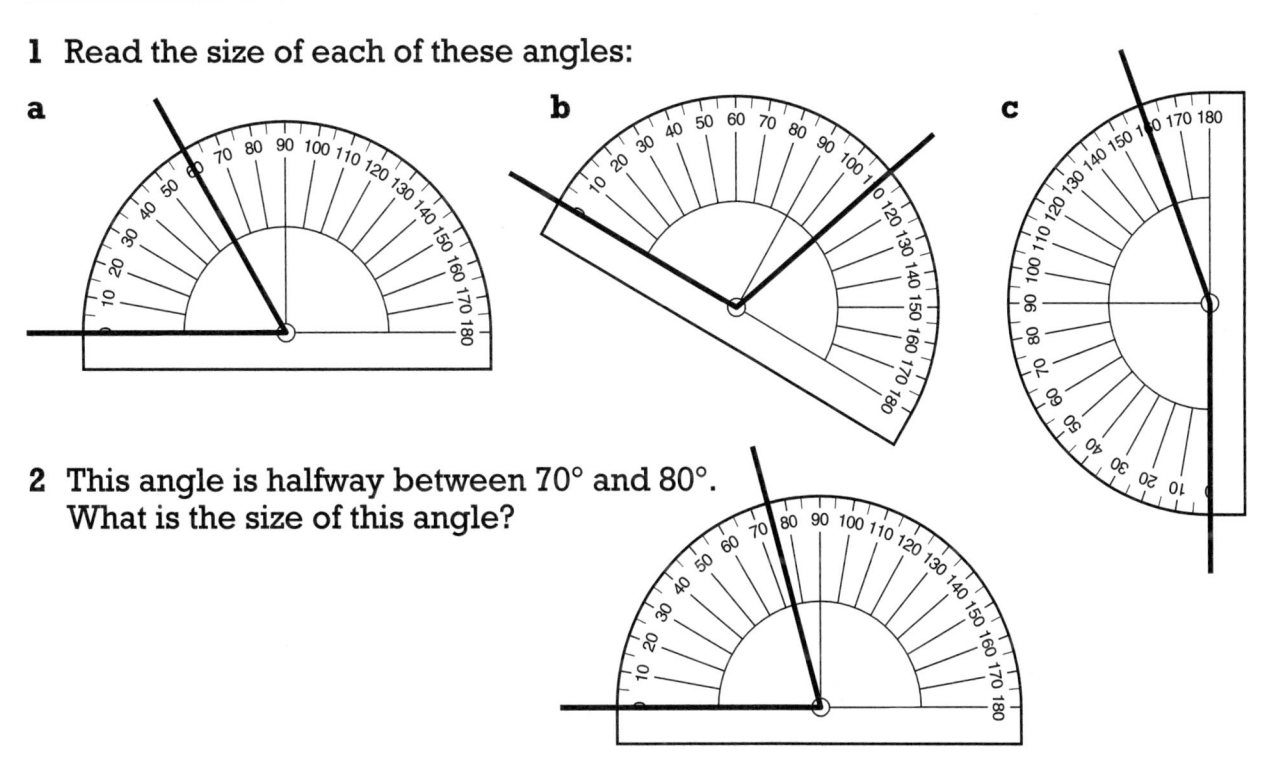

1. Read the size of each of these angles:

   a   b   c

2. This angle is halfway between 70° and 80°. What is the size of this angle?

3. Read the size of these angles:

   a   b   c

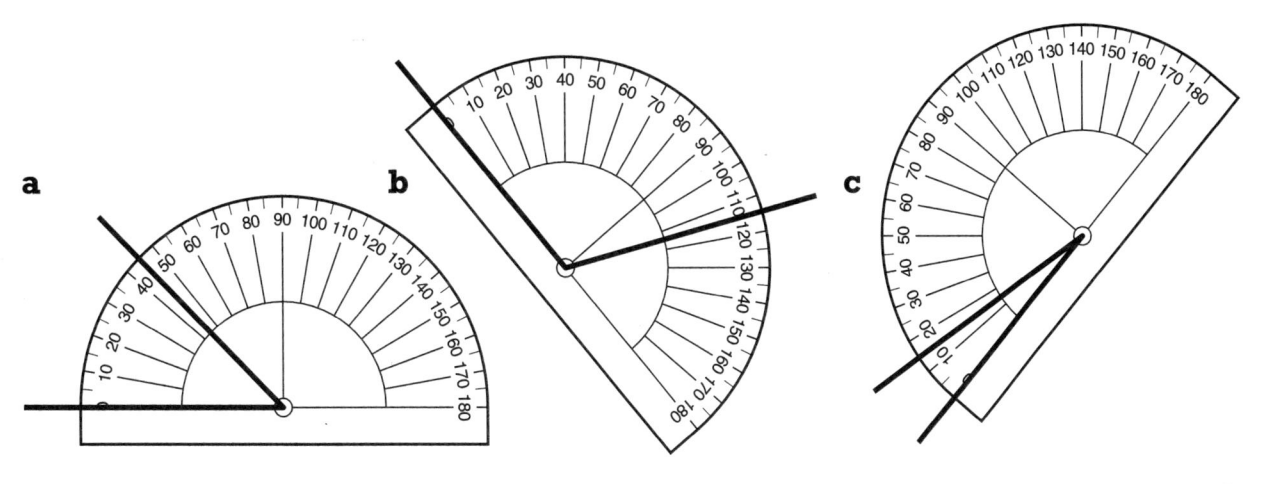

19

2 ALL ABOUT ANGLES

4 Now use a protractor to measure these angles.

a   b    c

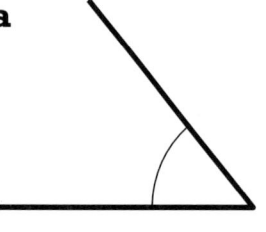

d 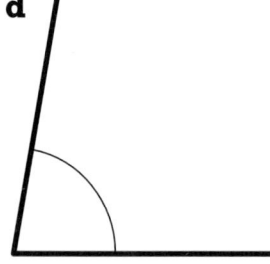   e 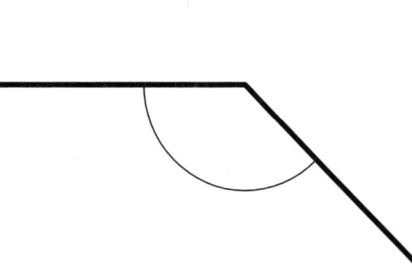   f

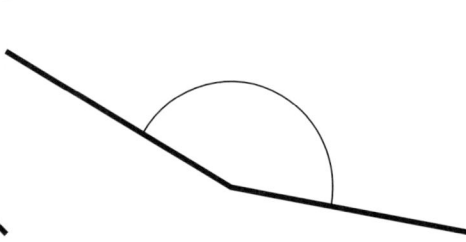

5 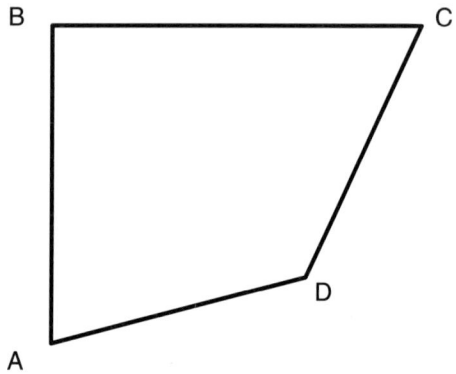 B   C   Measure the size of:

  a ∠ABC
  b ∠BCD
  c ∠CDA
  d ∠DAB

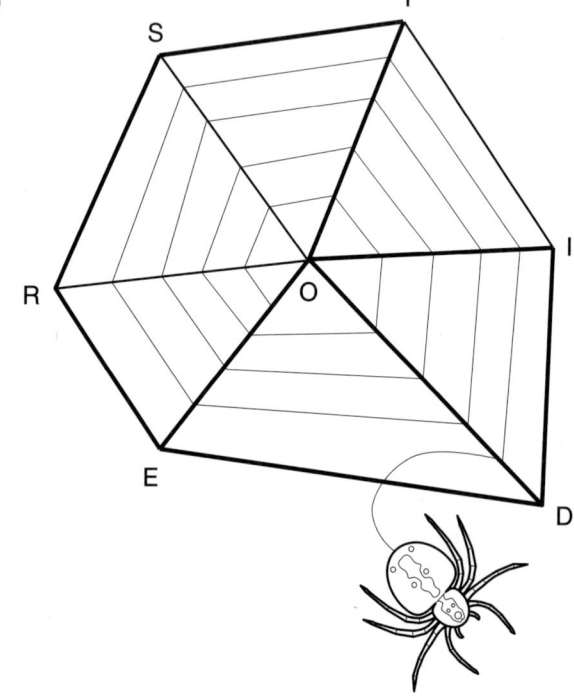

       D
A

6   P   Measure the size of:
    S
               a ∠SPO
               b ∠POI
               c ∠EOD
               d ∠IDE
               e ∠SRE
                I
R   O

  E   D

20

2 ALL ABOUT ANGLES

Drawing Angles with a Protractor

To draw an angle of 50°:

a Pick a point. Call it T. Draw a line from the point.

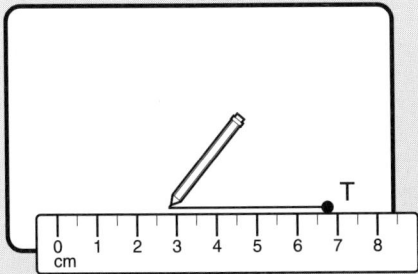

b Sit the protractor on the line. Put the centre on T and 0° on the line.

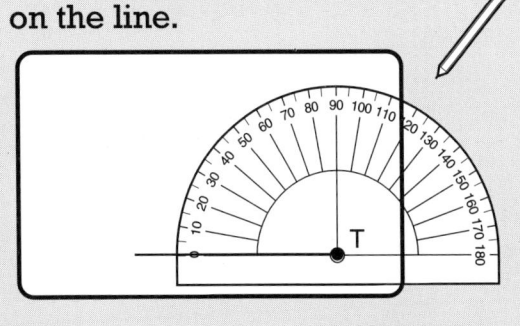

c Make a mark at 50°.

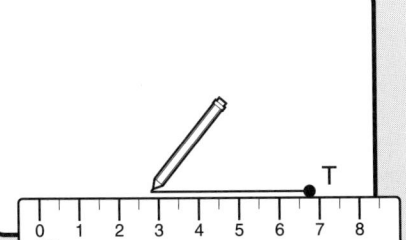

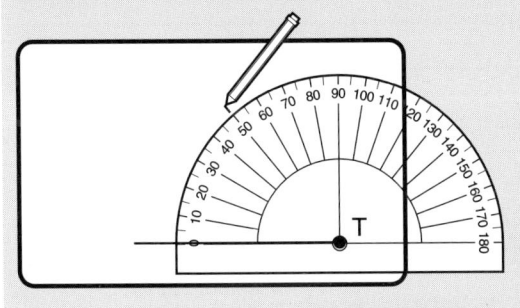

d Draw a line from T to the mark.

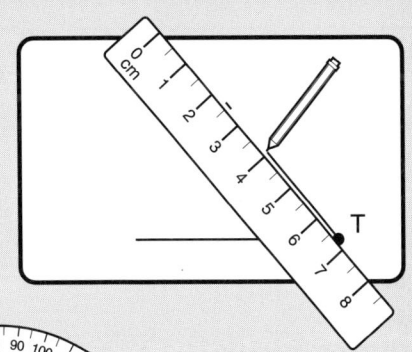

e You now have an angle of 50°.

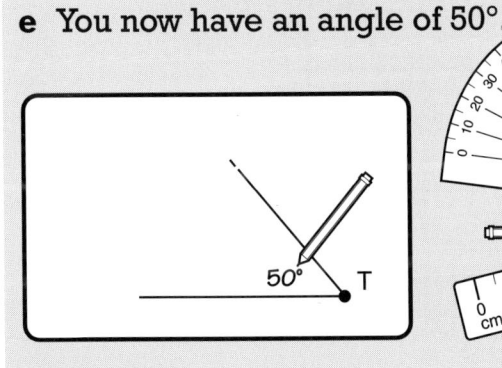

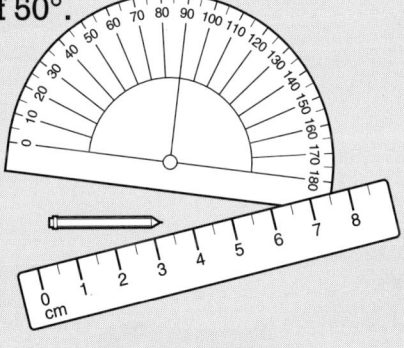

EXERCISE 4

1 Draw the following angles:

    a 30°   **b** 120°   **c** 75°   **d** 105°

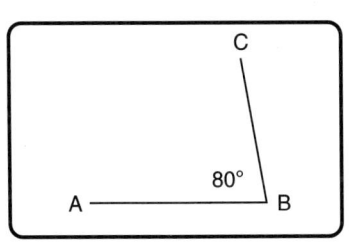

2 **a** Draw an angle of 80°.   **b** Label it as ∠ABC.

3 Now draw these angles.

    a ∠DEF = 55°   **b** ∠KLM = 160°   **c** ∠PQR = 135°

Describing Movement

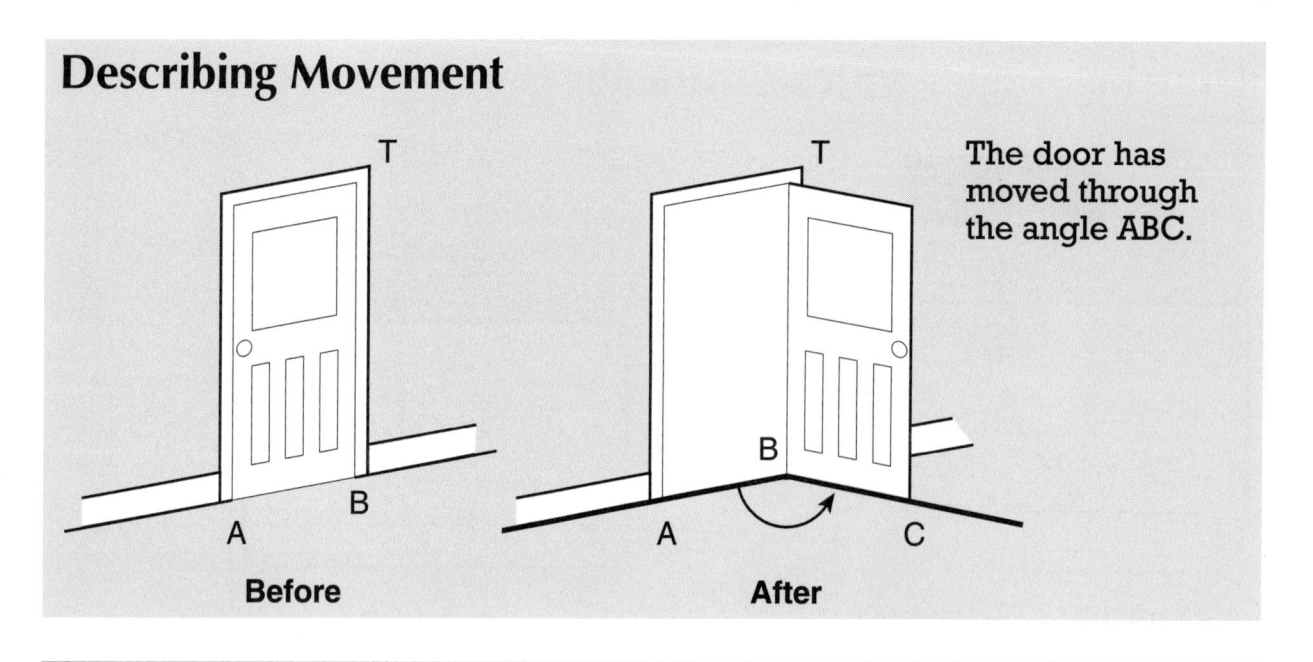

The door has moved through the angle ABC.

Before

After

EXERCISE 5

1 Name the angle:
   a the window turns through to open
   b the compasses move through to open
   c the scissors have opened through.

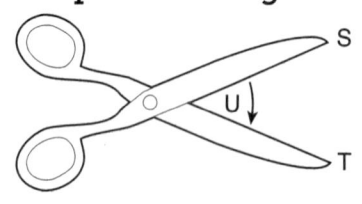

2 Mira turns her ruler. Use a protractor to measure the size of the angle at each position.

3 What size of angle will the pages turn through?

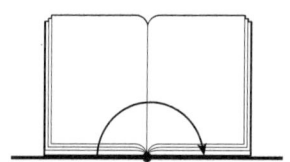

4 Jack had been looking at the fish. He turned to look at the crab. What angle did he turn through?

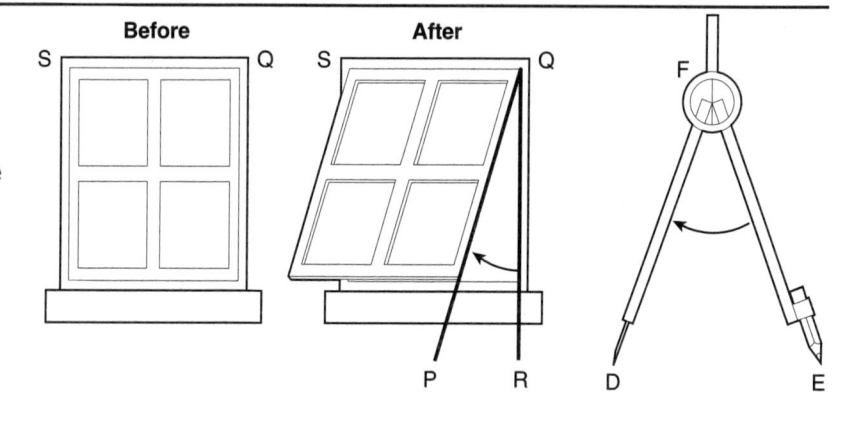

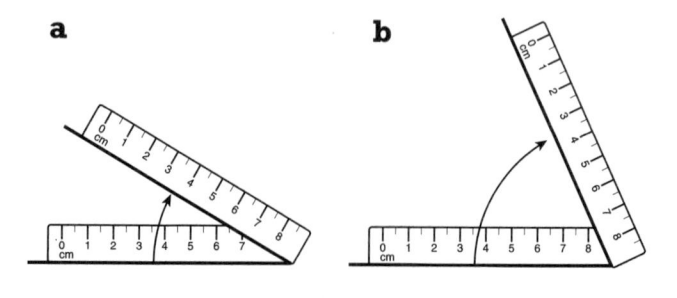

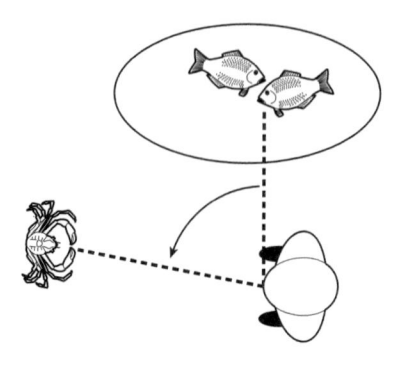

2 ALL ABOUT ANGLES

Describing Direction

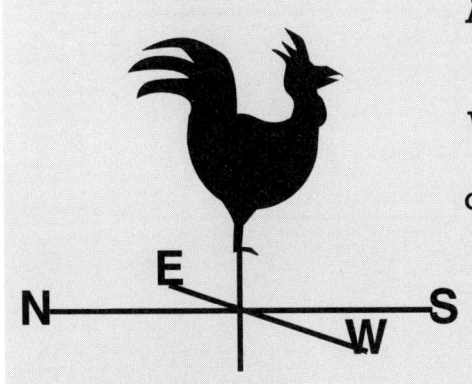

A compass will tell you where North is.

When you know where North is you can describe any direction.

This picture shows the eight main points of the compass.

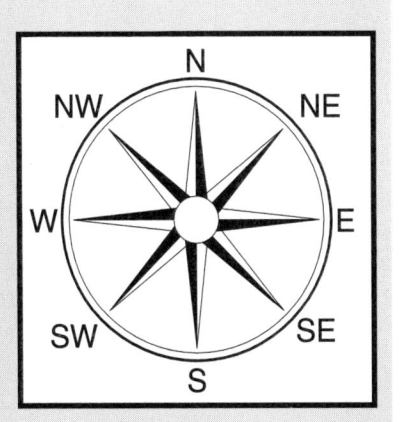

EXERCISE 6

1 Measure the size of the angle between:

   a North and East
   b South and North-west
   c East and South-east
   d East and West.

2 Which direction is opposite:

   a North
   b East
   c North-east
   d South-east?

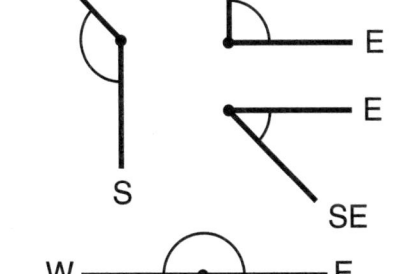

3 If North is towards the top of the page, in which direction is:

   a the lorry travelling
   b the car going
   c the bike facing?

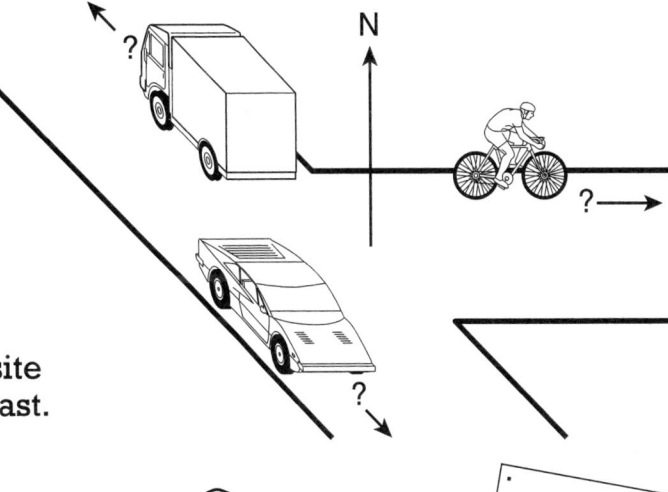

4 John and Bob are skiing in opposite directions. John is skiing North-east. In which direction is Bob skiing?

Do Worksheet 2

23

2 ALL ABOUT ANGLES

CHECK-UP ON ANGLES

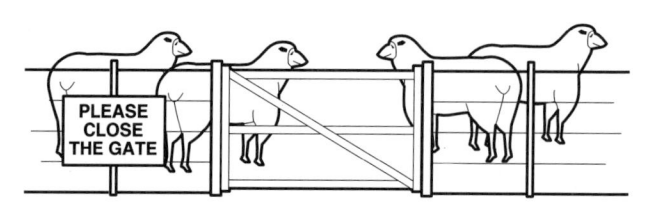

1
   a Name the marked angle.
   b What type of angle is it?
   c Name any acute angle on the gate.

2 Use your protractor to measure:
   a ∠SPQ
   b ∠PQR

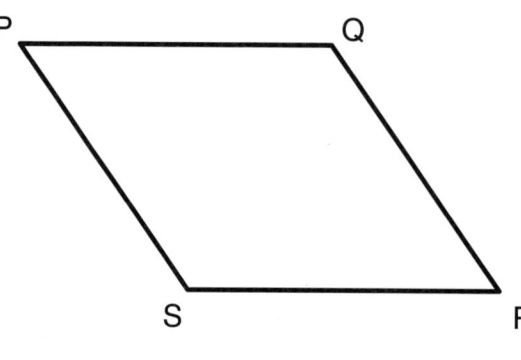

3 a (i) Draw a line 6 cm long and call it KL.
     (ii) Use your protractor to draw ∠KLM = 75°.
   b Draw an angle of 140°. Call it ∠VUW.

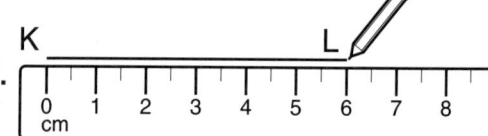

4 The guillotine blade shuts to cut paper. Name the angle it turns through.

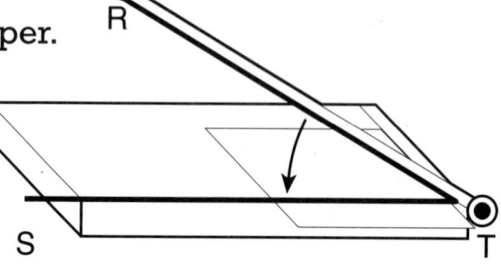

5 Two signs point in opposite directions. One points South-east. What is the direction on the other?

South-east   ?

24

3 LETTERS AND NUMBERS

Collecting Like Terms

Jack lists the plastic pieces in the geometry box: three circles and two triangles and five rectangles.

For a shorter method he writes: $3c + 2t + 5r$.

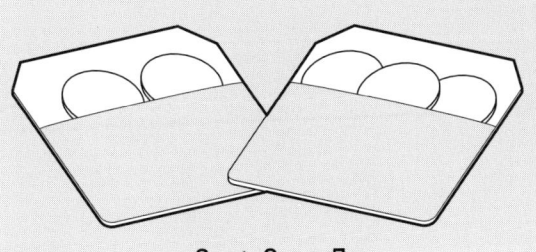

$2c + 3c = 5c$

Two circles from one folder and three circles from the other makes five circles in all.

EXERCISE 1

1 Mrs Jones is going shopping. Copy and complete the shorter version of her list.

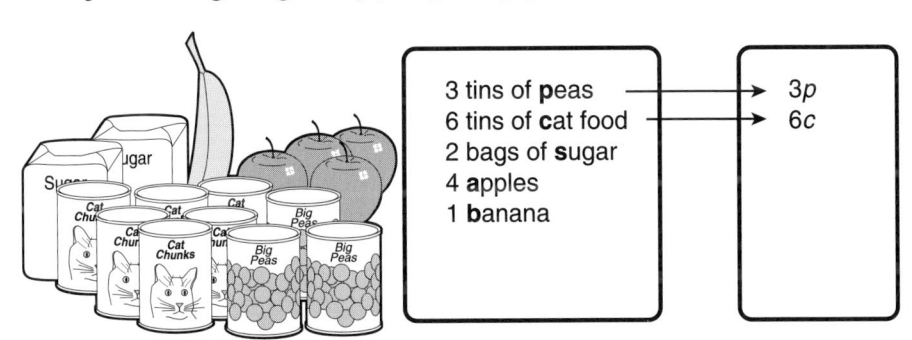

3 tins of **p**eas → $3p$
6 tins of **c**at food → $6c$
2 bags of **s**ugar
4 **a**pples
1 **b**anana

2 Sangeeta brought 3 **a**pples home.
Her husband brought 4 **a**pples.
There are now 7 **a**pples in the bowl.
Copy and complete this shorter version.
$3a + 4a = \boxed{}$

3 Write shorter versions of each of the following:

a 2 **p**rotractors and
4 **p**rotractors
make 6 **p**rotractors.

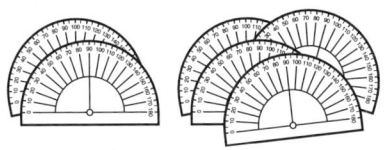

b 4 **p**encils and
5 **p**encils
make 9 **p**encils.

c 2 **f**rogs and
1 **f**rog
make 3 **f**rogs.

25

4 Write these in a shorter, simpler form. For example, $3a + 2a$ becomes $5a$.

- **a** $3x + 4x$
- **b** $4x + 6x$
- **c** $x + 5x$
- **d** $5y + 7y$
- **e** $3t + t$
- **f** $6k + 2k$
- **g** $r + 9r$
- **h** $8p + 5p$
- **i** $x + x$
- **j** $7x + 3x$
- **k** $3x + 4x + 4x$
- **l** $x + 4x + x$
- **m** $4f + 4f + 4f$
- **n** $2d + d + 3d$

Example

Eamon had six **h**ot dogs. Julie took one away. So now there are only five.

$6h - h = 5h$

5 Use letters to help you write these in shorter form.

a Three **t**rees. Two got blown down, leaving one **t**ree.

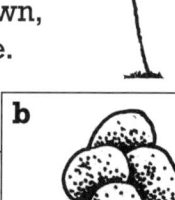

b Six **p**otatoes. Two got used for chips, leaving four **p**otatoes.

c One **e**gg sat on a wall. One **e**gg fell off, leaving none.

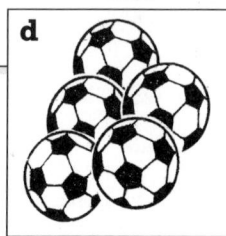

d Five **f**ootballs in the store. Three get taken away for games, leaving two **f**ootballs.

6 Write these in a shorter, simpler form. For example, $4b - b = 3b$.

- **a** $7c - c$
- **b** $3x - 2x$
- **c** $4d - 2d$
- **d** $5f - 2f$
- **e** $3a + 2a - a$
- **f** $6b - 2b + 3b$
- **g** $8x - x - 2x$

7 Now try these:

- **a** $a + a + a - a$
- **b** $3x + 2x - x$
- **c** $y + y + 4y - 2y$
- **d** $x + x - 2x$

3 LETTERS AND NUMBERS

We can only make things simpler when things are *like* each other.

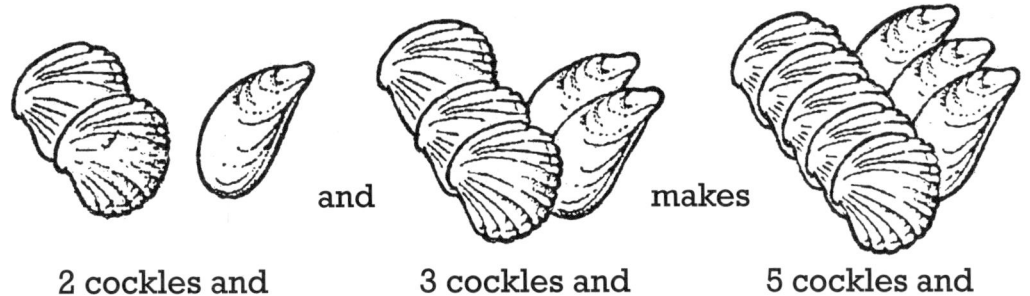

2 cockles and 1 mussel   and   3 cockles and 2 mussels   makes   5 cockles and 3 mussels

$$2c + m + 3c + 2m = 5c + 3m$$

8 Collect *like* terms to make each of the following as simple as possible.

a 2 helicopters and 2 planes   and   3 helicopters and 1 plane

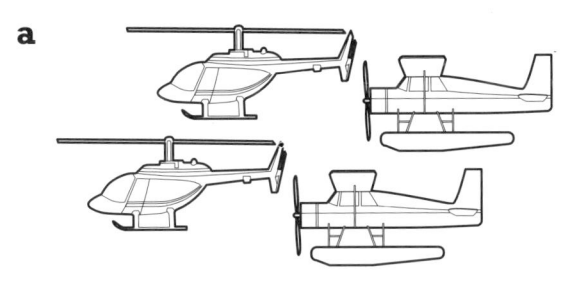

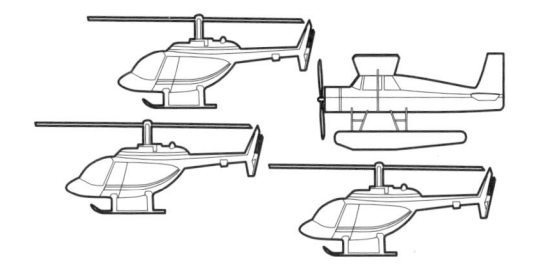

$$2h + 2p + 3h + p = ?$$

b 4 golf balls and 2 footballs   and   2 golf balls and 3 footballs

c a cat and a lamb   and   a cat and a lamb

9 Tidy up the following:

a $2a + 3b + 4a + 5b$ **b** $3x + 6y + x + 2y$ **c** $a + b + a + b$
d $5p + 5q + q + 6p$ **e** $4t + 2n + 2n + t$ **f** $2a + 4b + 3a + 5a$
g $2c + 5d + c + c$ **h** $6a + 4b - 2a - 2b$ **i** $2x + 3y - x$

27

3 LETTERS AND NUMBERS

Swapping Letters and Numbers

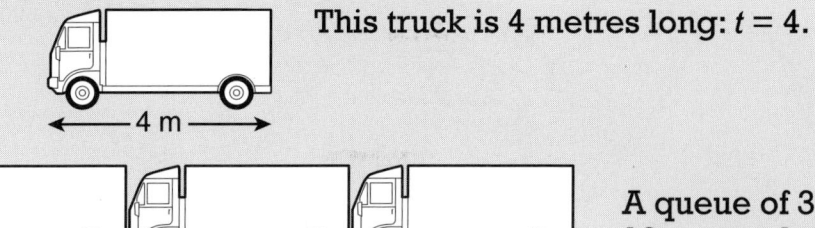

This truck is 4 metres long: $t = 4$.

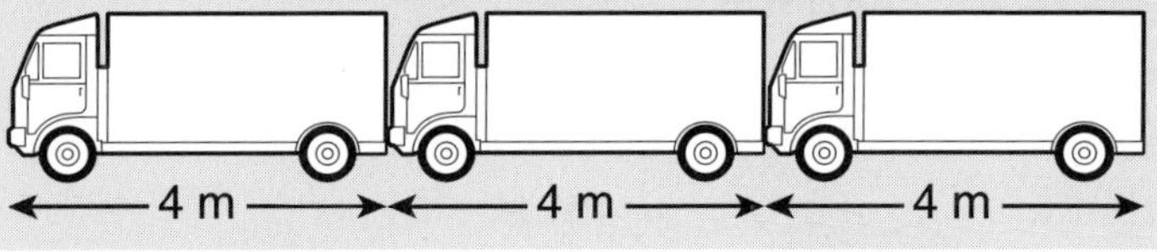

A queue of 3 trucks will be 12 metres long: $3t = 12$ because $3 \times 4 = 12$.

EXERCISE 2

1 a How long will each of these queues be? Answer like this: $4t = ...$
   (i) 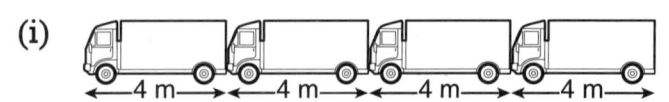
   (ii) 
   (iii)    (iv)

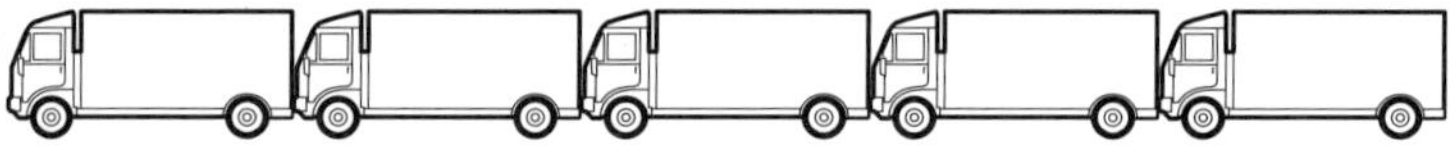

   b What length will these truck queues be?
   (i) $8t$ (ii) $7t$ (iii) $10t$

2 a Apples cost 10 pence each. Find the cost of the following:
   (i) 5 apples   (ii) 7 apples   (iii) 4 apples   (iv) 6 apples

   b What costs do these stand for?
   (i) $2a$ (ii) $8a$ (iii) $10a$

   $a = 10$

3 Bananas cost 8 pence each. What prices do these stand for?

   a $6b$ **b** $3b$ **c** $2b$ **d** $5b$ **e** $10b$ **f** $9b$

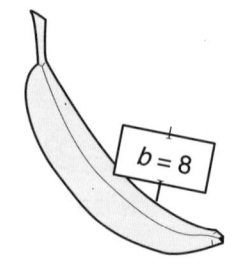

   $b = 8$

4 Baby corn cost 5 pence each. What are the following costs?

   a $3c$ **b** $4c$ **c** $2c$ **d** $8c$ **e** $10c$ **f** $7c$

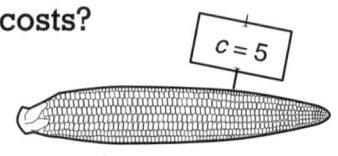

   $c = 5$

Multiplying and Dividing

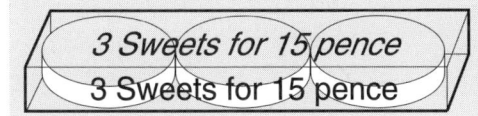

The label says '3 sweets for 15 pence'. $3s = 15$.
We can see that one sweet costs 5 pence because $3 \times 5 = 15$.
$3s = 15$ so $s = 5$.

EXERCISE 3

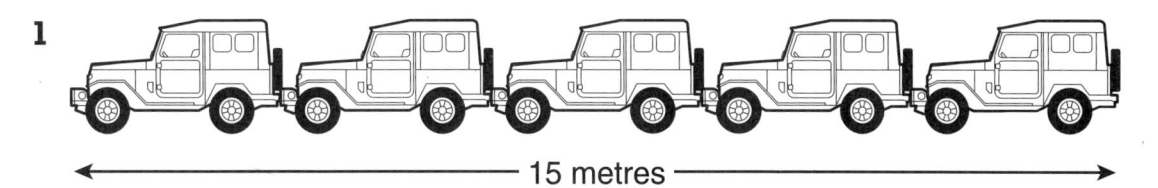

1 A queue of five cars is 15 metres. How long is one car?
Answer like this: $5c = 15$
so $c = ...$
A car's length is ...

2 Four buses in a row stretch for 24 metres. How long is one bus?

3 Five 'lost and found' golf balls are sold for £1. How much does each ball cost?

'Lost and found', 5 for a pound. Golf balls

4 The shopkeeper buys ten radios for £90. How much is each radio?

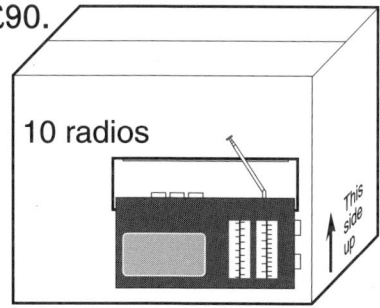

10 radios

5 Work out what each letter is worth:

   a $5x = 20$ **b** $4y = 32$ **c** $2z = 24$ **d** $6t = 18$ **e** $3q = 21$

3 LETTERS AND NUMBERS

Adding and Subtracting

James practises his putting.
He is 5 metres from the hole.
He only putts the ball 3 metres.
How far has he still to go?

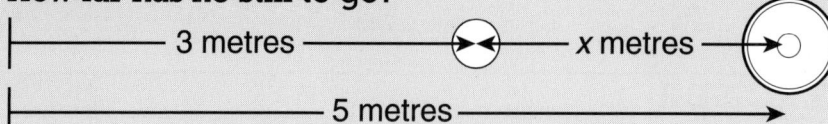

Answer like this: $3 + x = 5$ so $x = 2$.
He has 2 metres to go.

EXERCISE 4

1 Work out how far James has to putt to reach each hole.

a 4 metres, a metres; 7 metres

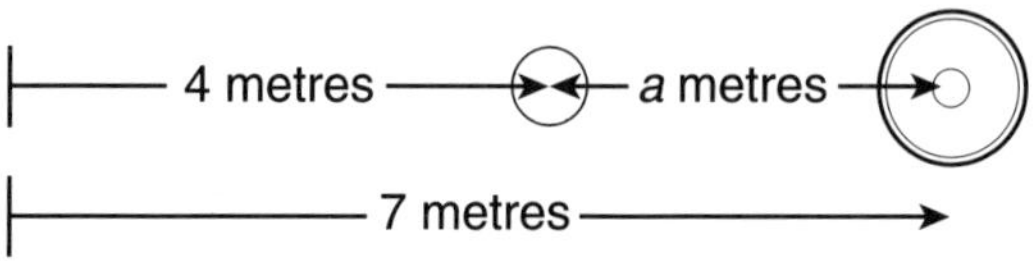

b 2 metres, b metres; 8 metres

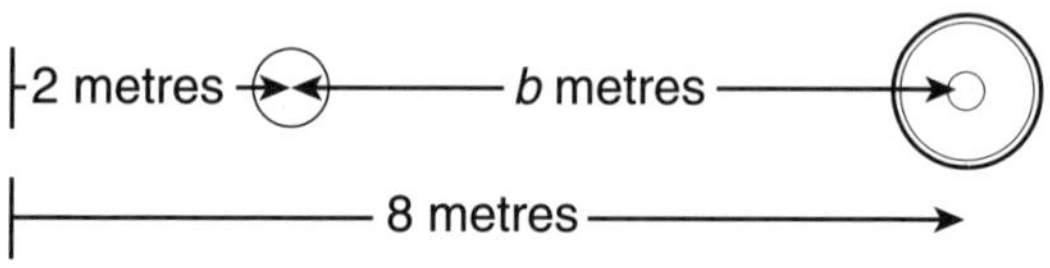

c 1 metre, c metres; 6 metres

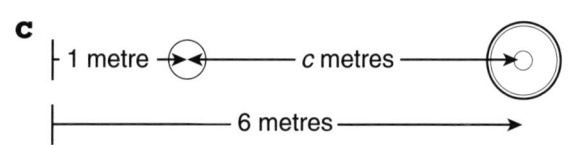

d 5 metres, d metres; 6 metres

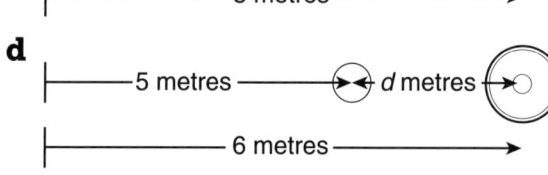

2 **a** 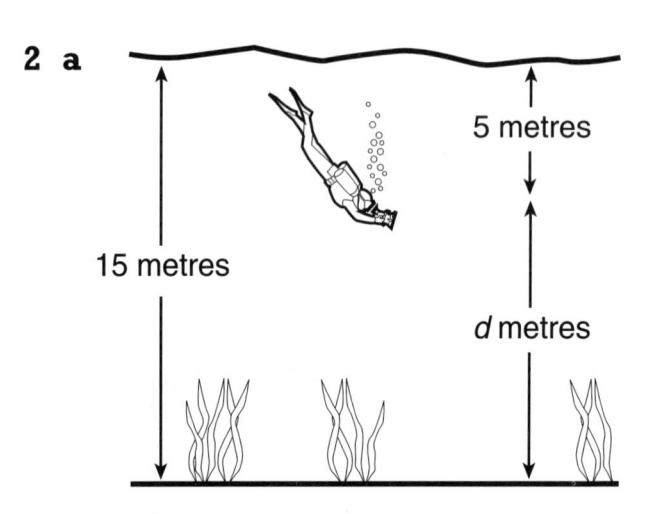 Sarah dives in 15 metres of water.
She is down 5 metres.
How far has she to go to reach the bottom?

Start your answer with $5 + d = 15$.

(15 metres total; 5 metres down; d metres to bottom)

Sarah makes other dives. Work out her depth in each case.

b 20 metres total; a metres depth; 7 metres to bottom

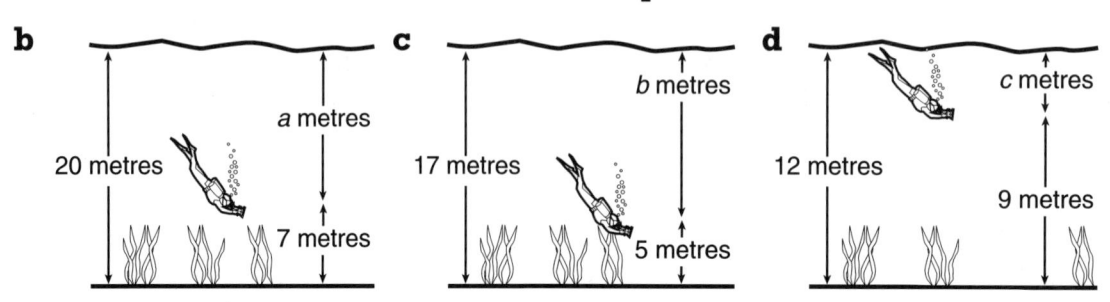

c 17 metres total; b metres depth; 5 metres to bottom

d 12 metres total; c metres depth; 9 metres to bottom

30

CHECK-UP ON LETTERS AND NUMBERS

1. Use letters to write this shopping list out in a shorter form.

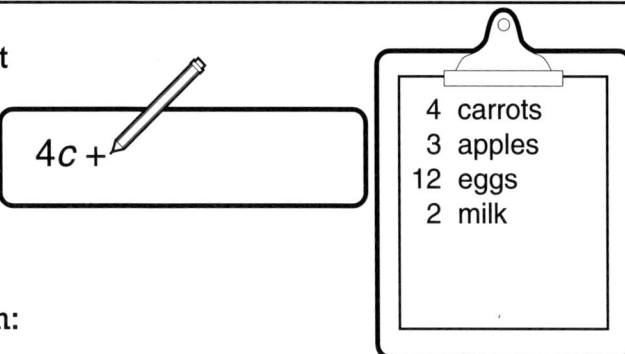

   4c +

   4 carrots
   3 apples
   12 eggs
   2 milk

2. Write the following in a shorter form:

   a $b + b + b$ **b** $2p + 6p$

3. Write these in a shorter, simpler way using letters and symbols.

   a There were two bees and one flew away, leaving one bee.

   b There were four coins and two were lost, leaving two coins.

4. Simplify the following:

   a $5a - 2a$ **b** $3a + 5a - 2a$

5. A toy truck costs £3.

   a What is the cost of:
   (i) 2 trucks   (ii) 6 trucks?
   b What prices do the following represent?
   (i) $3t$ (ii) $5t$ (iii) $10t$

   $t = 3$

6. An apple costs 10 pence, a banana costs 6 pence, a grapefruit costs 8 pence. Work out the cost of this shortened list: $5a + 4b + 3g$.

7. A queue of 3 buses is 36 metres long.
   How long is one bus?
   Start your answer $3b = 36$.

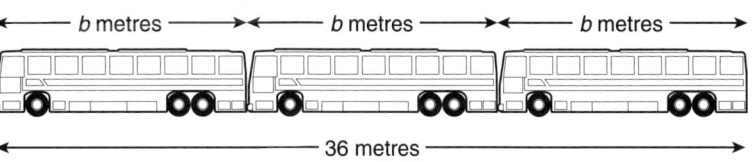

8. Mehmet climbs a 10 metre ladder. He has climbed 4 metres. How far from the top is he? Start with $x + 4 = 10$.

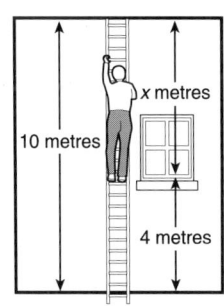

31

4 MAKING SENSE OF STATISTICS

Making Pictographs

Gail works in a music shop.
She makes a chart of sales, letting ⊙ stand for 4 sales.

She shows 3 sales as ◖ .

She shows 2 sales as ◗ .

So ⊙ ⊙ ◗ shows 4 + 4 + 2 = 10 sales.

EXERCISE 1

1 This pictograph shows the sales of CDs in the music shop one Saturday.

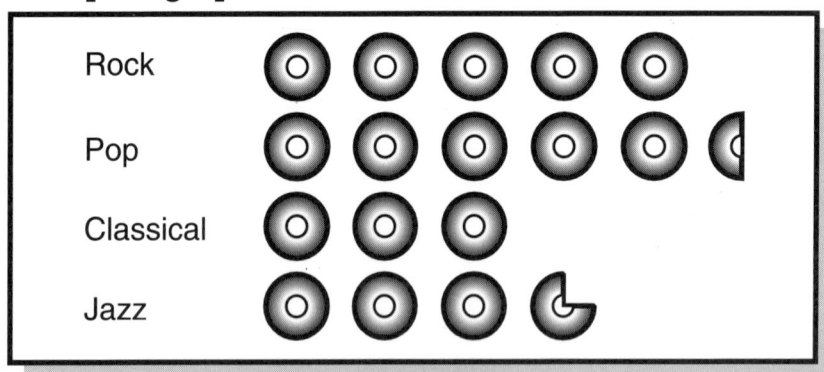

Rock	⊙ ⊙ ⊙ ⊙ ⊙
Pop	⊙ ⊙ ⊙ ⊙ ⊙ ◗
Classical	⊙ ⊙ ⊙
Jazz	⊙ ⊙ ⊙ ◖

⊙ = 4 compact discs

    a How many Rock CDs were sold?
    b Which was the least popular choice of music?
    c How many CDs were sold altogether?
    d How many more Pop CDs than Jazz ones were sold?

2 Here are the shop's CD sales the following Saturday:

Rock	Pop	Classical	Jazz
14	22	4	7

Draw a pictograph to illustrate these sales where ⊙ = 4 compact discs

32

3   The Music Shop

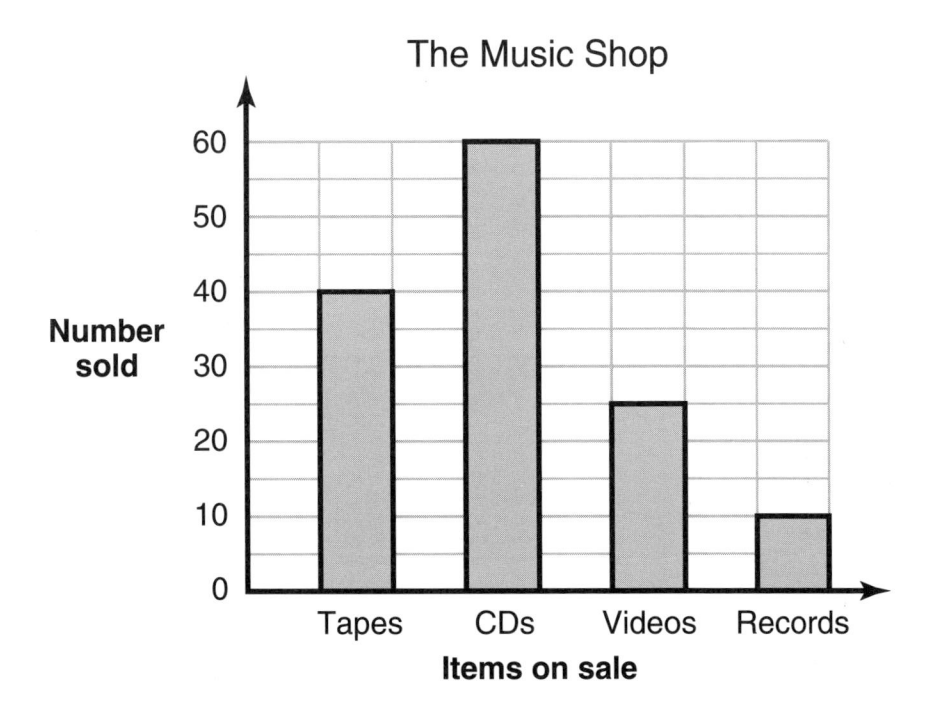

This bar graph shows the sales of different items on another day.

a List the items on sale.
b What is the best seller in the shop?
c How many tapes have been sold?
d How many more CDs than records have been sold?
e How many items have been sold altogether?

4 The shop also sells other items. This tally chart shows how well they are selling.

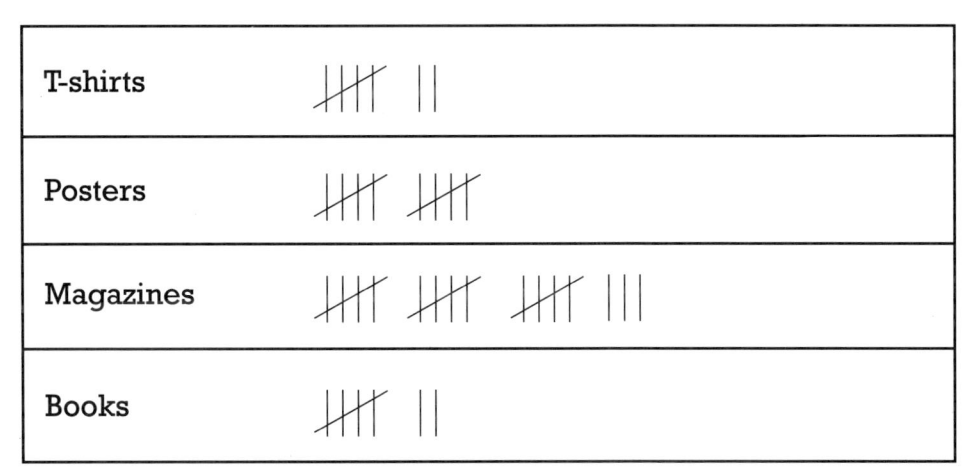

T-shirts							
Posters									
Magazines	|||| |||| |||| |||
Books							

a How many posters were sold?
b How many more magazines than books were sold?
c Which two items had equal sales?
d Fill in the table on Worksheet 1.
e Draw a bar graph of the table on your worksheet.

Get Worksheet 1

4 MAKING SENSE OF STATISTICS

Using Data to Make Decisions

Collecting data can often help us to make decisions.

EXERCISE 2

1. Is a bicycle shed needed for the school?
   The head teacher decided to do a survey on who cycles to school.
   She put the results in a bar graph.

   a How many 3rd year pupils cycle to school?
   b How many 5th year pupils cycle to school?
   c Which year has the most cyclists?
   d How many more 2nd year than 5th year pupils cycle to school?
   e How many pupils altogether cycle to school?
   f Should a cycle shed be built? Give reasons for your answer.

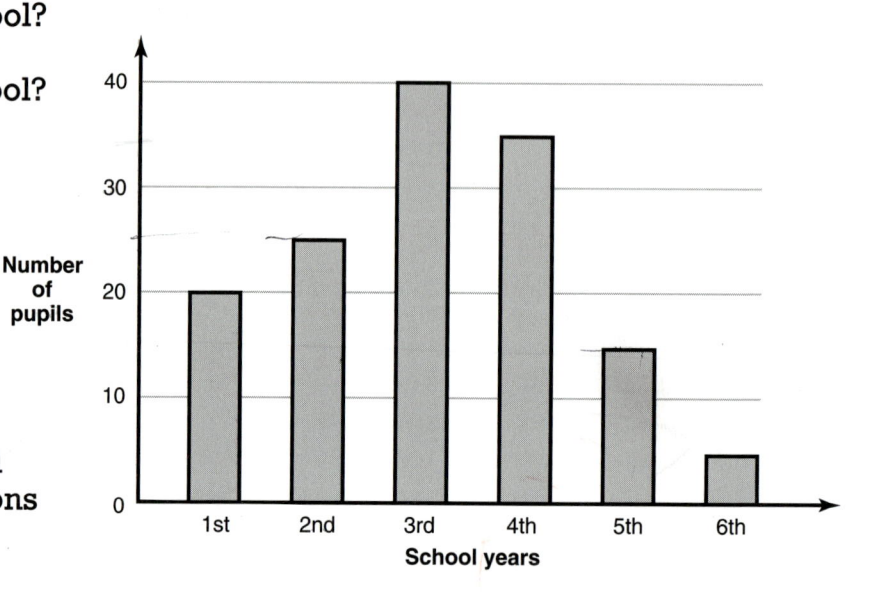

2. 500 people were asked to vote for their favourite type of computer game. The results were used to make the chart.

   a How many people does one square represent?
   b Which is the most popular type of game?
   c How many voted for a sports game?
   d How many altogether voted for a sci-fi and a mystery game?
   e Which two types of games got the same amount of votes?
   f List the games in order of popularity, putting the most popular first.

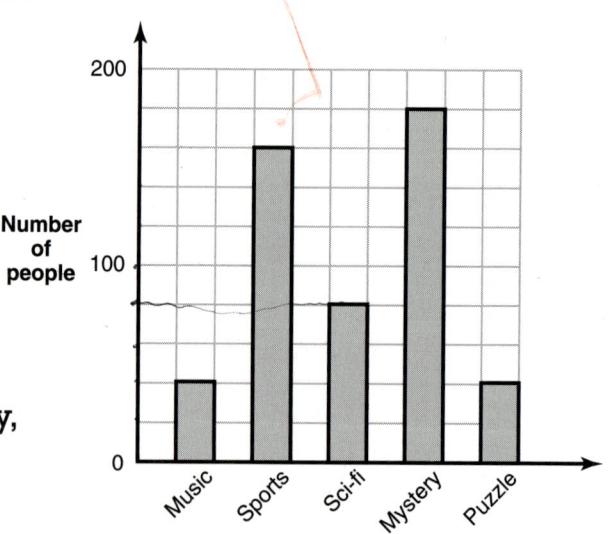

4 MAKING SENSE OF STATISTICS

3 Andrew repeated this survey with his class. Here are their 30 replies.

Music	Sci-fi	Music	Mystery	Sports
Mystery	Music	Sci-fi	Mystery	Music
Music	Puzzles	Mystery	Sports	Mystery
Sports	Sports	Sci-fi	Sports	Mystery
Sci-fi	Mystery	Puzzles	Mystery	Sports
Mystery	Sports	Sci-fi	Sports	Sci-fi

Use Worksheet 2 to help you sort them out and draw a graph.

Get Worksheet 2

4 At the school Hallowe'en disco a record was kept of the crisp sales.

To start with the school had 50 packets of each flavour.

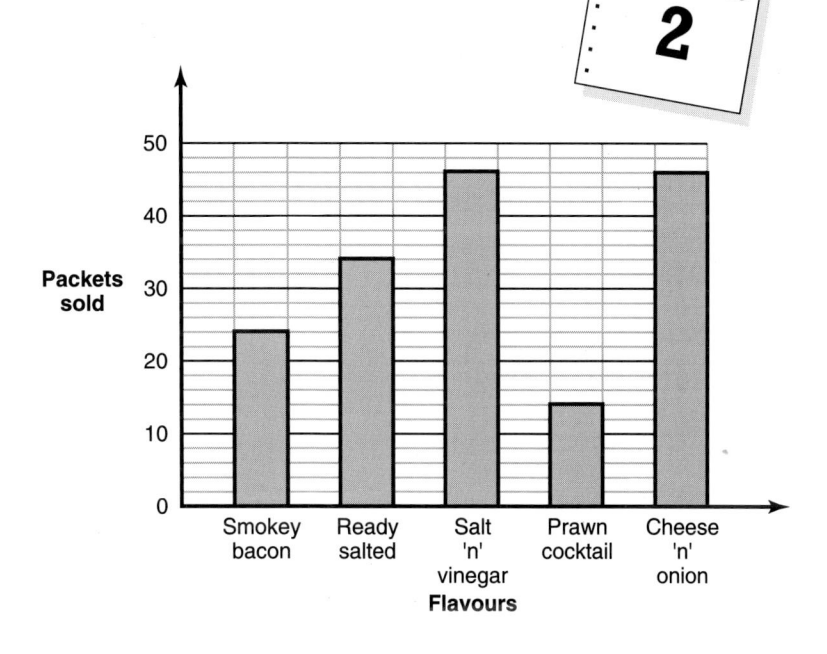

a Copy and complete the table below.

Flavours	**Number sold**	**Number left**
Smokey bacon	24	50 – 24 = **26**
Ready salted		
Salt 'n' vinegar		
Prawn cocktail		
Cheese 'n' onion		

b How many packets of crisps were sold altogether?
c How many packets of crisps were left?
d Is there a flavour you would not order for the next disco?

35

EXERCISE 3

1. The line graph shows the sales of the music shop in the ten weeks leading up to Christmas.
   Sales in week 2 made £400.

   a. How much money was made in week 3?
   b. How much money was made in week 9?
   c. In which week were the sales highest?
   d. In which week were the sales lowest?
   e. In which week was the money made on sales £300?
   f. Copy and complete this table. Use your calculator to add up the total sales.

Week	1	2	3	4	5	6	7	8	9	10	Total sales
Sales (£)	500	400	500								

2. Here is a line graph showing the temperature for one day during the heatwave.

   a. What was the temperature at 9 am?
   b. What was the temperature at 12 noon?
   c. At what time did the temperature reach its hottest?
   d. At what two times in the day was the temperature 28 °C?
   e. For how long did the temperature stay at 33 °C?
   f. What was the fall in temperature from 5 pm to 6 pm?
   g. What was:
      (i) the hottest temperature
      (ii) the coolest temperature?

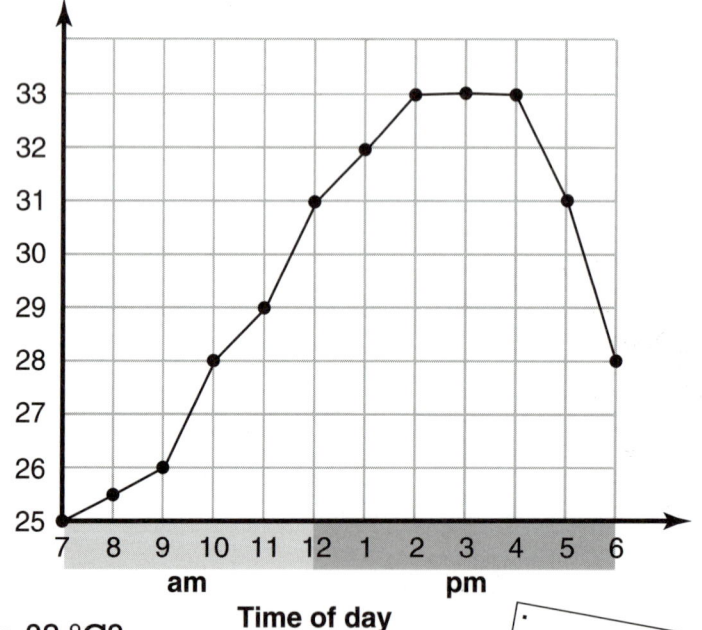

Do Worksheet 3

4 MAKING SENSE OF STATISTICS

Pie Charts

EXERCISE 4

Ask your teacher for a pie chart fractions template.

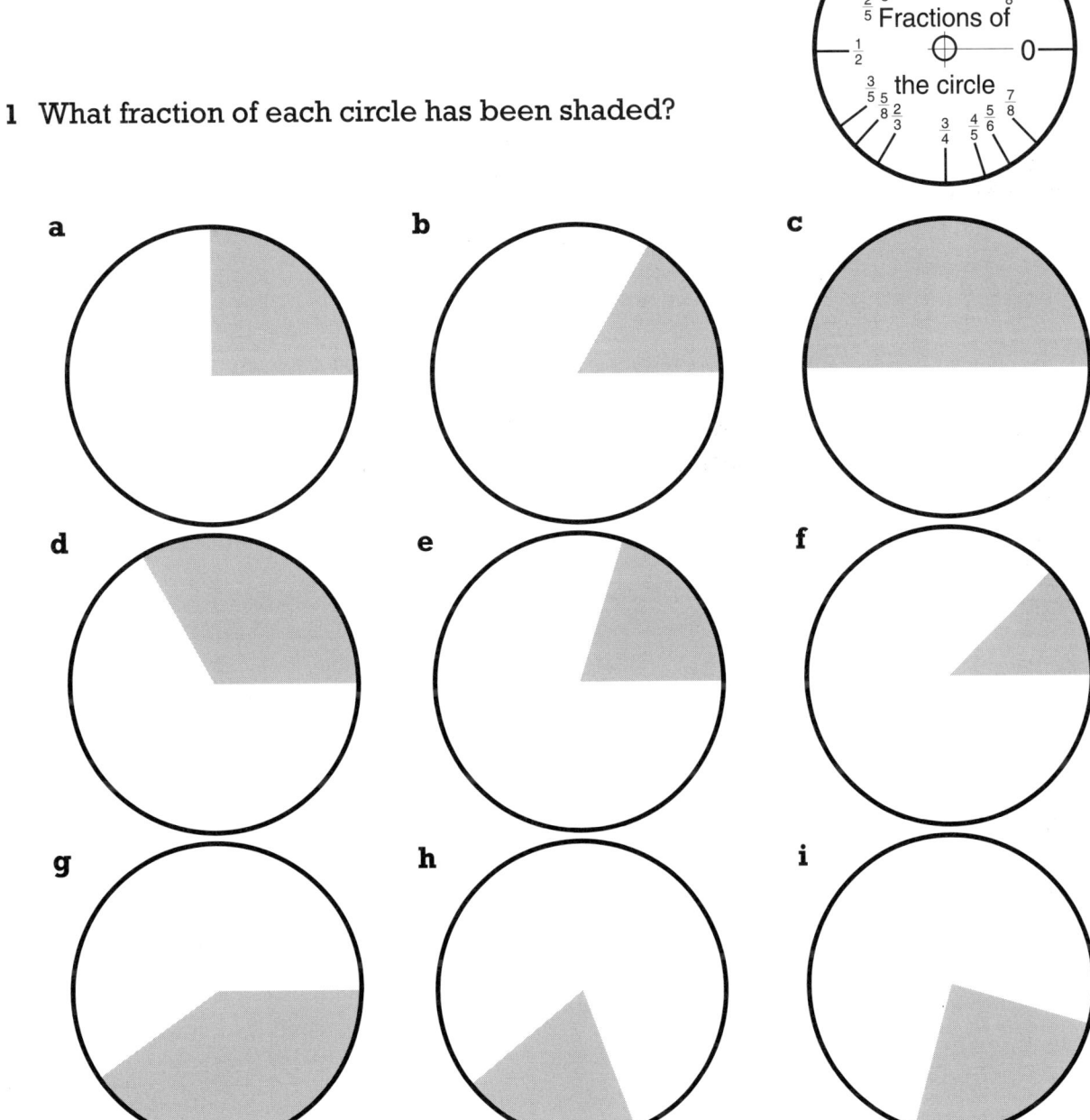

1 What fraction of each circle has been shaded?

a b c

d e f

g h i

37

4 MAKING SENSE OF STATISTICS

2 This pie chart shows how Hassan spends his pocket money.

Copy the sentences and fill in the blanks using the fractions below.

a Hassan spends .... of his pocket money on sweets and drinks.

b Hassan spends .... of his pocket money on comics.

c Hassan puts .... of his pocket money into his bank account.

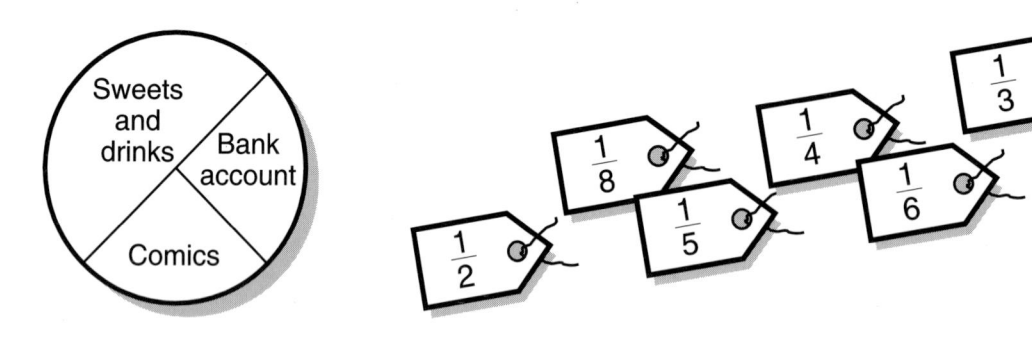

Fractions available: $\frac{1}{2}$, $\frac{1}{8}$, $\frac{1}{5}$, $\frac{1}{4}$, $\frac{1}{6}$, $\frac{1}{3}$

3 This pie chart shows how Mrs Smith spends her housekeeping money each week.

Copy and fill in the table below.

Item	Food	Bills	Rent	Clothes
Fraction				

4 Some pupils of Kelson High School were asked which flavour of ice-cream they preferred. Use the table below to draw a pie chart on Worksheet 4.

Flavour	Chocolate	Vanilla	Coffee	Mint	Strawberry
Fraction	$\frac{1}{3}$	$\frac{1}{4}$	$\frac{1}{8}$	$\frac{1}{6}$	$\frac{1}{8}$

Get Worksheet 4

CHECK-UP ON STATISTICS

1 This line graph shows the number of vehicles passing through a village on the outskirts of a large town at different times of the day.

   a How many vehicles were recorded at:
      (i) 7 am   (ii) 5 pm?
   b When were the busiest times of the day?
   c When was the quietest time of the day?
   d At what times were 250 vehicles recorded?

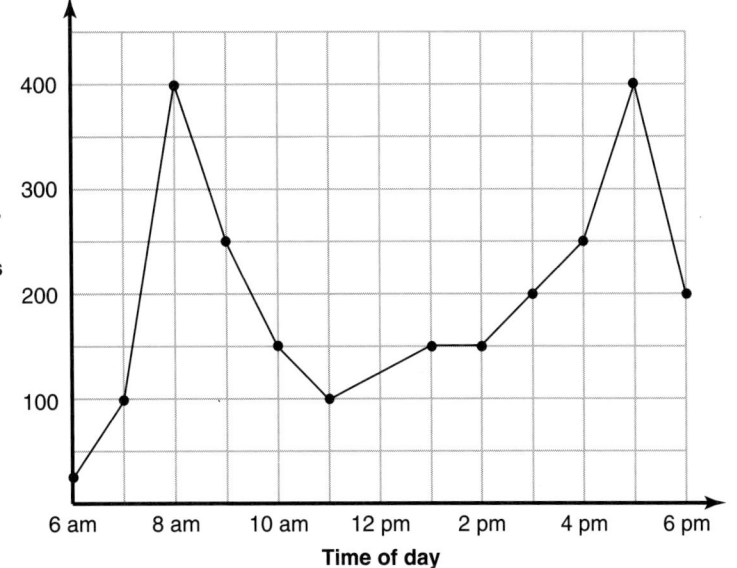

2 This bar graph shows how many cans of soft drinks were sold at the school Hallowe'en disco.

   a Which was the most popular drink?
   b How many cans of lemon were sold?
   c Which flavour sold the least number of cans?
   d How many more cans of cola than orange were sold?

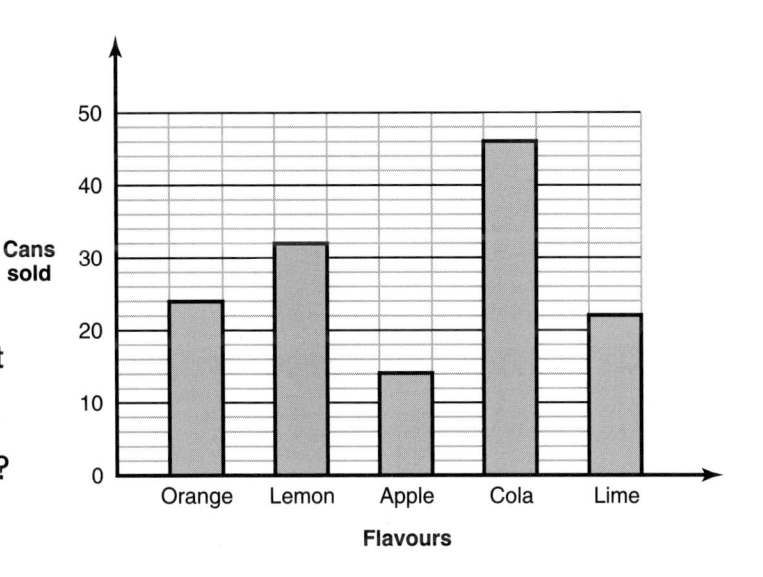

3 This pie chart shows eye colour in a class.

   a Which is the most common eye colour?
   b What fraction of the class has:
      (i) green eyes
      (ii) brown eyes?
   c If there are 30 pupils altogether, how many have blue eyes?

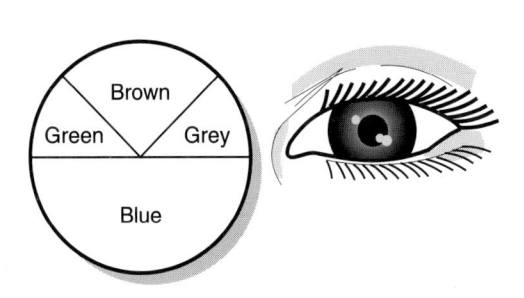

5 FRACTIONS, DECIMALS AND PERCENTAGES

Fractions

EXERCISE 1

Remember

1 part out of 3 is shaded.
We say one third of the circle is shaded.
We write: $\frac{1}{3}$ is shaded.

1 What fraction of this shape is shaded?

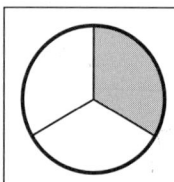

Remember

$\frac{1}{3}$ is shaded
$\frac{2}{3}$ is not shaded

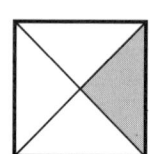

2 What fraction of this shape is not shaded?

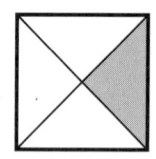

3 $\frac{2}{5}$ of another shape is shaded.

   What fraction of it is unshaded?

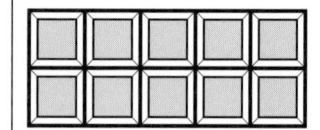

Remember

A chocolate bar has 10 squares.
Greg eats $\frac{1}{5}$ of the bar.
How many squares does he eat?

$\frac{1}{5}$ of 10 = 2 squares

4 Another chocolate bar has 12 squares.
   Julie eats $\frac{1}{4}$ of the bar.

   How many squares does she eat?

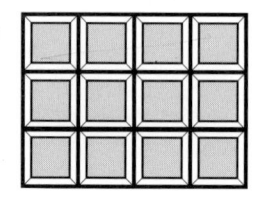

40

5 FRACTIONS, DECIMALS AND PERCENTAGES

Fraction Problems

A giant bar of chocolate has 20 squares.

Karen eats 1 square.

Karen eats $\frac{1}{20}$ of the bar.

$\frac{19}{20}$ of the bar is left.

EXERCISE 2

1. There are 50 stamps on the sheet. Mark tears 1 stamp off.

   a What fraction of the sheet of stamps does Mark tear off?
   b What fraction of the sheet is left?

2. A jar holds 20 sweets. Only 1 sweet are orange.

   a What fraction of the sweets is orange?
   b What fraction are not orange?

3. There are 30 Christmas stamps on the sheet. Rick tears 5 stamps off.

   a What fraction of the sheet of stamps does Rick tear off?
   b What fraction of the sheet is left?

4. There are 100 sweets in the jar. 20 of them are mints.

   a What fraction of the sweets are mints?
   b What fraction are not mints?

Do Worksheet 1

5 FRACTIONS, DECIMALS AND PERCENTAGES

Special Fractions – Percentages

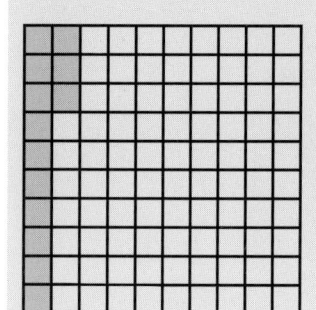

There are 100 squares here.
13 squares are shaded.
$\frac{13}{100}$ are shaded.
The fraction is 13 out of 100.
We often say **13 per cent** instead.
We write: **13%** of the big square is shaded.

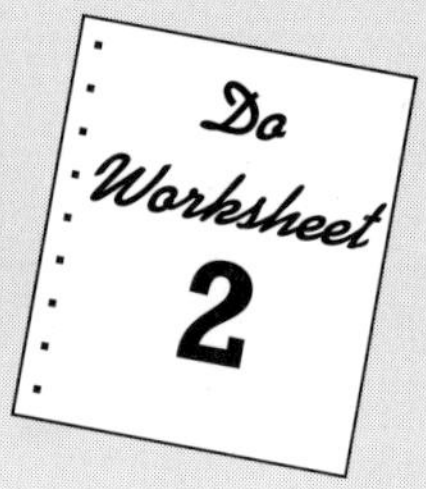

Do Worksheet 2

EXERCISE 3

1 a What percentage has been shaded?

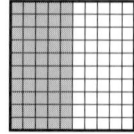

   b What fraction has been shaded?

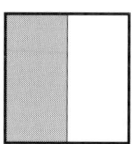

   c Can you see that 50% is the same as $\frac{1}{2}$?

2 a What percentage has been shaded?

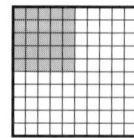

   b What fraction has been shaded?

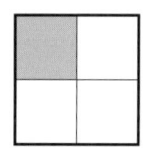

   c Can you see that 25% is the same as $\frac{1}{4}$?

3 Each pair of pictures below leads to similar findings.
   What does each pair show?

   a   b 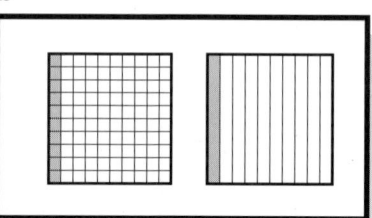   c

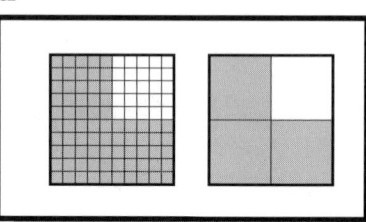

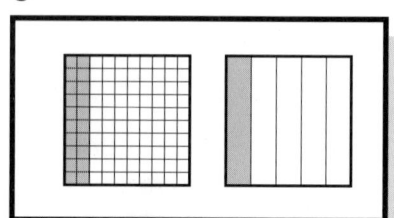

42

5 FRACTIONS, DECIMALS AND PERCENTAGES

Fractions and Percentages

We use these *links* to help us work out percentages without using a calculator.

$50\% = \frac{1}{2}$ $25\% = \frac{1}{4}$ $10\% = \frac{1}{10}$ $20\% = \frac{1}{5}$ $75\% = \frac{3}{4}$

Example

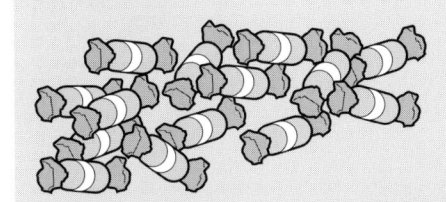

Sabrina has 14 sweets.
She says, 'You can have 50% of my sweets.'
How many would you get?

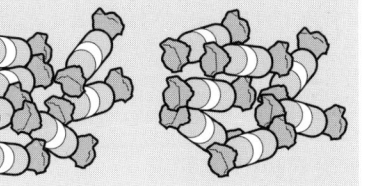

50% of 14 is the same as $\frac{1}{2}$ of 14.
So the answer is 7.

EXERCISE 4

1. Class 1B has 24 pupils in it.
   Mr Hardy said, '25% of the class is off today.'
   How many pupils are off school?

   Remember $25\% = \frac{1}{4}$

2. 50% of 18 sweets
   = $\frac{1}{2}$ of 18
   = 9 sweets

   Work out the following in the same way:

   a 50% of £40   b 50% of 36 pencils
   c 50% of 30 pence   d 50% of 4 people

3. 10% of 40 sweets
   = $\frac{1}{10}$ of 40
   = 4 sweets

   Work out the following in a similar way:

   a 25% of 20 pence   b 10% of £50   c 20% of £35
   d 25% of 16 pence   e 10% of £60   f 20% of £20
   g 25% of 40 pence   h 10% of £10   i 20% of £40

Do Worksheet 3

43

5 FRACTIONS, DECIMALS AND PERCENTAGES

Fractions into Decimals

Calculator work
We know that **1 split into 2 equal parts**  gives the answer $\frac{1}{2}$.
If we key in [1] [÷] [2] [=] the answer is [0.5]
$\frac{1}{2}$ **is the same as 0.5**.

We can turn **fractions** into **decimals** by **dividing**.
$\frac{3}{4}$ is changed by working out [3] [÷] [4] [=]
$\frac{3}{4} = 0.75$

EXERCISE 5

1 Use your calculator to change these fractions into decimals.

- **a** $\frac{1}{5}$
- **b** $\frac{1}{8}$
- **c** $\frac{1}{4}$
- **d** $\frac{1}{10}$
- **e** $\frac{7}{10}$
- **f** $\frac{3}{5}$
- **g** $\frac{11}{20}$
- **h** $\frac{4}{5}$
- **i** $\frac{22}{50}$
- **j** $\frac{45}{50}$
- **k** $\frac{1}{20}$
- **l** $\frac{9}{25}$

2 a Use your calculator to show that $\frac{1}{2}$ and $\frac{3}{6}$ both equal 0.5.
 b Use your calculator to find which of the following are equal to $\frac{1}{4}$:
  (i) $\frac{2}{8}$ (ii) $\frac{5}{20}$ (iii) $\frac{6}{9}$ (iv) $\frac{7}{25}$ (v) $\frac{8}{32}$

3 Eight pupils are each asked to write down a fraction.
Use your calculator to find who wrote equal fractions.

Ann $\frac{12}{30}$ Jim $\frac{2}{5}$ Declan $\frac{3}{4}$ Ella $\frac{7}{10}$ Dan $\frac{15}{20}$ Amy $\frac{21}{30}$ Philip $\frac{5}{10}$ Dionne $\frac{1}{2}$

4 Use your calculator to match up the following cards in pairs.

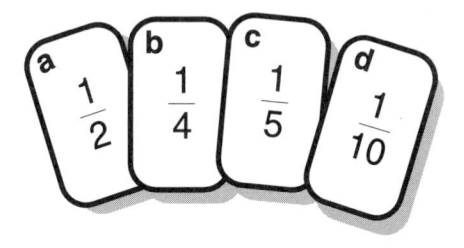

- **a** $\frac{1}{2}$
- **b** $\frac{1}{4}$
- **c** $\frac{1}{5}$
- **d** $\frac{1}{10}$
- **e** $\frac{20}{100}$
- **f** $\frac{50}{100}$
- **g** $\frac{25}{100}$
- **h** $\frac{10}{100}$

44

5 FRACTIONS, DECIMALS AND PERCENTAGES

Percentages into Decimals

We can change percentages into decimals in the same way.

17% mean $\frac{17}{100}$ so we change it by pressing [17] [÷] [100] [=]

17% = 0.17

EXERCISE 6

Use your calculator to change these percentages into decimals.

1. 24%   [24] [÷] [100] [=]
2. 37%   [37] [÷] [100] [=]
3. 16%   [16] [÷] [100] [=]
4. 9%   [9] [÷] [100] [=]
5. 45%
6. 53%
7. 82%
8. 11%
9. 96%
10. 1%
11. 57%
12. 7%

'of' means '×'

Example

There are 25 pupils in Class 2T.
$\frac{3}{5}$ of Class 2T walk to school.
How many pupils is this?
For $\frac{3}{5}$ of 25 we do this: [3] [÷] [5] [×] [2] [5] [=] 15 pupils

EXERCISE 7

1. Use your calculator to work these out.

   a. $\frac{2}{5}$ of £120   [2] [÷] [5] [×] [1] [2] [0] [=]

   b. $\frac{3}{4}$ of £36
   c. $\frac{5}{8}$ of £160
   d. $\frac{1}{20}$ of £720
   e. $\frac{4}{5}$ of 1450 people

   f. $\frac{2}{5}$ of 35 pence
   g. $\frac{3}{4}$ of 84 metres
   h. $\frac{5}{6}$ of 108 sweets

2. There were 2560 people at a Rovers v United football match. $\frac{3}{5}$ of the people supported Rovers. How many supported Rovers?

3. Eva won £2000 in a competition. She spent $\frac{3}{4}$ of the money on a computer. How much did the computer cost?

4. $\frac{3}{8}$ of the jelly beans are red. The jar holds 744 jelly beans. How many red ones are there?

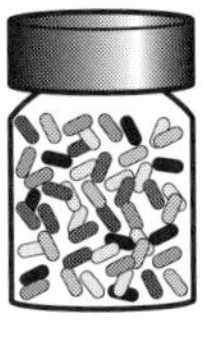

5. Katya had a piece of ribbon 4 metres long. She used $\frac{3}{8}$ of it to decorate a parcel. How much ribbon did she use?

CHECK-UP ON FRACTIONS, DECIMALS AND PERCENTAGES

1 This chocolate bar had 20 pieces.

What fraction is broken off?

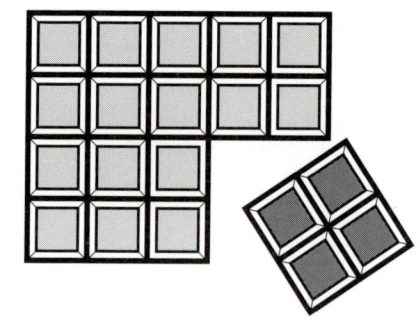

2 Copy this rectangle onto squared paper.

    a Colour $\frac{3}{20}$ of it red.

    b Colour $\frac{8}{20}$ of it yellow.

    c What fraction is left unshaded?

3 What percentage of this shape is shaded?

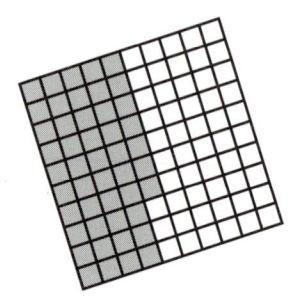

4 Copy and complete this table.

Fraction	$\frac{1}{2}$	$\frac{1}{4}$	$\frac{3}{4}$	
Percentage	50%			10%

5 a Change these fractions into decimals.

    (i) $\frac{1}{2}$ (ii) $\frac{3}{5}$ (iii) $\frac{9}{10}$

  b Change these percentages into decimals.

    (i) 17%   (ii) 85%   (iii) 7%

6 There are 125 bricks in a wall.
$\frac{2}{5}$ of the bricks are red.

How many red bricks are there?

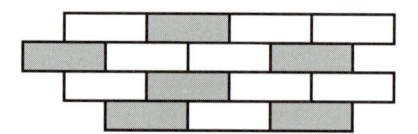

7 There are 460 coins in the money box.
$\frac{3}{20}$ of the coins are silver coins.

How many silver coins are there?

46

6 DISTANCES AND DIRECTIONS

Measuring and Recording

EXERCISE 1

1 Measure the length and breadth of this rectangle in centimetres.

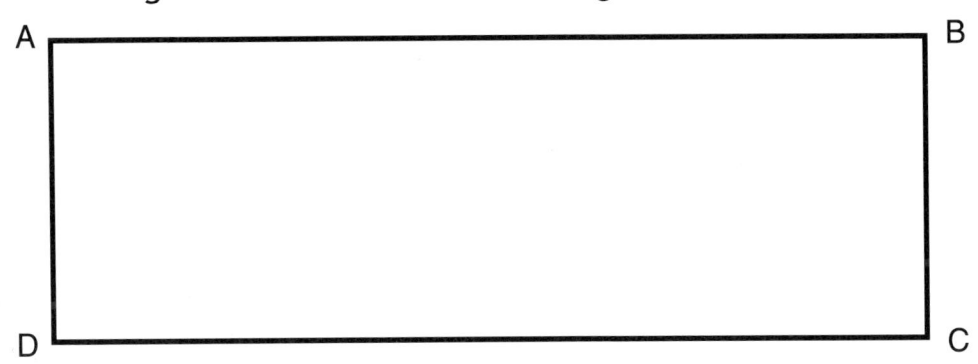

2 Draw a square with sides of 70 mm.

3 a Measure the sides of triangle XYZ in millimetres.
   (i) XY
   (ii) YZ
   (iii) ZX
  b Measure the size of the angles.
   (i) ∠XYZ
   (ii) ∠ZXY
   (iii) ∠YZX
  c Which two sides are the same size?
  d Which two angles are the same size?

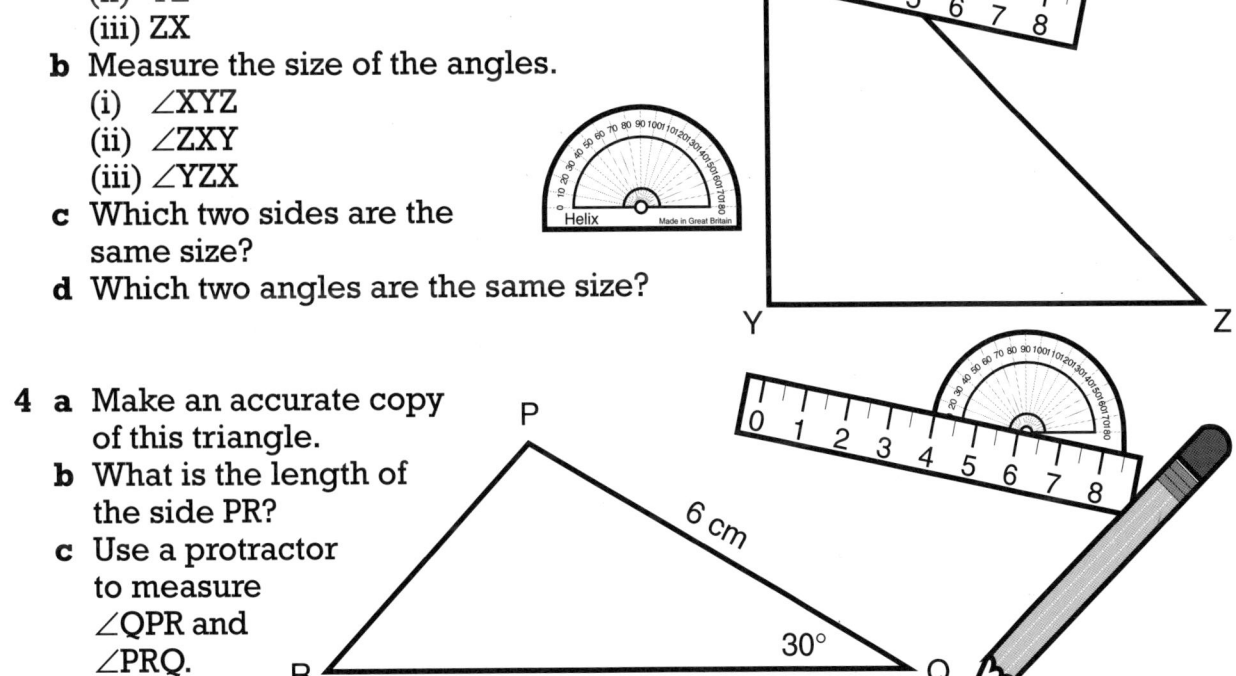

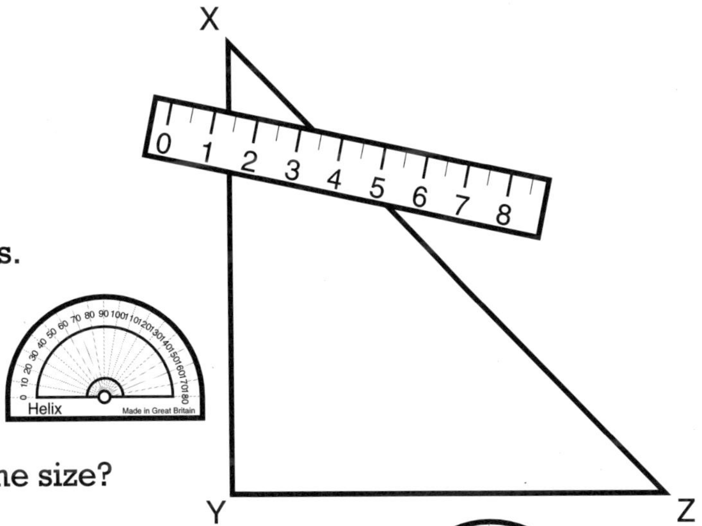

4 a Make an accurate copy of this triangle.
  b What is the length of the side PR?
  c Use a protractor to measure ∠QPR and ∠PRQ.

6 DISTANCES AND DIRECTIONS

5 Draw these shapes the correct size.

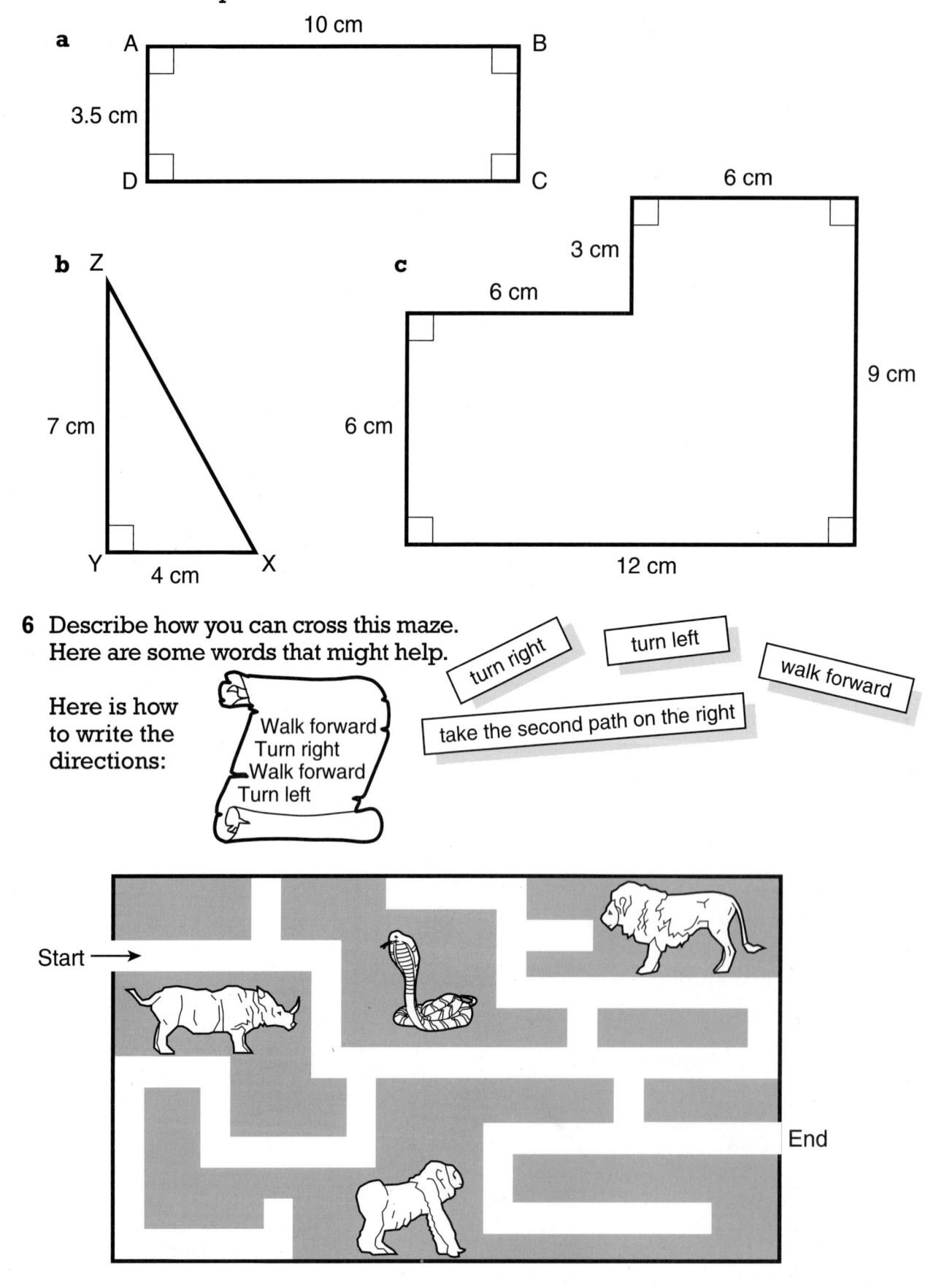

a Rectangle ABCD: AB = 10 cm, AD = 3.5 cm

b Triangle XYZ: ZY = 7 cm, YX = 4 cm, right angle at Y

c Shape with sides: 6 cm, 3 cm, 6 cm, 9 cm, 12 cm, 6 cm

6 Describe how you can cross this maze. Here are some words that might help.

turn right   turn left   walk forward
take the second path on the right

Here is how to write the directions:

Walk forward
Turn right
Walk forward
Turn left

Start → ... End

48

Directions

Remember

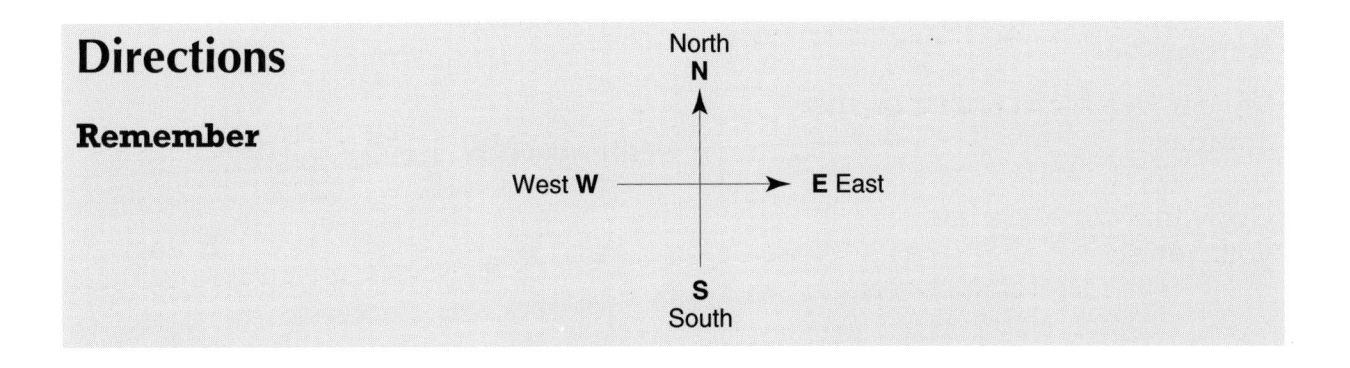

```
        North
          N
          ↑
West W ———→ E East
          ↓
          S
        South
```

EXERCISE 2

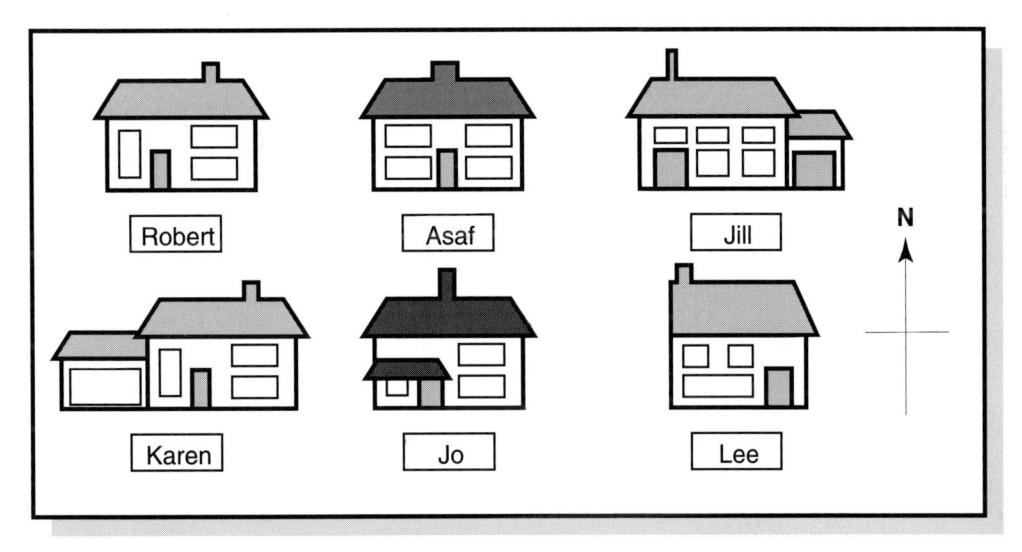

[Map showing six houses arranged in two rows of three, with a compass indicating North pointing up. Top row: Robert, Asaf, Jill. Bottom row: Karen, Jo, Lee.]

1. **a** Who lives to the **north** of Lee?
   b Who lives to the **south** of Robert?
   c Who lives to the **west** of Jo?
   d Who lives to the **north** of Karen?
   e Who lives to the **east** of Asaf?
   f Who lives to the **south** of Jill?
   g Who lives to the **east** of Jo?
   h Who lives to the **west** of Asaf?

2. **a** Lee's best friend lives in the house to the north of Karen.
   Who is Lee's best friend?
   b Asaf is the same age as the person who lives to the east of him.
   Who is the same age as Asaf?

3. Copy and complete: *(North, West, East, South)*

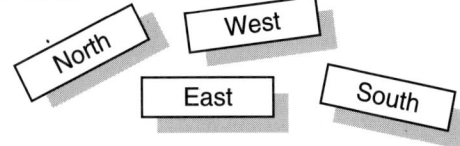

   a Jo lives to the .... of Asaf and to the .... of Karen.
   b Lee lives to the .... of Jo and to the .... of Jill.
   c Robert lives to the .... of Karen and to the .... of Asaf.
   d Asaf lives to the .... of Robert and to the .... of Jill.

49

6 DISTANCES AND DIRECTIONS

Remember

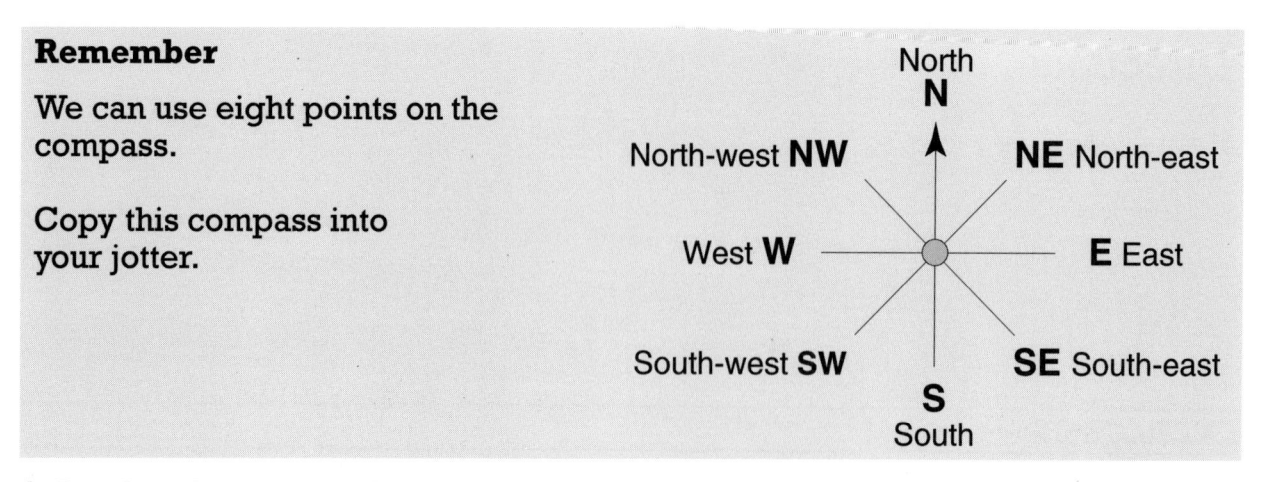

We can use eight points on the compass.

Copy this compass into your jotter.

North-west **NW** — **N** North — **NE** North-east
West **W** — **E** East
South-west **SW** — **S** South — **SE** South-east

4 Read each sentence. Look at the map. Decide if the sentence is true or false.

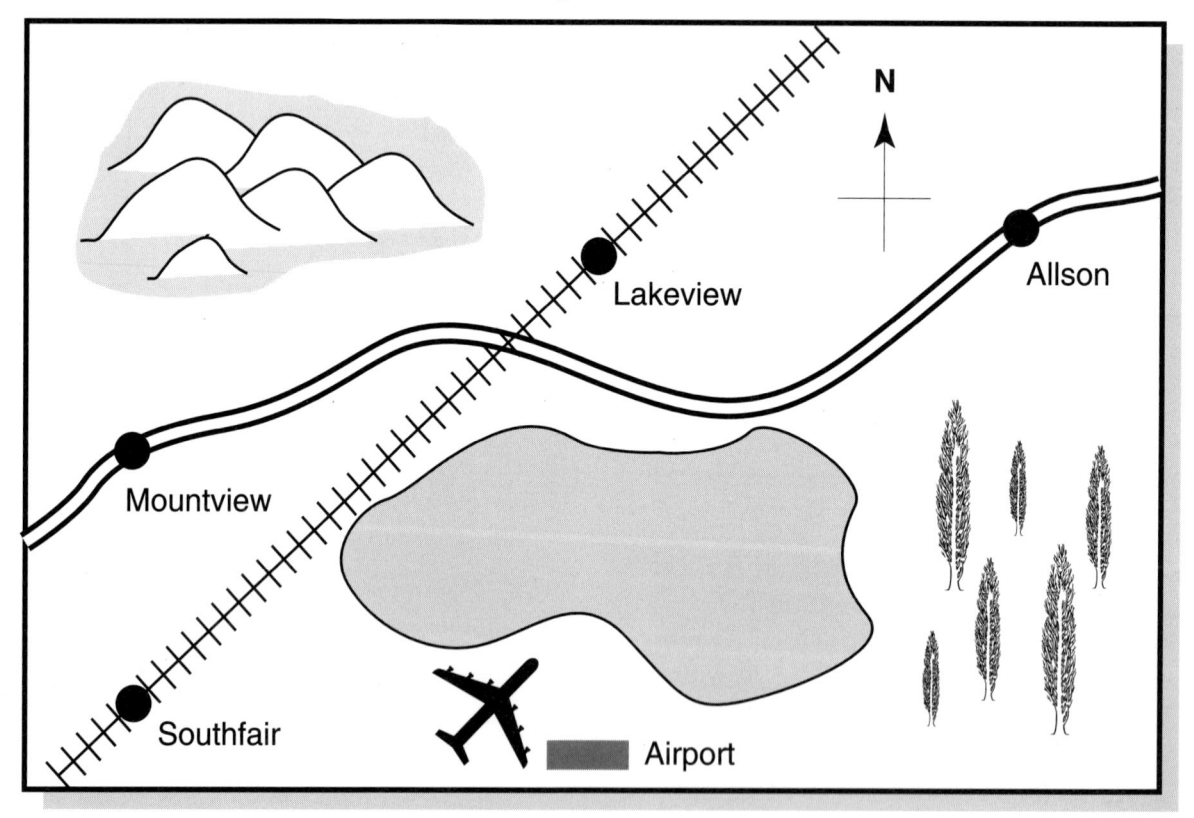

 a The airport lies south of the lake.
 b The railway runs south-west to north-east.
 c The forest lies west of the lake.
 d Mountview lies to the south-west of the airport.
 e The mountains lie to the west of Allson.
 f Lakeview lies to the north-west of Southfair.
 g The airport lies to the south-east of the mountains.
 h Allson lies to the north-west of the airport.
 i The forest lies to the south-east of the mountains.

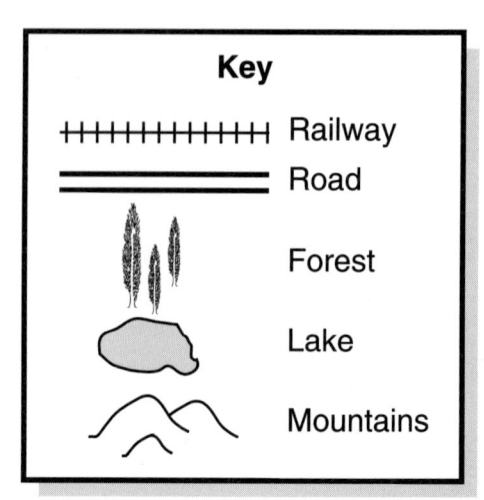

Key

++++++++ Railway
═══════ Road
Forest
Lake
Mountains

5

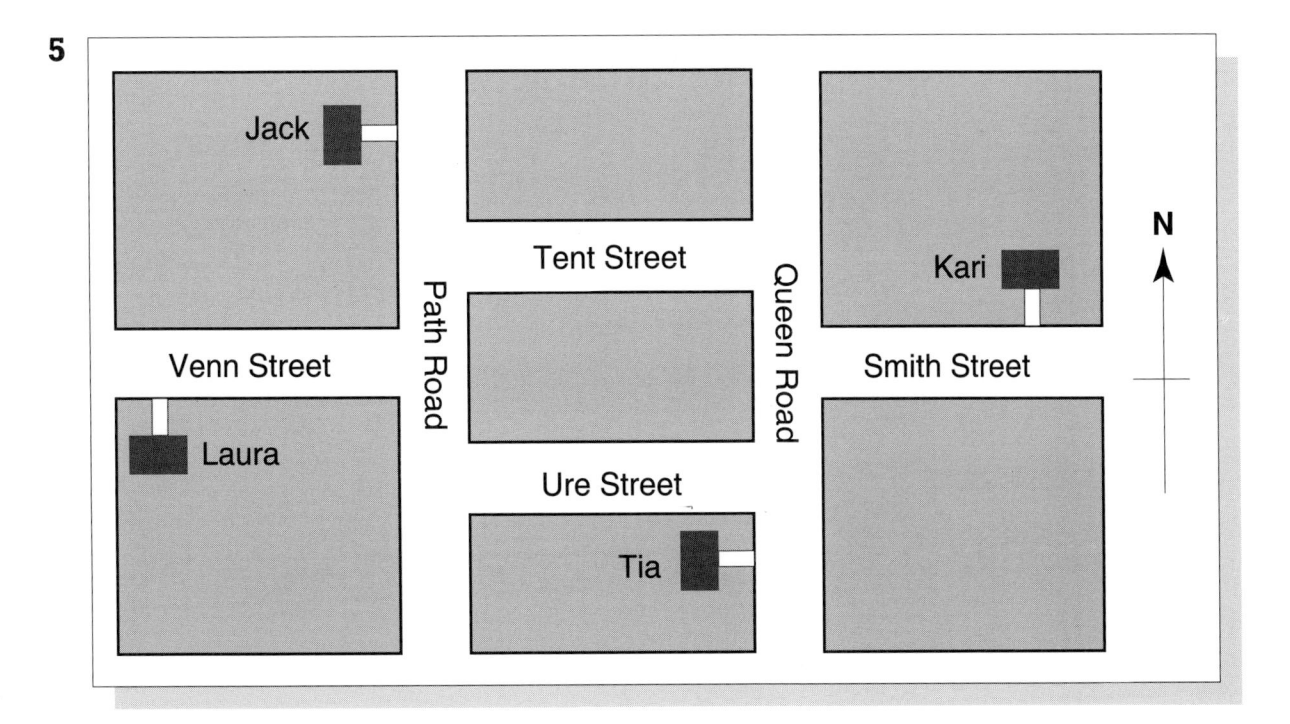

Use street names and compass points to help you answer each of the following.

a Describe how Jack gets from his house to Tia's house.
b How does Laura get from her house to Kari's house?

6 Describe your journey from **home** to **school**.

7 a Jayshree is driving along Ann Street towards the roundabout. In what direction is she travelling?
b Bill is driving along Gill Road towards the roundabout. In what direction is he travelling?
c Which road runs due east from the roundabout?
d Which road runs south-west to north-east?
e Which road runs north to the roundabout?

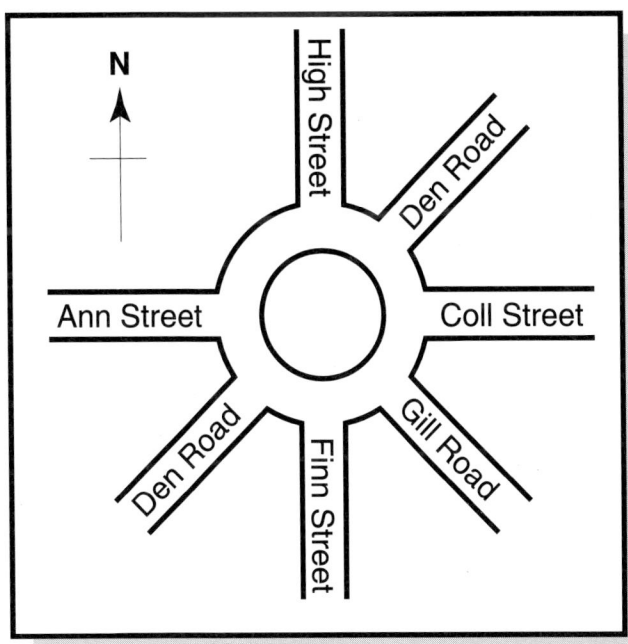

6 DISTANCES AND DIRECTIONS

Changing Direction: Turning Through Angles

Remember

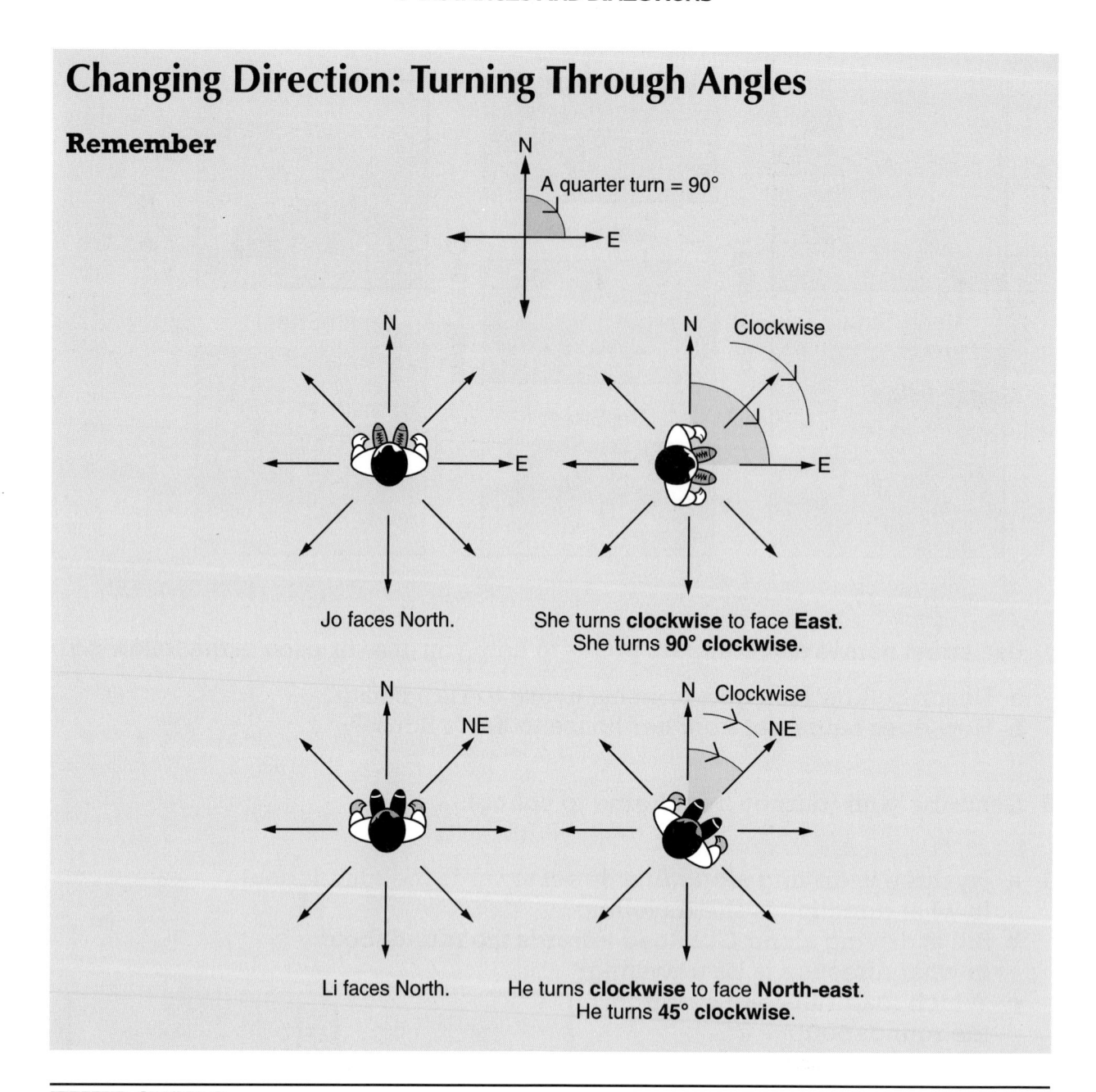

A quarter turn = 90°

Jo faces North.

She turns **clockwise** to face **East**.
She turns **90° clockwise**.

Li faces North.

He turns **clockwise** to face **North-east**.
He turns **45° clockwise**.

EXERCISE 3

1 What angle is turned through here?

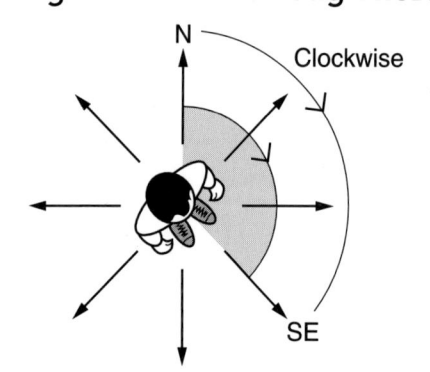

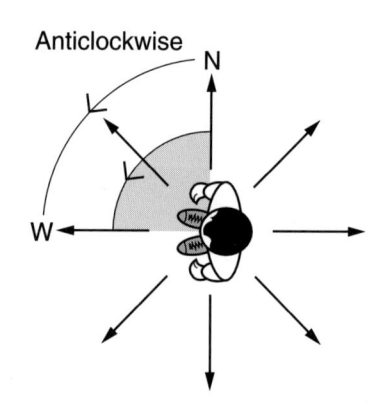

a From North to South-east clockwise **b** From North to West anticlockwise c From West to South-east anticlockwise 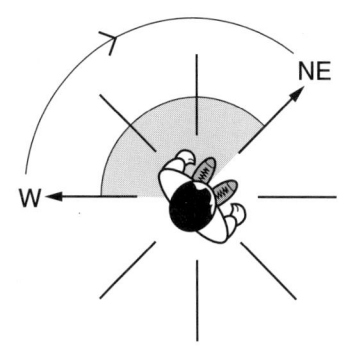   d From West to North-east clockwise

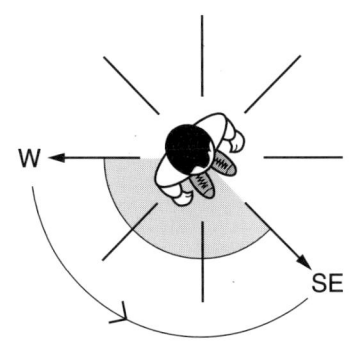

2 Describe the angle turned through. Use the word clockwise.

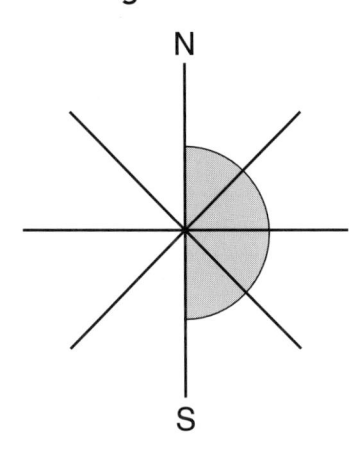

a From North to South 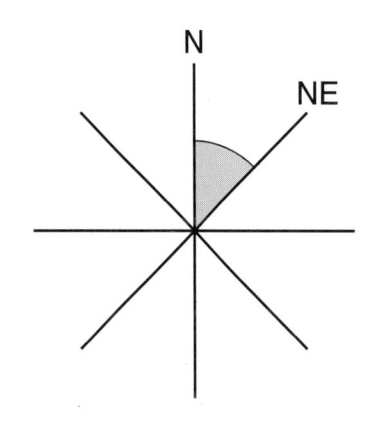   b From North to North-east

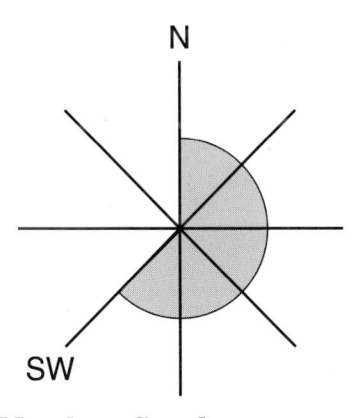

c From North to South-west 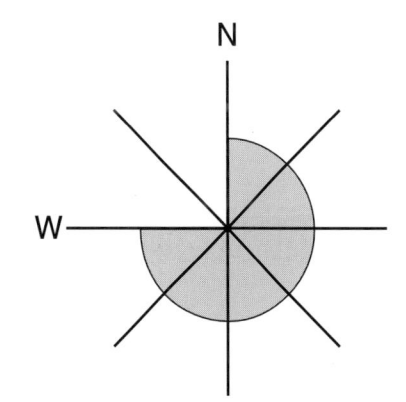   d From North to West

3 Use the compass to calculate the angle turned.
   a From North to West anticlockwise
   b From East to South-west clockwise
   c From North-east to West clockwise
   d From East to South anticlockwise
   e From West to North-west clockwise
   f From West to North-west anticlockwise
   g From South to North-west clockwise

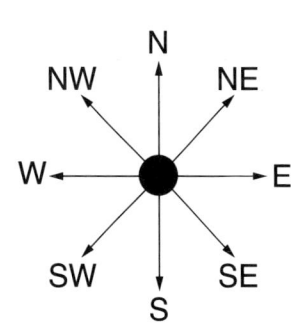

4 Follow the instructions and write down the new direction.

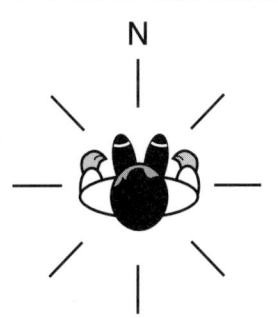

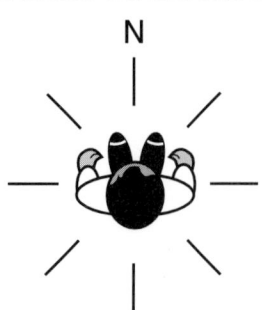

a Face North. Turn **90° clockwise**.

b Face North. Turn **270° clockwise**.

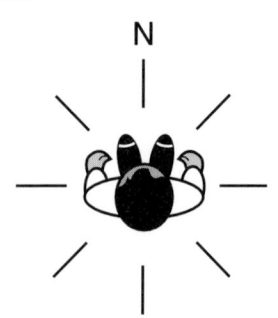

c Face North. Turn **135° clockwise**.

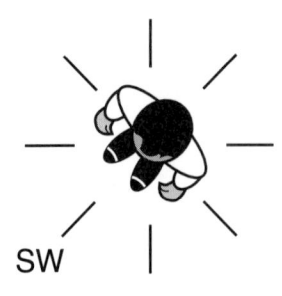

d Face South-west. Turn **90° clockwise**.

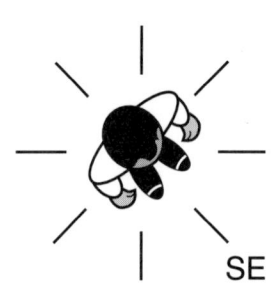

e Face South-east. Turn **180° clockwise**.

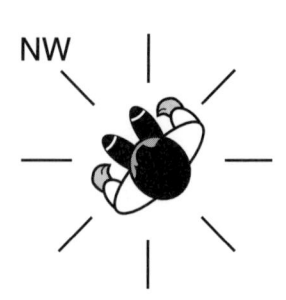

f Face North-west. Turn **90° anticlockwise**.

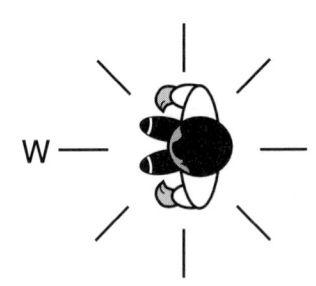

g Face West. Turn **135° anticlockwise**.

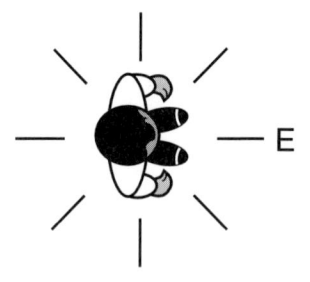

h Face East. Turn **315° clockwise**.

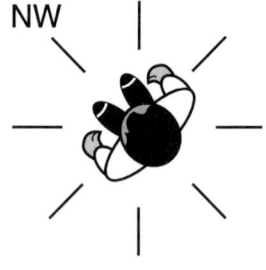

i Face North-west. Turn **360° clockwise**.

5 What turn is needed?

Remember to give the direction – **clockwise** or **anticlockwise**.

Example: I'm facing **North**. I want to face **South**.
Answer: **Turn 180° clockwise**.

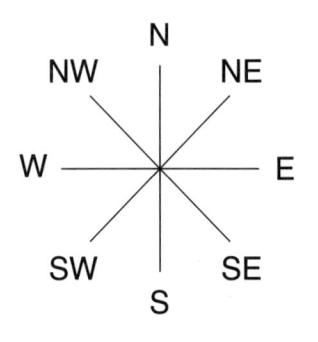

a I'm facing **East**. I want to face **South-west**.
b I'm facing **East**. I want to face **North**.
c I'm facing **West**. I want to face **South**.
d I'm facing **North-east**. I want to face **East**.
e I'm facing **North-west**. I want to face **South**.
f I'm facing **South**. I want to face **East**.
g I'm facing **West**. I want to face **South-east**.
h I'm facing **North**. I want to face **South-west**.

Three-figure Bearings

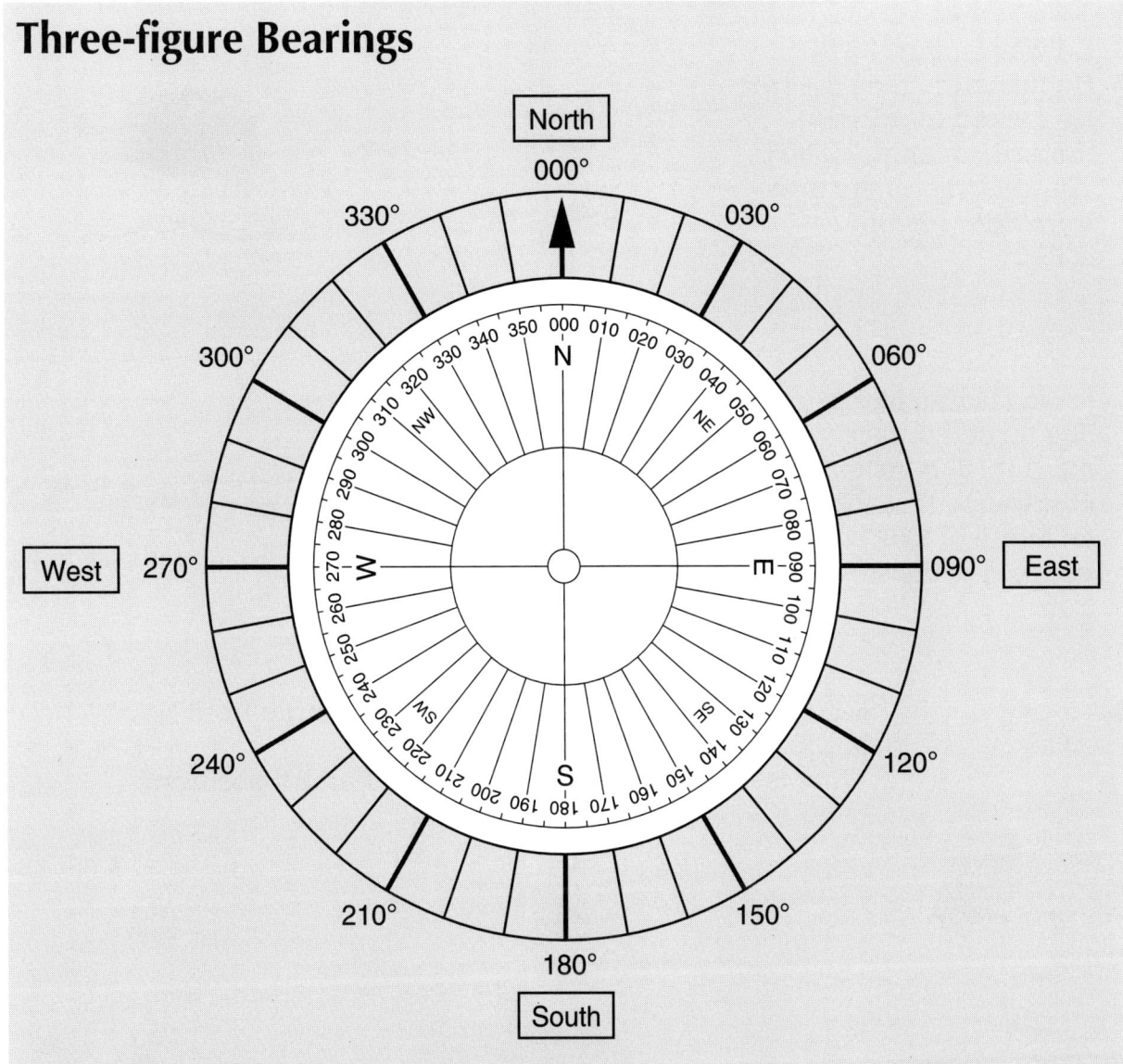

We can describe direction using **angle only**.

We measure the angle from **North**.

We **always** measure **clockwise**.

The 3-figure bearing for North is 000°.

EXERCISE 4

Use the diagram above to answer these questions.

1 What is the 3-figure bearing for East?

2 What is the 3-figure bearing for South?

3 What is the 3-figure bearing for West?

6 DISTANCES AND DIRECTIONS

Ed was facing North. He turned to face the tree. He turned **clockwise** through an angle of **90°**. The bearing of the tree from Ed's position is **090°**.

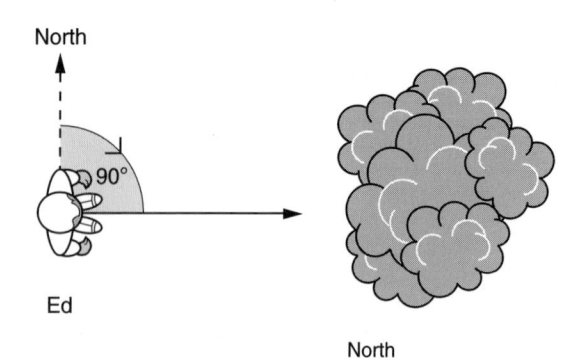

Jo was facing North. She turned to face the tree. She turned **clockwise** through an angle of **270°**. The bearing of the tree from Jo's position is **270°**.

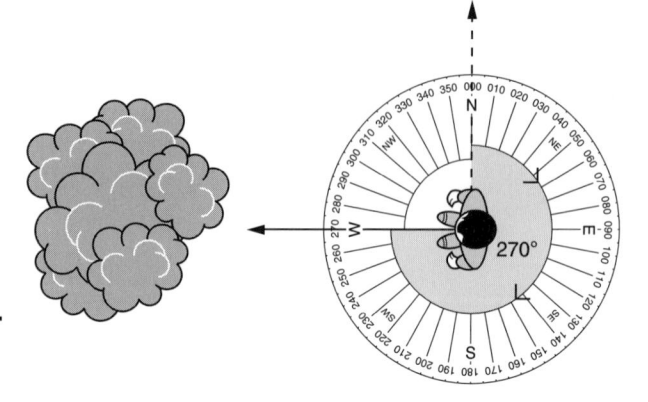

4 Kamil is facing the car. The clockwise angle from North is 180°.
What is the bearing of the car from Kamil's position?

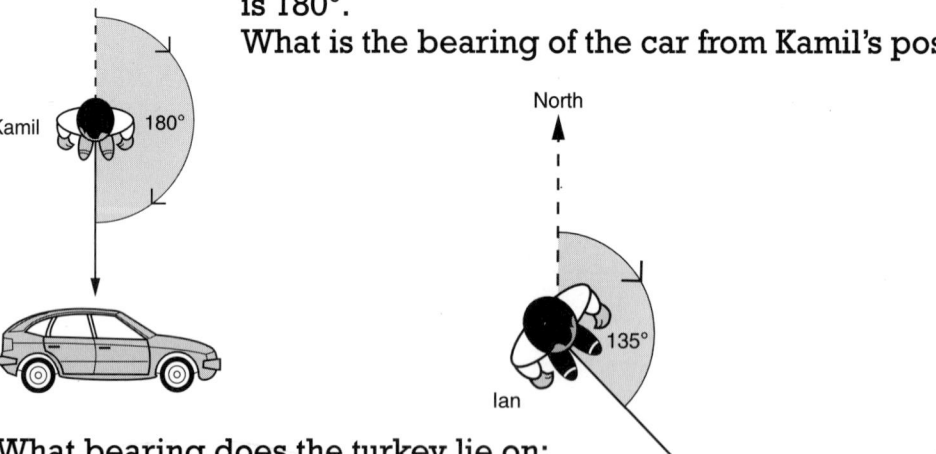

5 What bearing does the turkey lie on:

   a from Ian's position
   b from Glen's position?

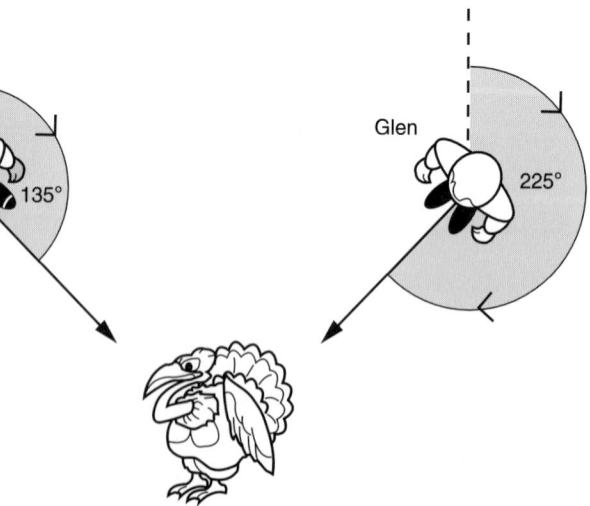

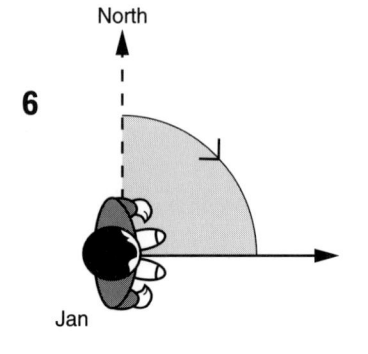

6 What bearing does the church lie on from Jan's position?

Remember a bearing must have 3 figures.

56

6 DISTANCES AND DIRECTIONS

7 Gemma, Jack, Liam and Toni are visiting a theme park.
From different points they take bearings to the top of the castle.

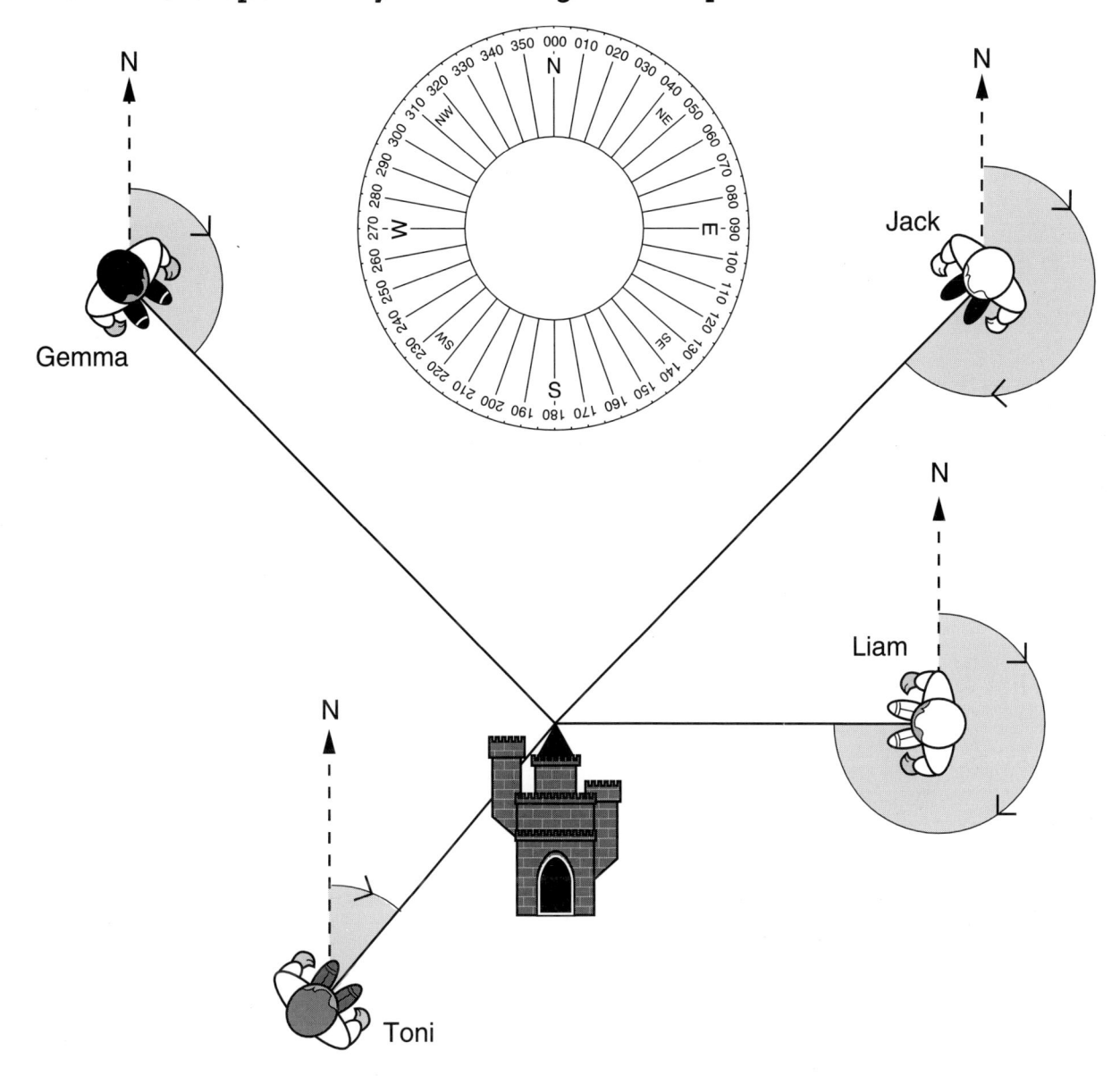

a Estimate the bearing from each position.
b Copy and complete the table by measuring the angles.

Position	Estimate	Angle (clockwise from N)	3-figure bearing
Gemma			
Jack			
Liam			
Toni			

57

CHECK-UP ON DISTANCES AND DIRECTIONS

1 a Draw these shapes the correct size.

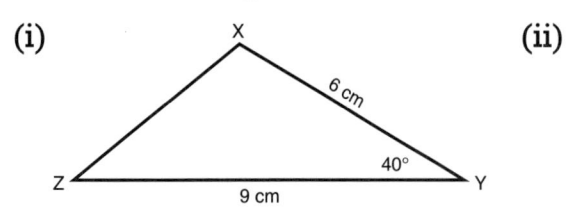

(i) Triangle XYZ with XY = 6 cm, ZY = 9 cm, angle at Y = 40°.

(ii) Stepped shape with sides 4 cm, 4 cm, 4 cm, 4 cm, 2 cm, 4 cm, 10 cm, 12 cm.

b Measure the size of the angles.
(i) ∠XZY   (ii) ∠YXZ

2 Describe this path using compass points.

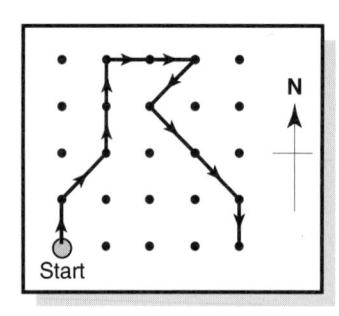

3 What angles have been turned through in these pictures?

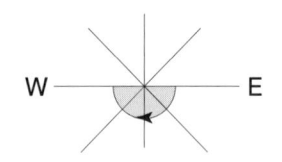

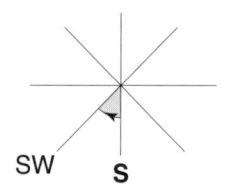

a From East to West clockwise.   **b** From South to South-west clockwise.

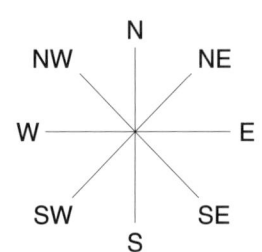

4 Describe what turn is needed.

a I'm facing North. I want to face East.
b I'm facing West. I want to face South-east.

5 What bearing does the church lie on:

a from Sven's position
b from Uma's position?

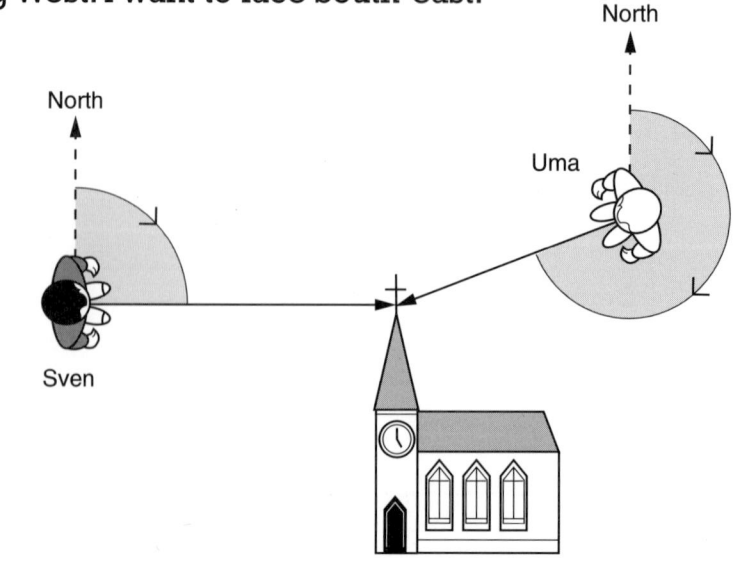

58

7 POSITIVE AND NEGATIVE NUMBERS: TEMPERATURE

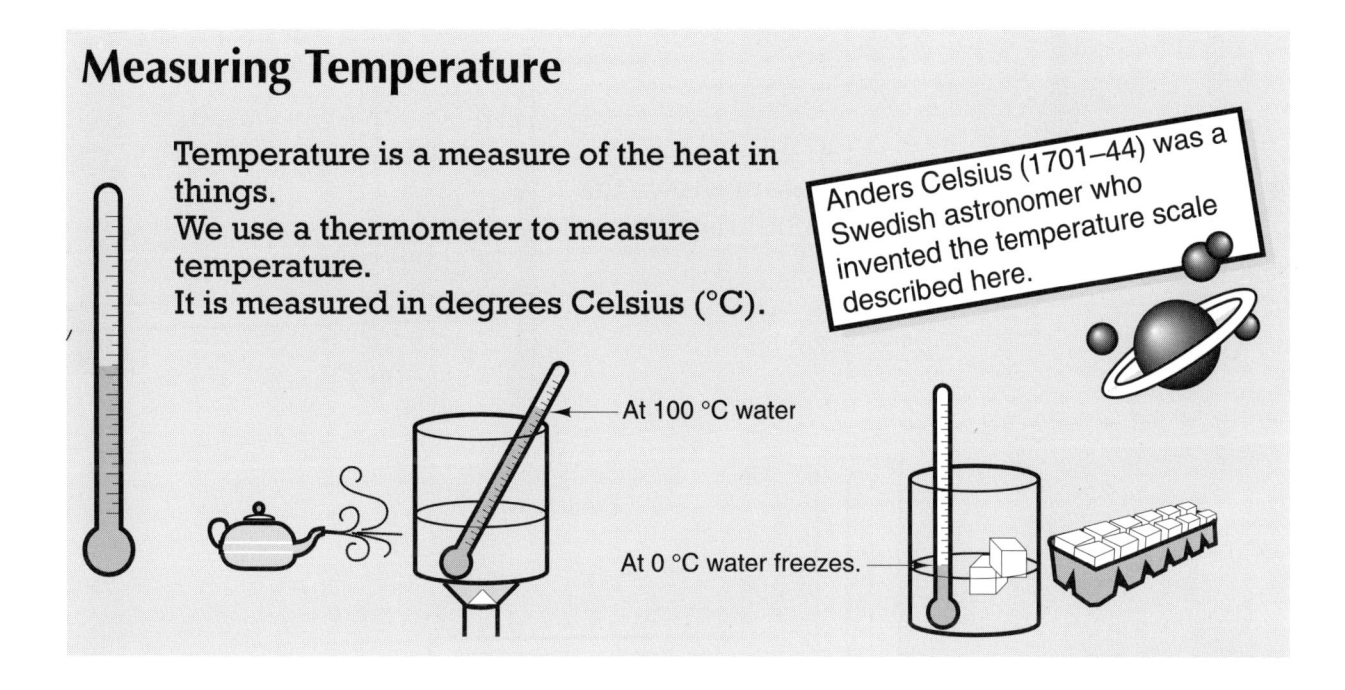

Measuring Temperature

Temperature is a measure of the heat in things.
We use a thermometer to measure temperature.
It is measured in degrees Celsius (°C).

At 100 °C water

At 0 °C water freezes.

Anders Celsius (1701–44) was a Swedish astronomer who invented the temperature scale described here.

EXERCISE 1

1

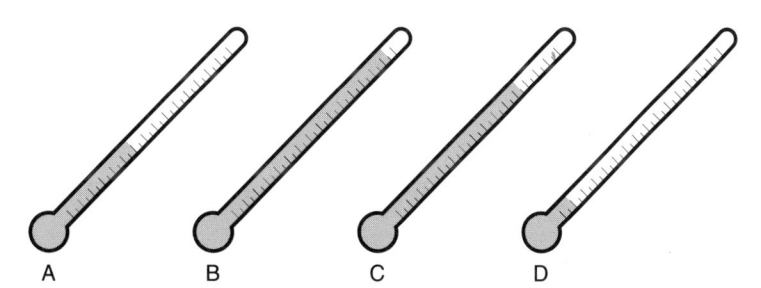

a Which thermometer shows the highest temperature?
b Which one shows the lowest temperature?

2

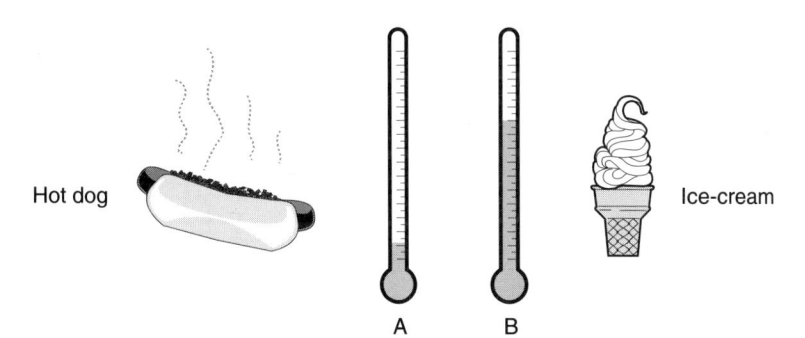

Match up the thermometer with the right food.

7 POSITIVE AND NEGATIVE NUMBERS: TEMPERATURE

3 Which of these two thermometers shows the best temperature for a skiing holiday?

4 Which of these two thermometers shows the best temperature for a beach holiday?

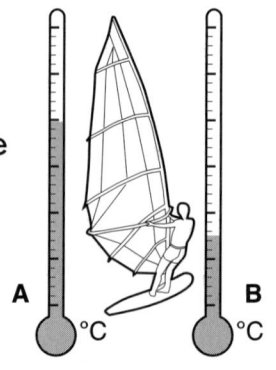

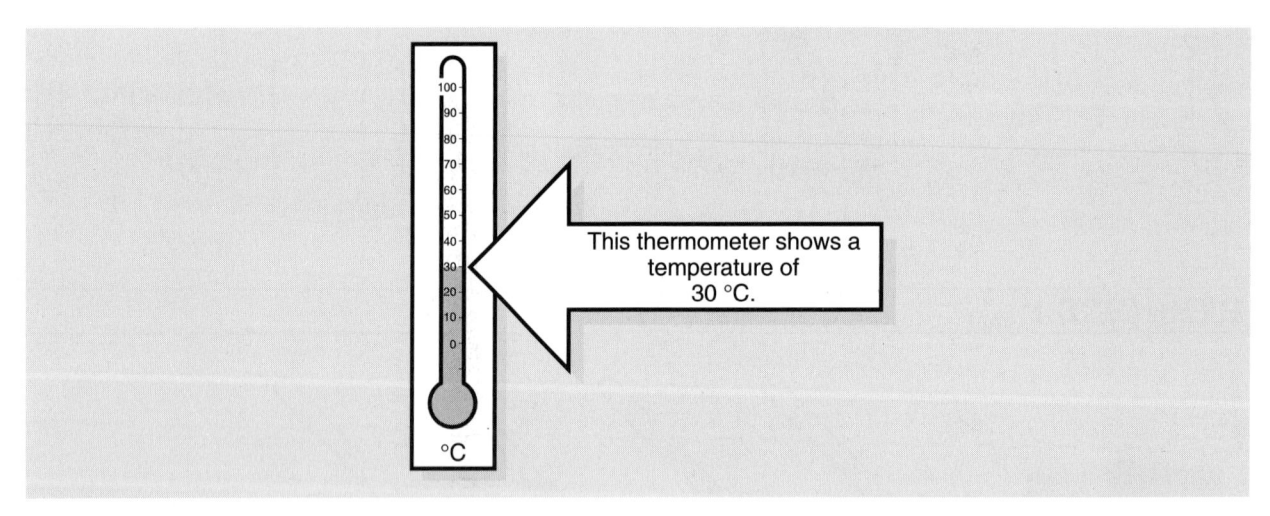

This thermometer shows a temperature of 30 °C.

EXERCISE 2

1 Write down each of these temperature readings.

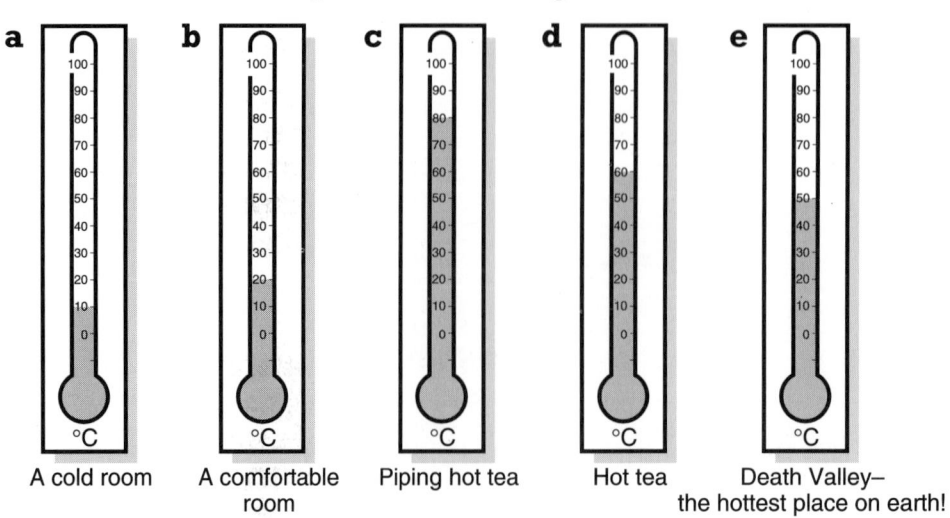

a A cold room
b A comfortable room
c Piping hot tea
d Hot tea
e Death Valley– the hottest place on earth!

60

7 POSITIVE AND NEGATIVE NUMBERS: TEMPERATURE

2 This reading is halfway between 20 °C and 30 °C.
It shows a temperature of 25 °C.
Read the following thermometers.

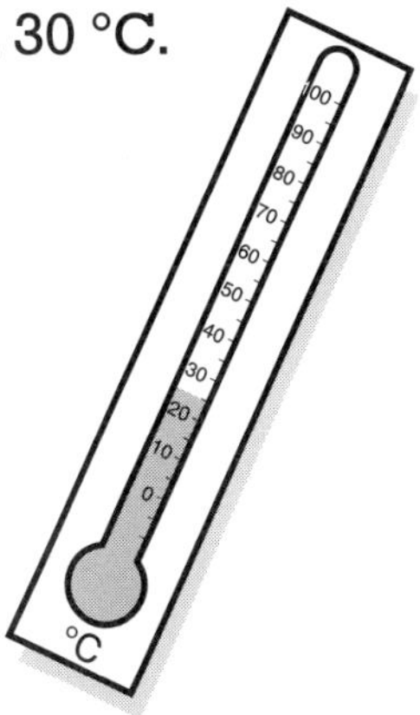

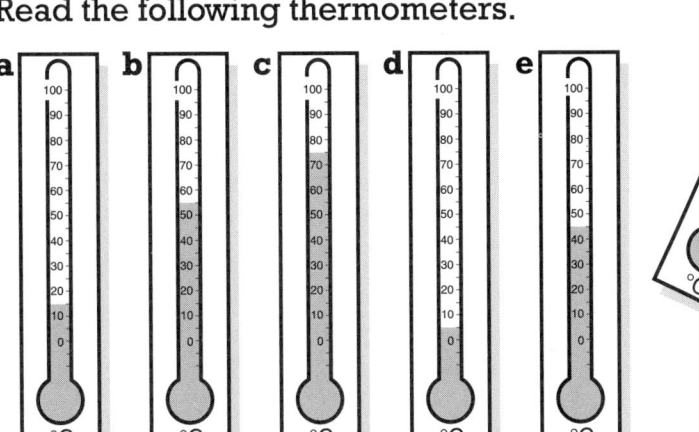

3 Mike's temperature is low.
The thermometer reads 35 °C.

What will it read if his temperature rises by 5 °C?

4 The beaker of water is at 55 °C.
It is cooling down.

What will the thermometer read when the water has cooled by 15 °C?

5 In this close-up you can see 10 spaces between 20 °C and 30 °C.
Each space shows 1 °C.
This thermometer is reading 22 °C.

Read the following thermometers.

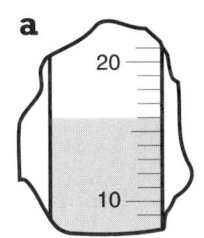

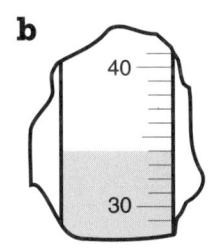

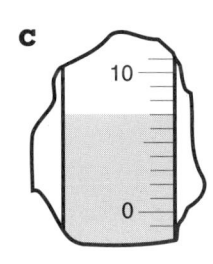

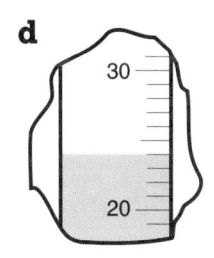

6 Here is a different thermometer.

   a How many spaces are marked between 10 °C and 20 °C?
   b How many degrees does each space show?
   c What temperature is showing on this thermometer?

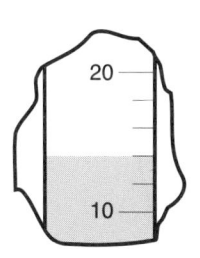

61

7 POSITIVE AND NEGATIVE NUMBERS: TEMPERATURE

7

Holidays Abroad

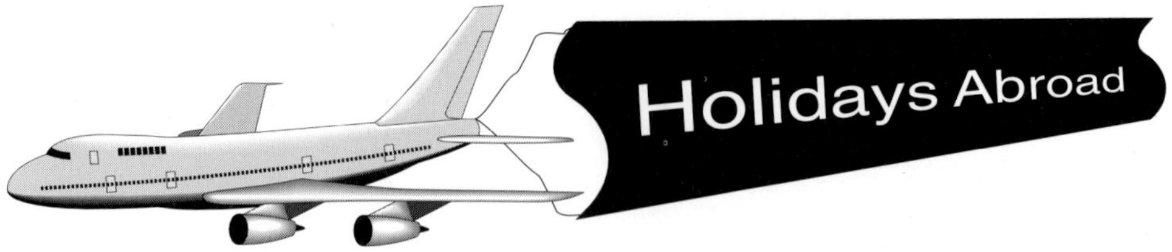

Write down the temperature for each of the following places.

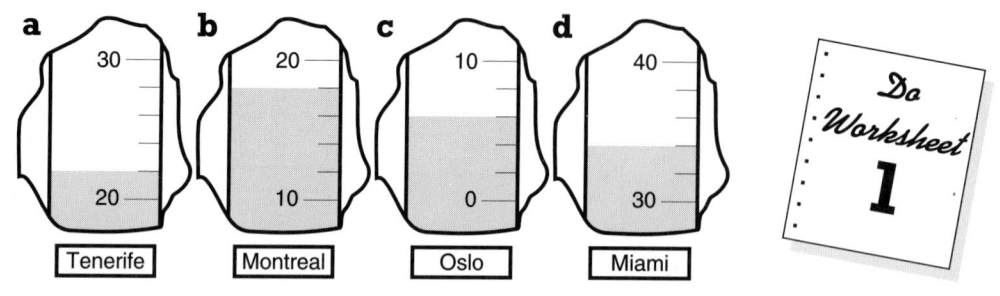

a Tenerife
b Montreal
c Oslo
d Miami

Do Worksheet 1

Negative Numbers

At 0 °C water freezes

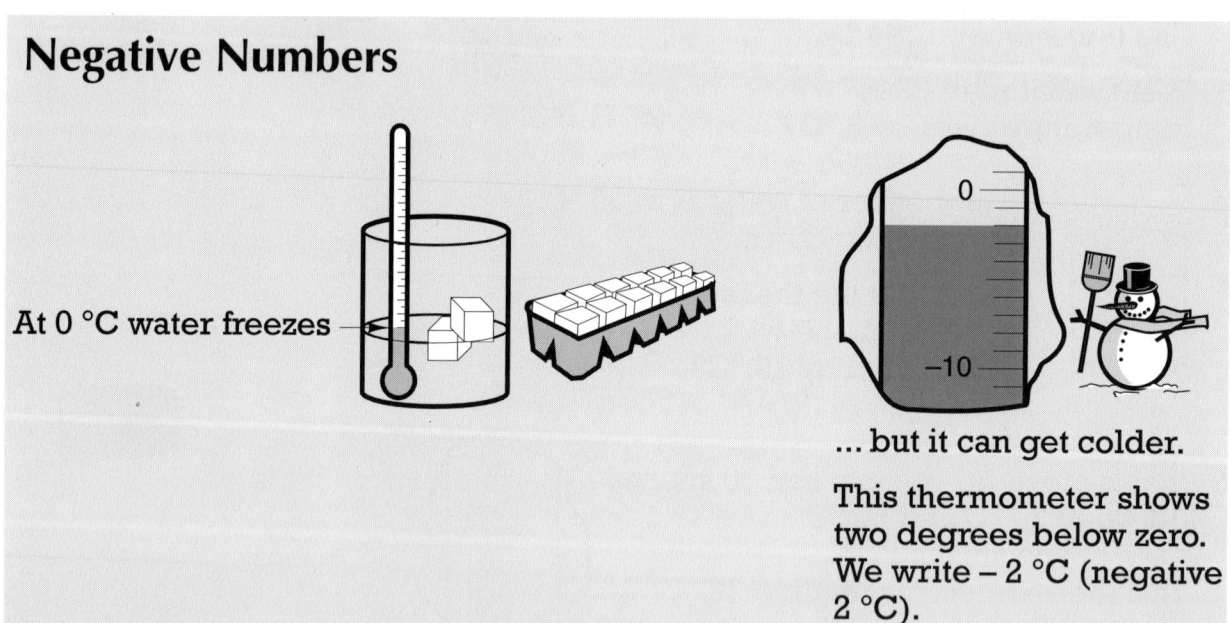

... but it can get colder.

This thermometer shows two degrees below zero. We write – 2 °C (negative 2 °C).

EXERCISE 3

1 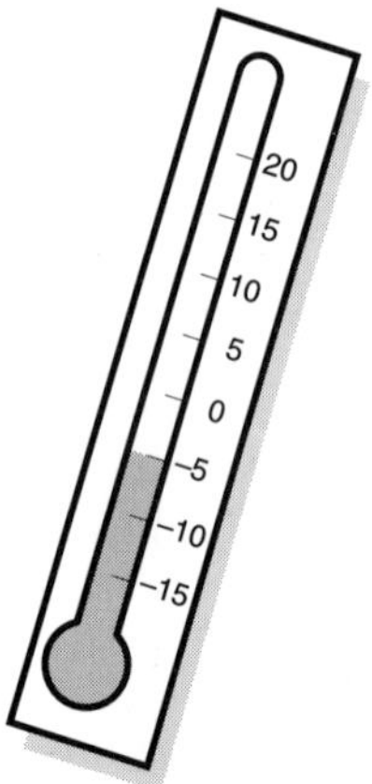
    a This thermometer shows – 5 °C.

       How many degrees below zero is this?

    b Now it shows – 10 °C.

       (i) How many degrees below zero is this?
       (ii) Which is colder, – 10 °C or – 5 °C?

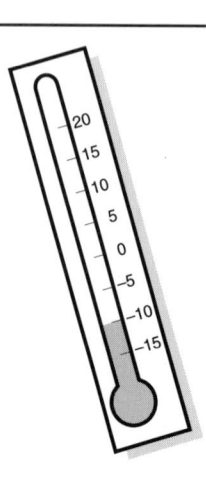

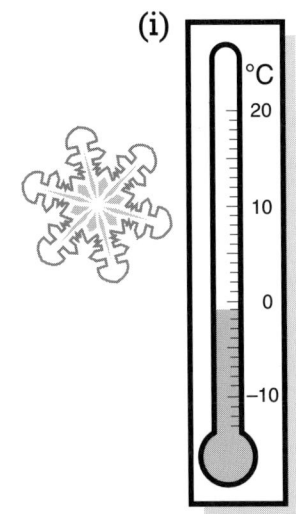

7 POSITIVE AND NEGATIVE NUMBERS: TEMPERATURE

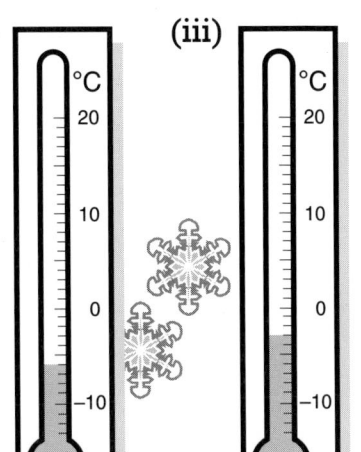

2

(i) (ii) (iii) (iv)

   a Give the reading on each of these thermometers.
   b Which thermometer shows the coldest temperature?

3 Which temperature is colder?

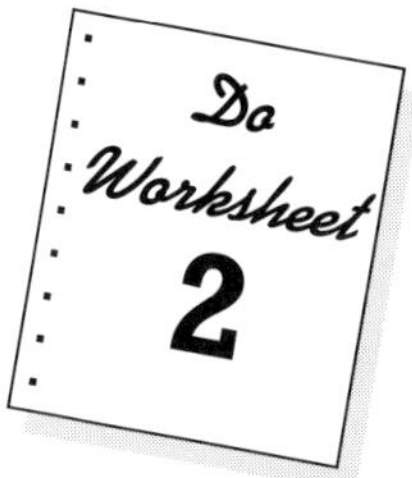

   a 2 °C or − 2 °C
   b − 3 °C or − 5 °C
   c − 10 °C or − 12 °C

Do Worksheet 2

4 The thermometer reads − 2 °C.
The temperature falls by 1 °C.

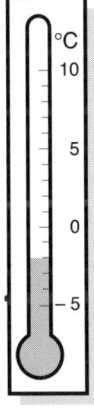

What is the new reading?

5 The thermometer on the freezer reads − 5 °C.

There is a rise of 1 °C.

What does it read now?

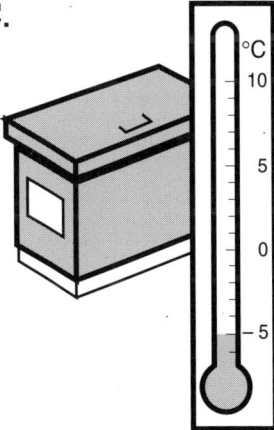

63

7 POSITIVE AND NEGATIVE NUMBERS: TEMPERATURE

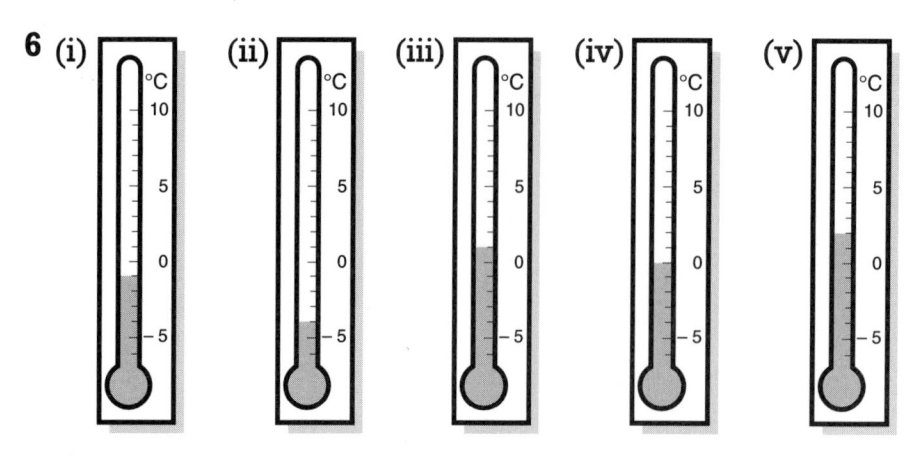

6 (i) (ii) (iii) (iv) (v)

a What does each of these thermometers read?
b What will they each read after a drop in temperature of 2 °C?

7 What will the following become after a rise in temperature of 3 °C?
   a −8 °C   b −5 °C   c −3 °C   d −1 °C   e 0 °C

8 What will the following become after a drop in temperature of 4 °C?
   a −2 °C   b −5 °C   c −1 °C   d 0 °C   e 2 °C

9 Jack brought a snowball into the room to melt.
The ball was at a temperature of −3 °C.
Once melted, it was a pool of water at 18 °C.

What was its rise in temperature?

10 Louise was in Athens for Christmas. The temperature there was 14 °C.
She flew home to Glasgow and a temperature of −4 °C.

What was the drop in temperature?

Ordering Positive and Negative Numbers

Example

Put the following numbers in order, **smallest first**: −4, 6, −2

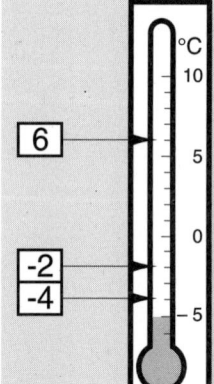

Find them on the thermometer.

The higher the numbers on the scale, the bigger they are.

Write them out from the bottom up: −4, −2, 6.

64

7 POSITIVE AND NEGATIVE NUMBERS: TEMPERATURE

EXERCISE 4

Use the thermometer on the right to help you with these questions.

1. **a** Which temperature is higher, – 5 °C or – 2 °C?
   b Which number is bigger, – 5 or – 2?

2. Find which number is higher in each of the following pairs:

   a – 4 or – 1   **b** – 2 or – 9   **c** 0 or – 5
   d 3 or – 6   **e** – 2 or 2   **f** – 6 or – 5

3. Put the following sets of numbers in order, smallest first.

   a – 3, 8, – 4   **b** – 4, 0, – 6   **c** – 6, – 9, – 2
   d – 1, 0 – 2   **e** – 9, 10, – 11   **f** – 5, – 7, – 6

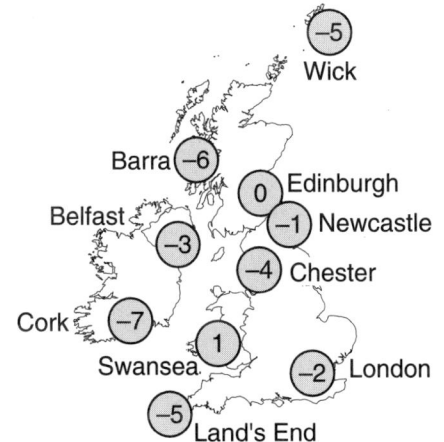

4. The weather report gives the temperatures (in °C) for various places in the British Isles.

   Arrange the following lists of places, putting the warmest first.

   a Newcastle, Chester, London
   b Edinburgh, Barra, Swansea
   c Wick, Belfast, Cork

5. As the temperature rises by 1 °C at a time, the readings form a pattern: – 5 °C, – 4 °C, – 3 °C, ...

   Copy the pattern and continue it for another five readings.

6. Copy and continue these patterns of numbers for another three numbers:

   a – 3, – 2, – 1, ...
   b 2, 1, 0, – 1, ...
   c – 8, – 6, – 4, – 2, ...
   d – 20, – 15, – 10, ...

65

7 POSITIVE AND NEGATIVE NUMBERS: TEMPERATURE

CHECK-UP ON TEMPERATURE

1 Which thermometer shows the coldest temperature?

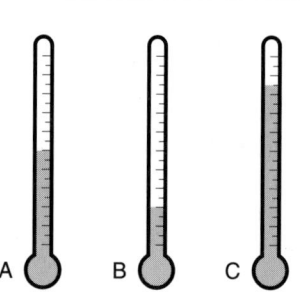

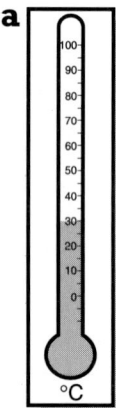

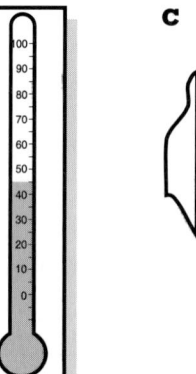

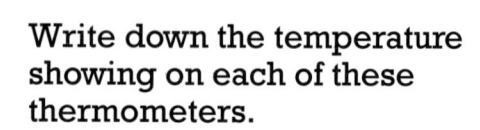

2 Write down the temperature showing on each of these thermometers.

3 How do we write down a temperature that is five degrees below zero?

4 What are the readings on the two thermometers here?

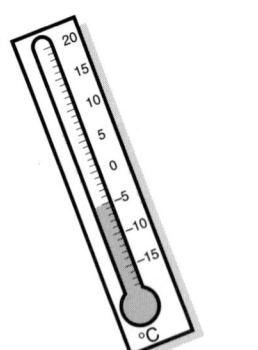

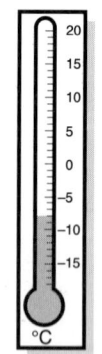

5 Which temperature is warmer, −8 °C or −2 °C?

6 a A thermometer reads 3 °C. There is a drop of 7 °C.
      What is the new reading?

   b A thermometer reads −2 °C. There is a drop of 4 °C.
      What is the new reading?

7 James takes some ravioli out of the freezer and heats it in the microwave oven.

   Its temperature goes from −10 °C to 80 °C.

   What is the rise in temperature?

8 ROUND IN CIRCLES

Recognising Circles

Mary is playing with a hula-hoop. The hoop is a circle.

At the park, Jim is on the roundabout.
He stays the same distance from the centre as he goes round.
He goes round in a circle.

EXERCISE 1

1 Look at this picture. Make a list of all the circles you can find.

2 Some parts of these objects are **circular** (like circles).
   Can you find them?

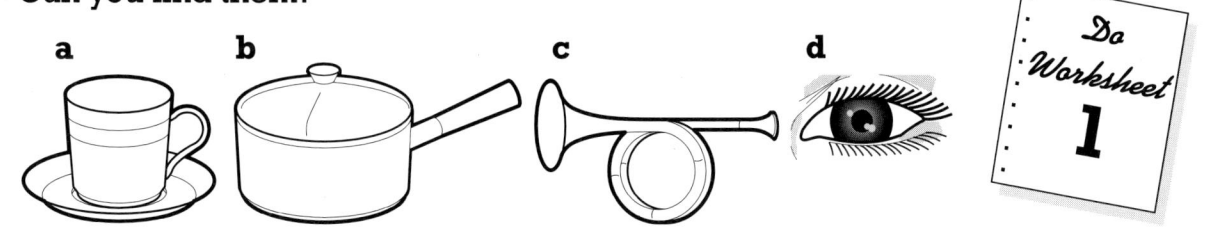

   a   b   c   d

Do Worksheet 1

67

Drawing Circles

Use a rope and sticks.

Draw round a circular object.

Use a pair of compasses.

When you draw round an object to make a circle, you don't know where its centre is. A 'Centre Finder' helps. Ask your teacher for a 'Centre Finder'.

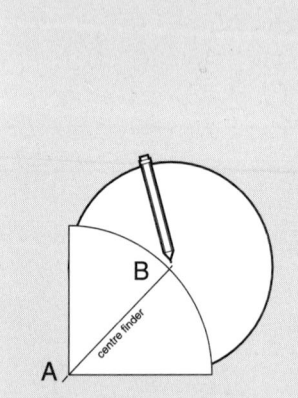

Sit the 'Centre Finder' on the circle as shown. Mark A and B.

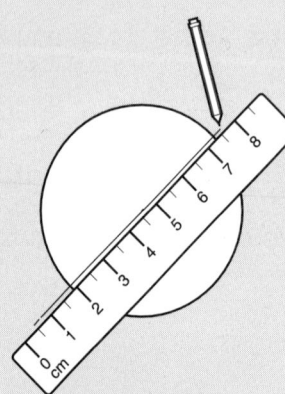

Draw a line through A and B.

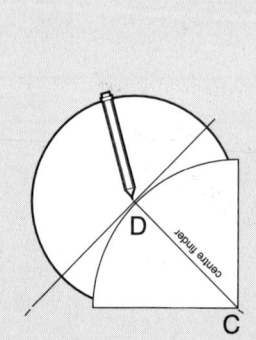

Change the position of the finder. Mark C and D.

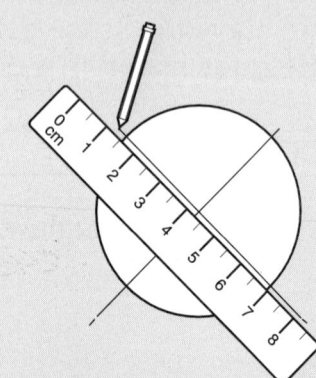

Draw a line through C and D. The centre is where the two lines cross.

EXERCISE 2

1 Which coins are suitable for drawing circles?

2 **a** Get a coin and use it to draw a circle.
   b Find the centre of the circle.
   c Repeat parts **a** and **b** using larger round objects.

3 Draw a circle using compasses.
   Use the 'Centre Finder' to check the drawing.

Do Worksheet 2

Naming the Parts of a Circle

The boundary of the circle is called the **circumference**.

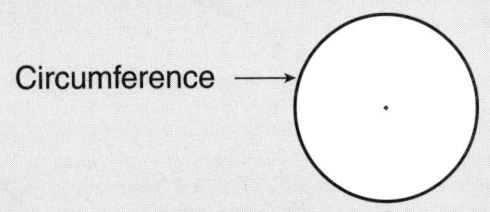

Circumference ⟶

This straight line is a **diameter**.
It goes through the **centre** to touch the circumference at two points.

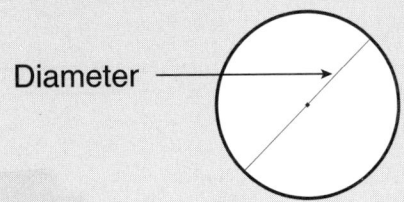

Diameter ⟶

This straight line is a **radius**.
It goes from the centre to any point on the circumference.

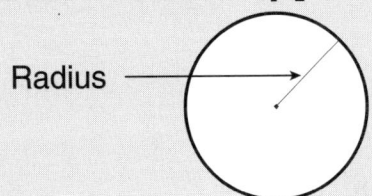

Radius ⟶

EXERCISE 3

1 Name the labelled parts in these shapes:

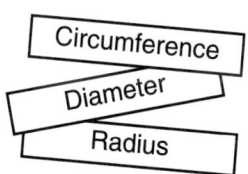

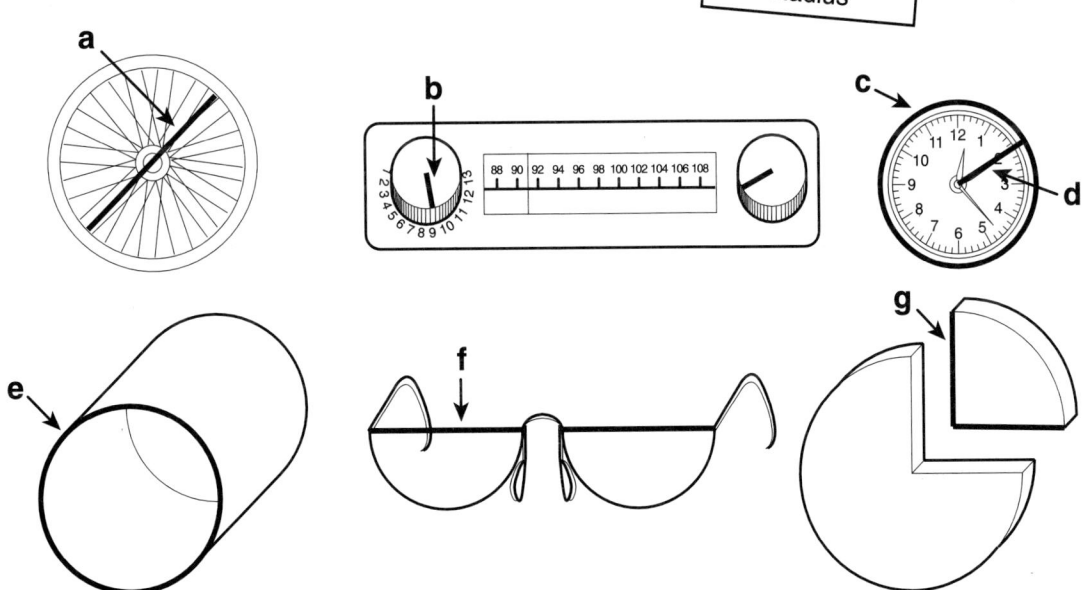

Circumference
Diameter
Radius

8 ROUND IN CIRCLES

2 Measure the length of:

(i) the radius
(ii) the diameter

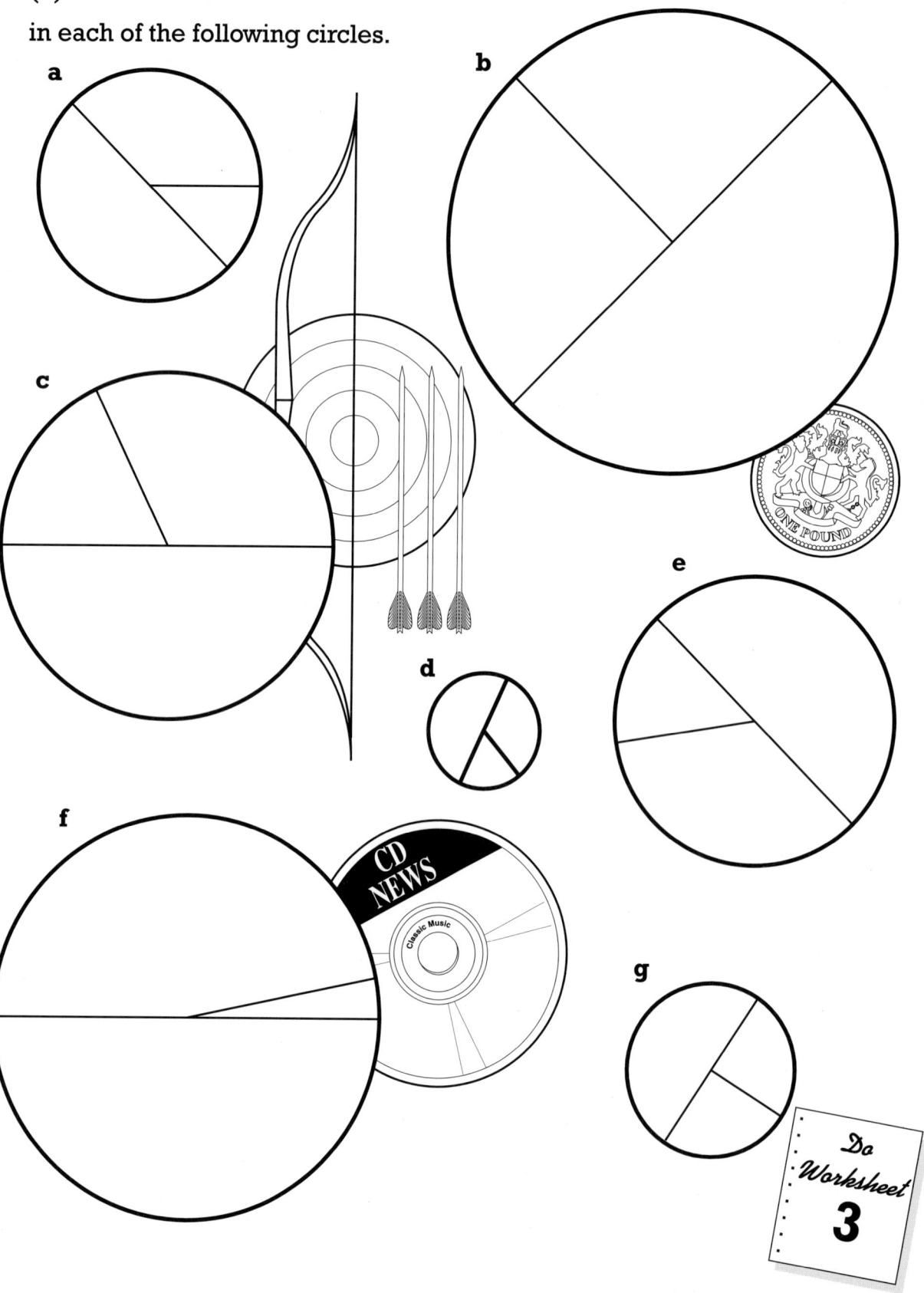

in each of the following circles.

a

b

c

d

e

f

g

Do Worksheet **3**

70

8 ROUND IN CIRCLES

Working out the Radius or Diameter

Diameter = 2 × radius

EXERCISE 4

Copy and complete the sentences below. (The circles are not actual size.)

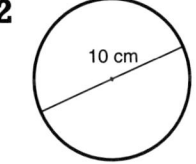

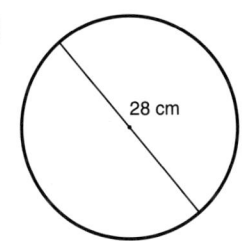

1 The diameter of this circle is ...... cm
(6 cm)

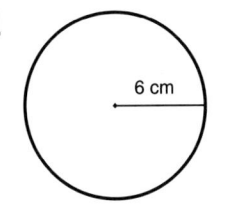

2 The radius of this circle is ...... cm
(10 cm)

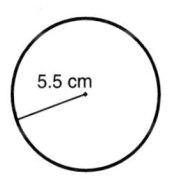

3 The radius of this circle is ...... cm
(28 cm)

4 The diameter of this circle is ...... cm
(5.5 cm)

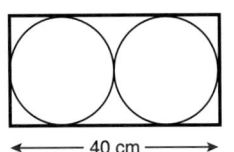

5 These two circles are the same size.
    a The diameter of each circle is ...... cm.
    b The radius of each circle is ...... cm.
(40 cm)

6 These circles are the same size.
    a The diameter of each circle is ...... cm.
    b The radius of each circle is ...... cm.
(30 cm)

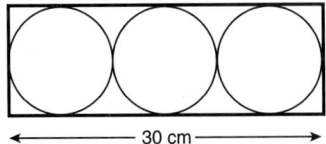

7 The two small circles are the same size.
    a The diameter of the large circle is ...... cm
    b The diameter of each of the small circles is ...... cm
    c The radius of each of the small circles is ...... cm
(4 cm)

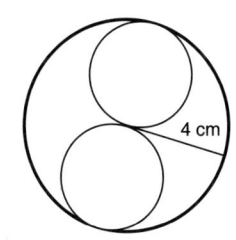

71

Constructing a Circle

Example: constructing a circle with a radius of 5 cm.

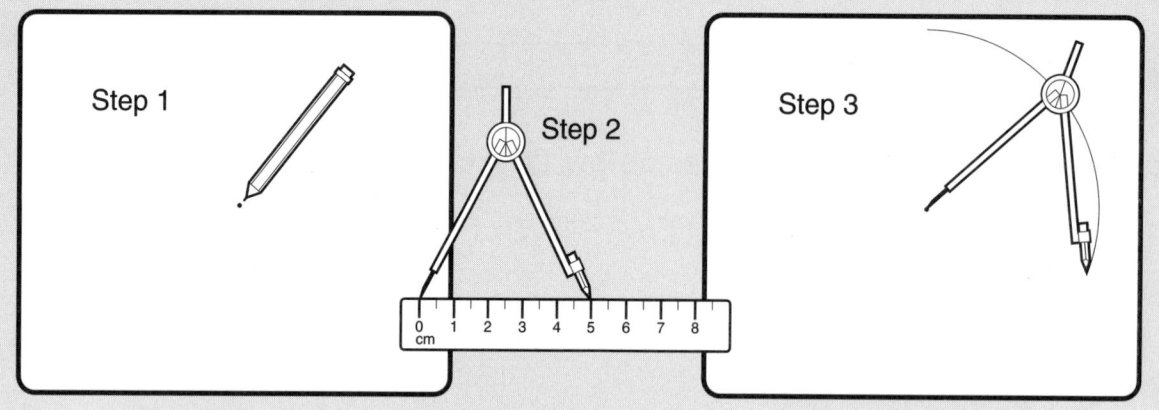

Step 1 Mark a centre point on your page (well away from the edges).

Step 2 Set the distance between the compass point and pencil point to 5 cm.

Step 3 Put the compass point on your marked centre point and carefully draw your circle.

EXERCISE 5

1 Construct a circle with radius:

   a 4 cm   **b** 3 cm   **c** 2 cm   **d** 4.5 cm.

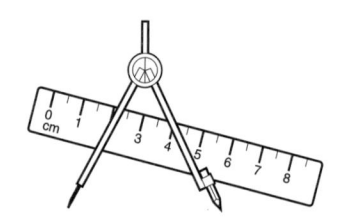

2 Copy and complete the table. Remember: diameter = 2 × radius.

Radius	1 cm			5 m	4.5 m	
Diameter		6 cm	4 mm			15 cm

3 For each diameter below:
   (i) work out the radius
   (ii) draw the circle.

   a 10 cm   **b** 12 cm   **c** 5 cm   **d** 11 cm

4 Draw a circle with:

   a radius 7 cm   **b** diameter 7 cm   **c** radius 6.5 cm.

5 Here is a simple pattern made from a square and five circles.

To make it:
- **a** draw a square of side 10 cm
- **b** at each corner draw a circle of radius 5 cm
- **c** find the **centre** and **radius** of the circle which is **inside** the square.

Do Worksheet 4

EXERCISE 6

1 Collect some circular objects from the classroom.

   a Measure the diameter.
   b Measure round the circumference.
   (You can use the scale from Worksheet 4.)
   c Make a table of your results.

   Notice that: **circumference = 3 × diameter** (roughly).

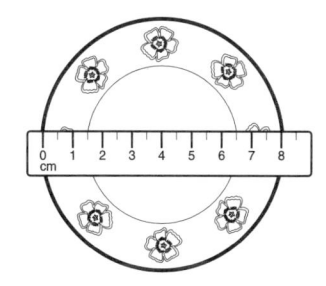

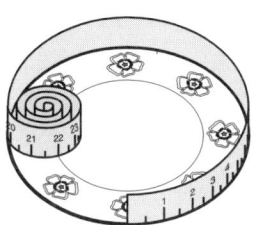

2 Work out roughly the circumference of each of the following circles.

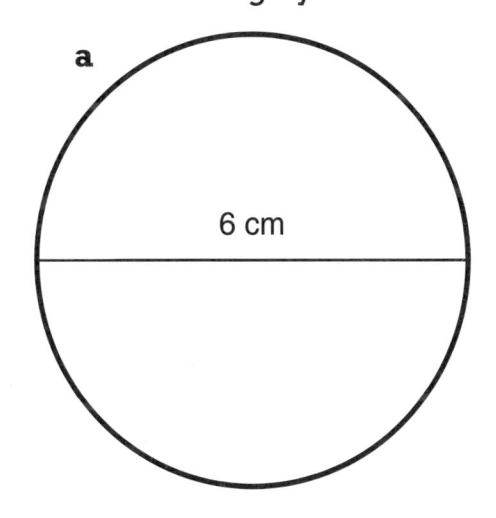

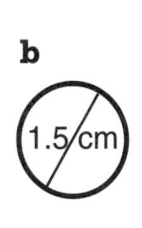

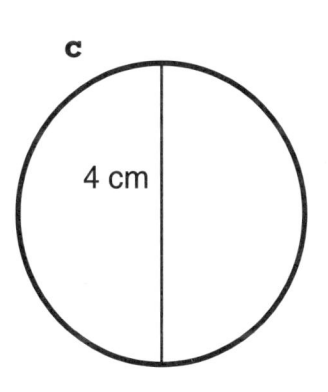

   a 6 cm
   b 1.5 cm
   c 4 cm

3 **a** There is a pattern round the rim of the cup.
     Work out roughly the circumference of the rim.
   b What is the circumference of the rim of the saucer?

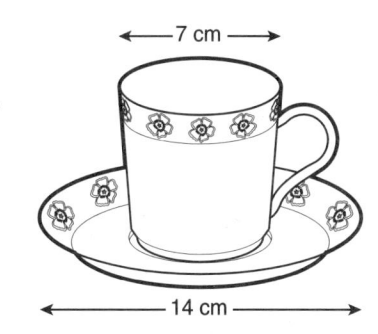

   7 cm
   14 cm

73

Using Circles to Draw Patterns

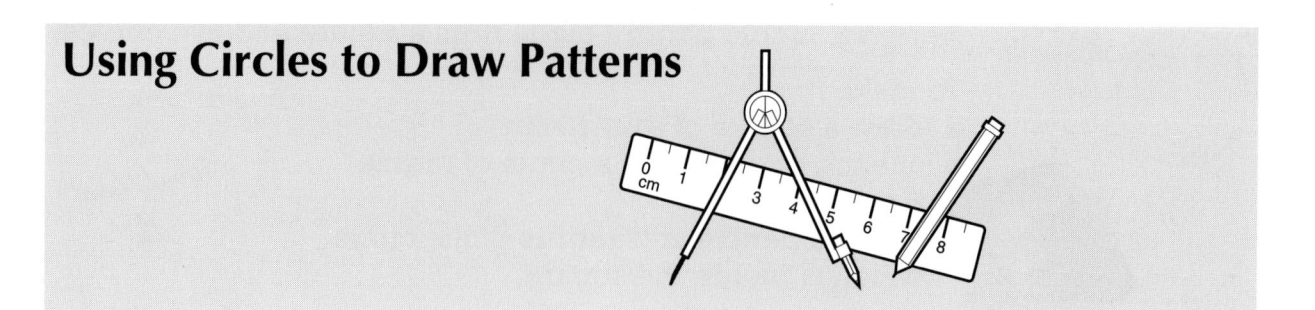

EXERCISE 7

Draw the following circle patterns using a ruler and a pair of compasses. (The squares are only there to help you plan.)

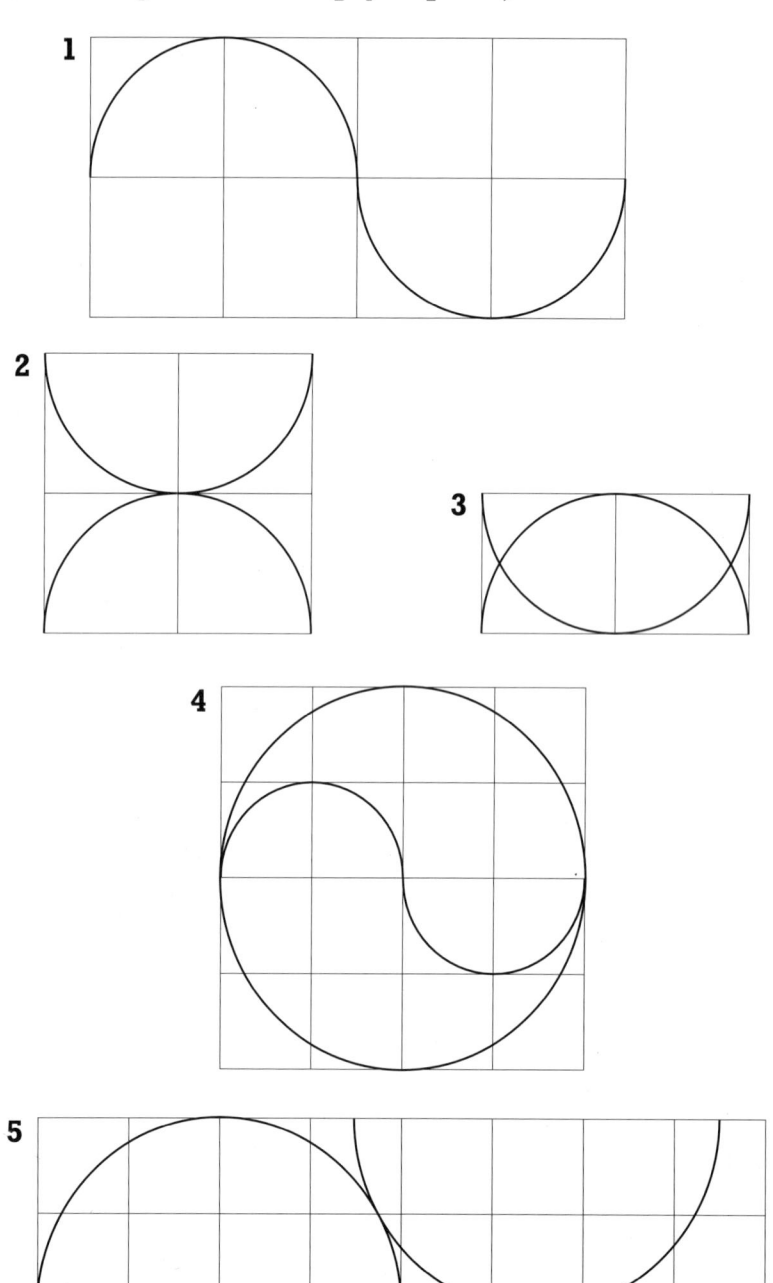

CHECK-UP ON CIRCLES

1 Name the labelled parts in the following diagrams.

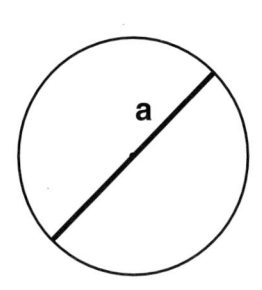

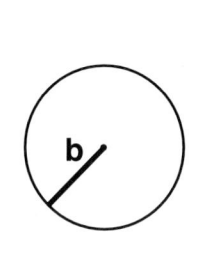

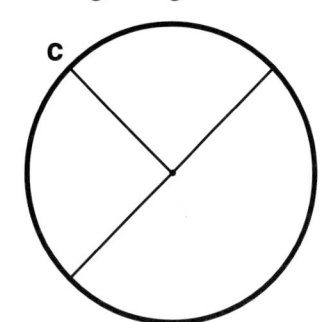

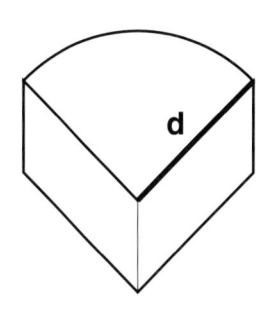

2 For this circle, measure:
   a the diameter
   b the radius.

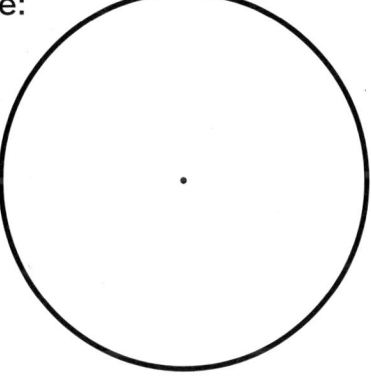

3 Copy and complete this table.

Radius	3 cm		2.5 mm
Diameter		8 cm	

4 a Draw a circle with a radius of 5 cm.
  b Write down the diameter of this circle.

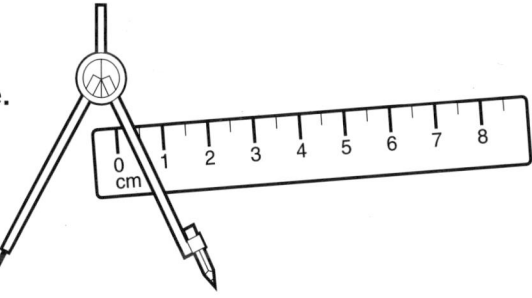

5 These circles are not drawn to scale. Copy the sentences and fill in the blanks.

   a   3 cm   The diameter of this circle is ......

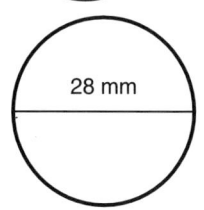

   b   28 mm   The radius of this circle is ......

6 These circles are the same size.

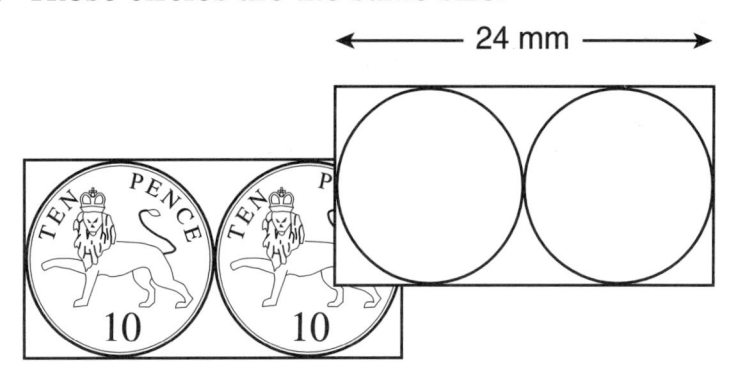

← 24 mm →

a What is the diameter of one circle?
b What is the radius of one circle?

7 These circles are not drawn to scale.

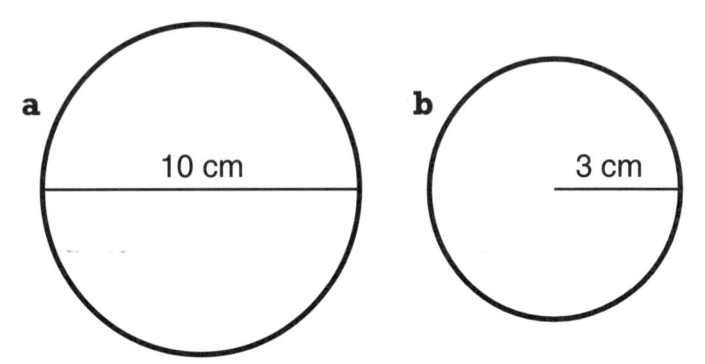

a 10 cm

b 3 cm

Write down (roughly) the circumference of each circle.

8 Mary's hoop is 1 m in diameter. It was made by bending a length of plastic in a circle. Roughly how long was the length of plastic?

9 COORDINATES

Position and Movement

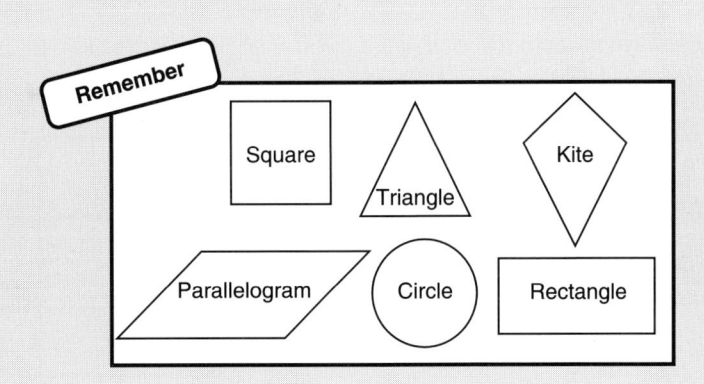

Remember

Square, Triangle, Kite, Parallelogram, Circle, Rectangle

EXERCISE 1

1. The circle is **in front of** the triangle.
   The triangle is **to the left of** the kite.

   a Which shape is in front of the kite?
   b Which shape is to the left of the triangle?
   c Which shape is to the right of the circle?
   d Which shape is behind the parallelogram?

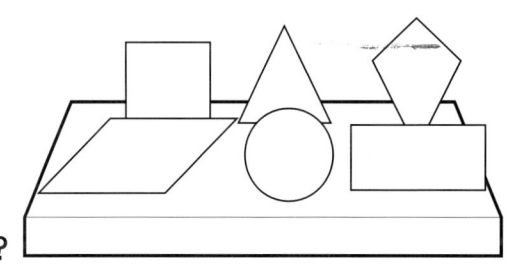

2. Anticlockwise   Clockwise

   Four friends are playing 'Spin the Bottle'.

   The bottle points to Anne.

   a It is given a **quarter turn clockwise**.
     To whom is it now pointing?
   b The bottle is pointing to Anne again.
     It is given a **half turn anticlockwise**.
     To whom is it now pointing?

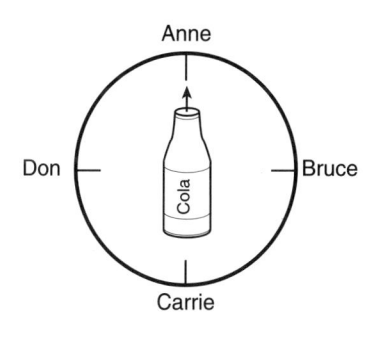

77

9 COORDINATES

3

	A	B	C	D
3	Selina	Maggie	Jo	Yasmin
2	Katya	Ben	Jean	Ali
1	Binta	Scott	Chris	Oliver

Ben is sitting in seat **B2**.

a Who is sitting in **D3**?
b In what seat is Katya sitting?

4 Charles is fixing the broken panes of glass in his greenhouse. He is about to replace **B3**.

Make a list of the other broken panes.

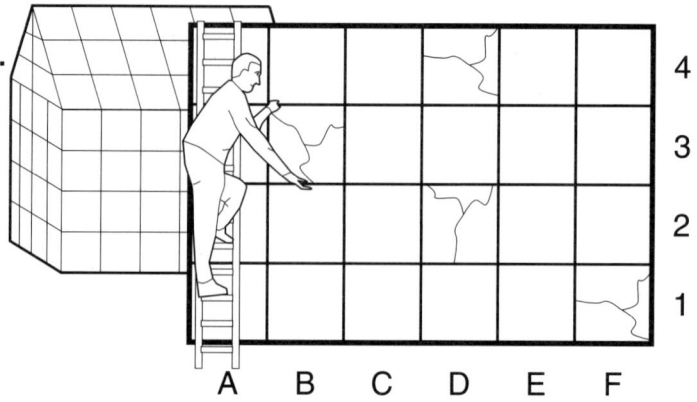

5 Rob has tied the apple tree to a grid of garden canes. He has put ties at C1, C2 and C3.

List the other places where he has put ties.

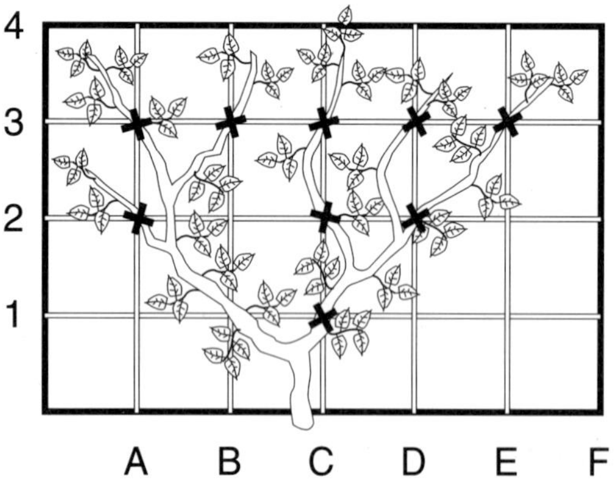

6 Grace is pulling the weeds out between the patio slabs.

List the places where there are weeds.

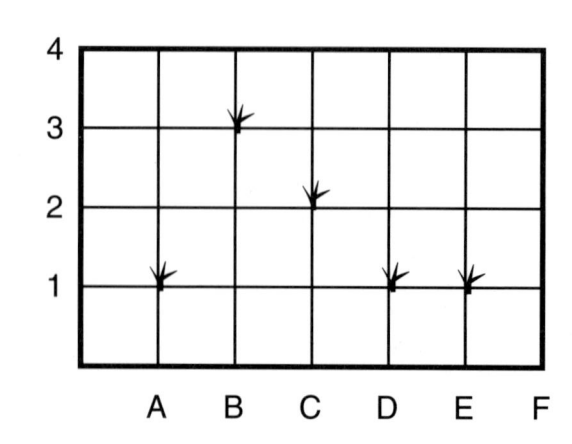

78

9 COORDINATES

Writing Coordinates

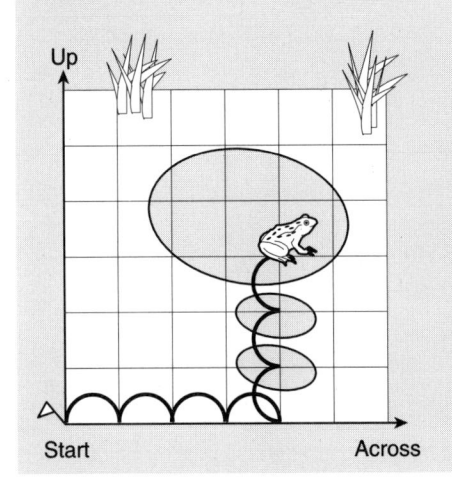

Maria is watching a frog in the garden pond.
She *imagines* a grid on the pond.

The frog starts at the flag.
He makes **4 hops across, then 3 hops up**.
He ends up on the big lily-pad.

Maria notes this position as (4,3).

EXERCISE 2

1. Frog 2 starts at the flag. He makes **3 hops across, then 1 hop up**. The cross shows where the frog stopped.

   How will Maria record this position?

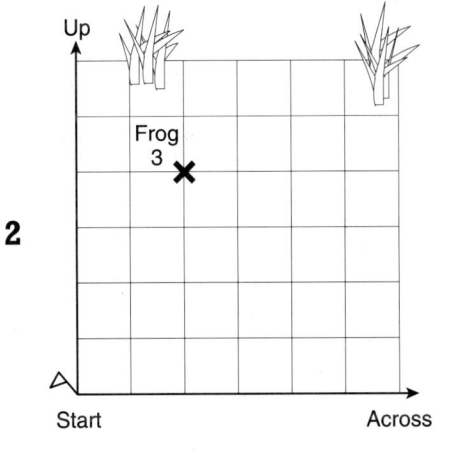

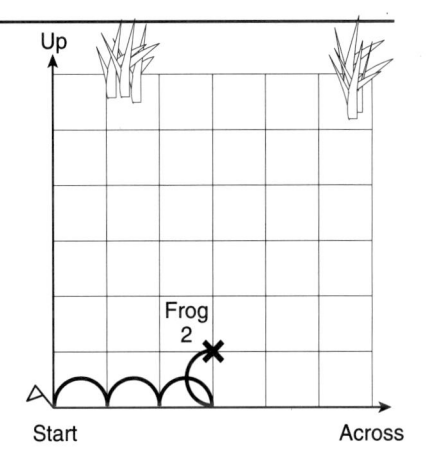

2. Frog 3 starts at the flag and makes **2 hops across, then 4 hops up**.
   The cross shows where the frog landed.

   How will Maria record this?

3. Here is a picture with four more frogs.
   A is at position (2,4).

   List the other three positions in the same way.

   Do Worksheet 1

   Ask to play the 'Hopping Mad' game.

79

Coordinates

Adam does it the right way.

Bruno does it the wrong way!

→ **across** then ↑ **up**

The point A is **4** lines **across**, then **3** lines **up**.

We say '**The coordinates of A are 4,3.**'

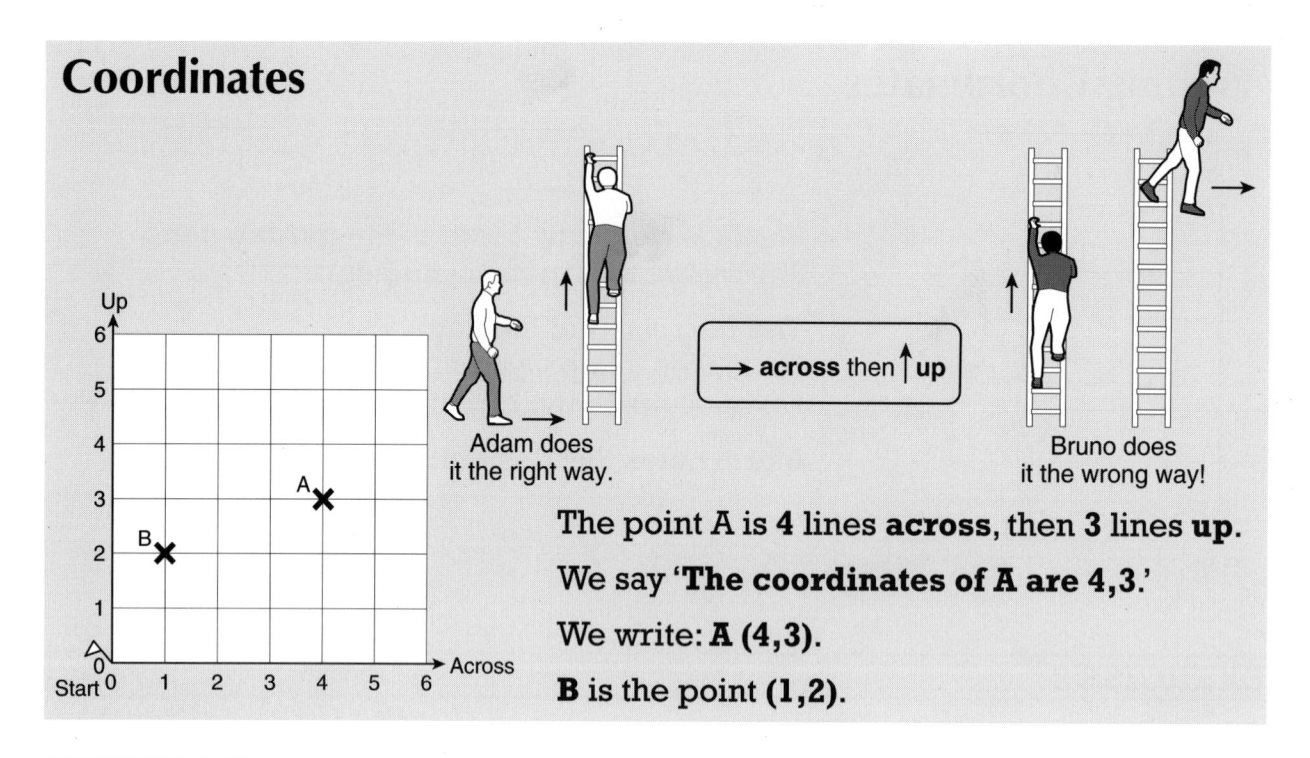

We write: **A (4,3)**.

B is the point **(1,2)**.

EXERCISE 3

1 **C** is the point **(1,5)**.
Copy and complete this list:

D (4,...)
E (...,4)
F (...,...)
G (...,...)
H (...,0)
I (...,...)
J (0,...)

→ **across** then ↑ **up**

2 Jan makes a larger picture of the lamb by drawing a grid on it and noting some points.

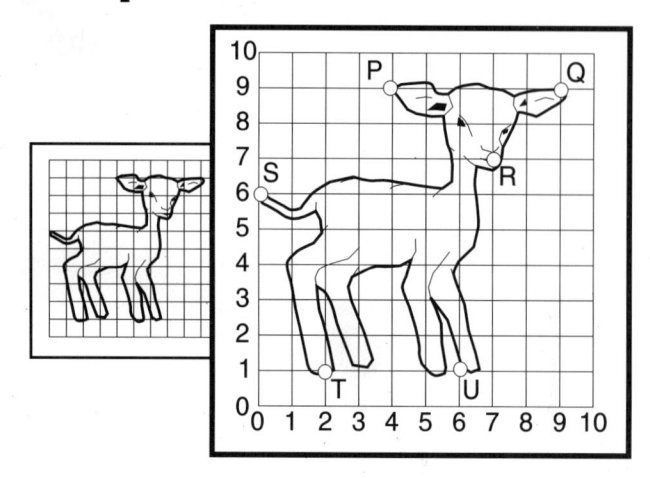

Write down the coordinates of:

a P **b** Q **c** R
d S **e** T **f** U

9 COORDINATES

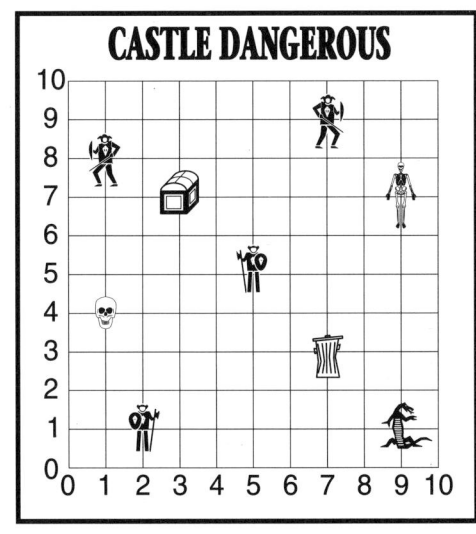

3 Mike has an adventure game called 'Castle Dangerous'.

a There are four warriors on the board. One of them is at (2,1). Where are the other three?

b What is at these points?
(i) (1,4)   (ii) (9,7)

c What is the position of:
(i) the treasure chest
(ii) the dustbin?

(Be careful!)

4 A poster advertises some of the activities in the sports centre.

a Name the activity drawn at these points:
(i) (1,1)   (ii) (1,4)

b Name the point where there is:
(i) a couple dancing
(ii) a ballet dancer.

c The basketball picture covers two points. What are they?

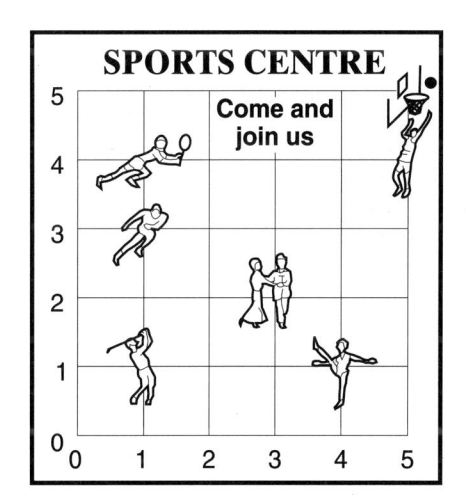

5 The geography teacher is showing the class a map.

a Give the coordinates of:
(i) Ayton
(ii) Beeton

b Name the town at:
(i) (2,4)
(ii) (4,2)

c (i) What town is closest to Eton?
(ii) Give its coordinates.

Do Worksheet 2

Ask to play 'Three in a Row'.

81

Coordinate Quadrilaterals

These are all **quadrilaterals** or **four-sided shapes**.
You should be able to name them.

Square   Rectangle   Rhombus

Parallelogram   Kite   Trapezium

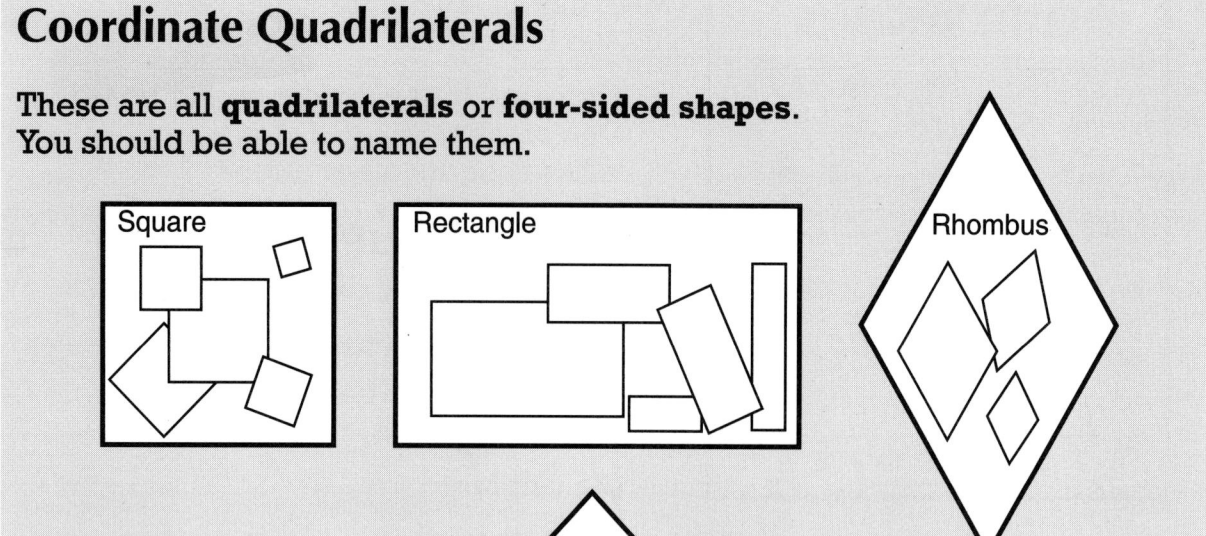

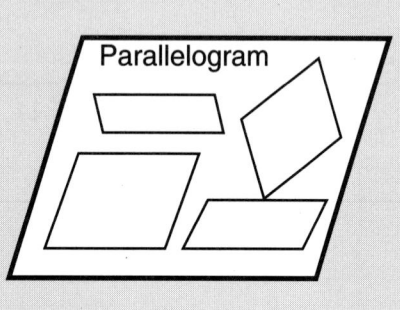

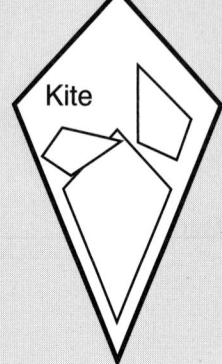

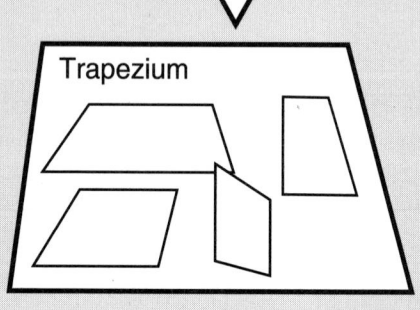

EXERCISE 4

You will need a Grid Sheet.

1 Plot each set of points on a grid and join them up in the order given. Write down the name of the shape you have drawn.

Example:

P(1,1) → Q(2,4) → R(4,4) → S(6,1) → P

The shape is a **trapezium**.

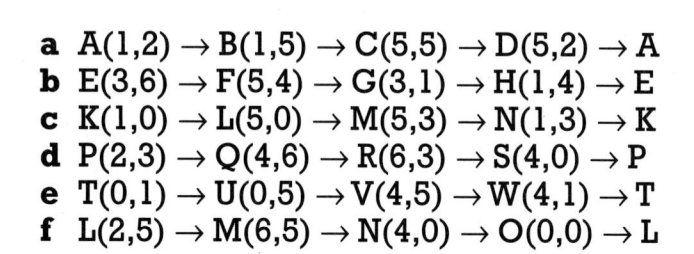

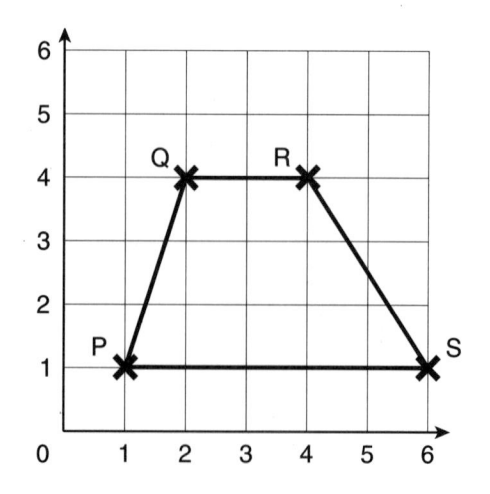

   a A(1,2) → B(1,5) → C(5,5) → D(5,2) → A
   b E(3,6) → F(5,4) → G(3,1) → H(1,4) → E
   c K(1,0) → L(5,0) → M(5,3) → N(1,3) → K
   d P(2,3) → Q(4,6) → R(6,3) → S(4,0) → P
   e T(0,1) → U(0,5) → V(4,5) → W(4,1) → T
   f L(2,5) → M(6,5) → N(4,0) → O(0,0) → L

9 COORDINATES

2 (i) Plot the three points given.
(ii) Find the fourth point to make the shape asked for.
(iii) Write down the **coordinates** of the fourth point.

Example:

A(4,1) → B(3,3) → C(4,5) → D (?,?).

Find D so that ABCD is a **rhombus**.

D is the point (5,3).

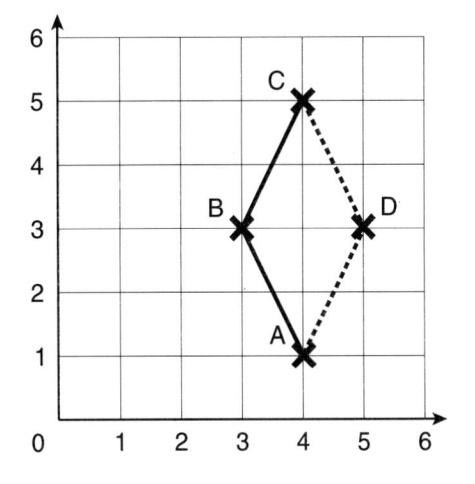

a Plot P(1,6) → Q(4,6) → R(4,3) → S (?,?).
Find S so that PQRS is a **square**. Write down the coordinates of S.
b Plot E(2,5) → F(5,5) → G(6,2) → H (?,?).
Find H so that EFGH is a **parallelogram**. Write down the coordinates of H.
c Plot S(3,1) → T(1,4) → U(3,5) → V (?,?).
Find V so that STUV is a **kite**. Write down the coordinates of V.
d Plot W(1,1) → X(1,5) → Y(4,5) → Z (?,?).
Find Z so that WXYZ is a **rectangle**. Write down the coordinates of Z.

More than Four Sides

3 A **pentagon** has **five** sides.
Plot these points to make a pentagon:

A(2,1) → B(4,1) → C(5,3) → D(3,5) → E(1,3) → A.

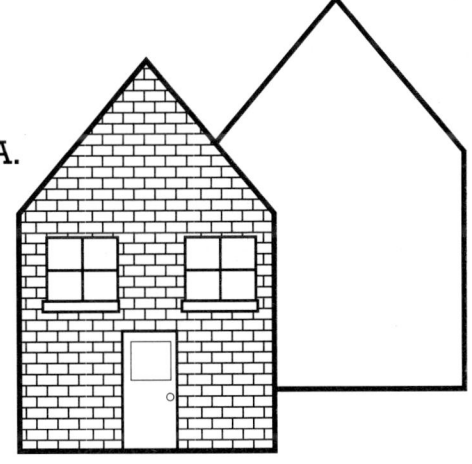

4 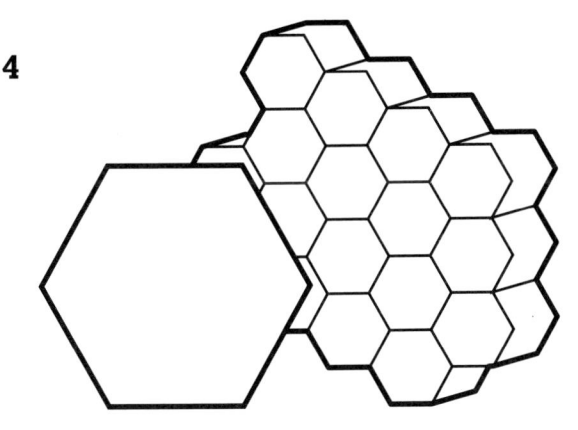 A **hexagon** has **six** sides.
Plot these points to make a hexagon:

P(3,0) → Q(5,0) → R(6,2) → S(5,4) → T(3,4) → U(2,2) → P.

Do Worksheet 3

83

Names

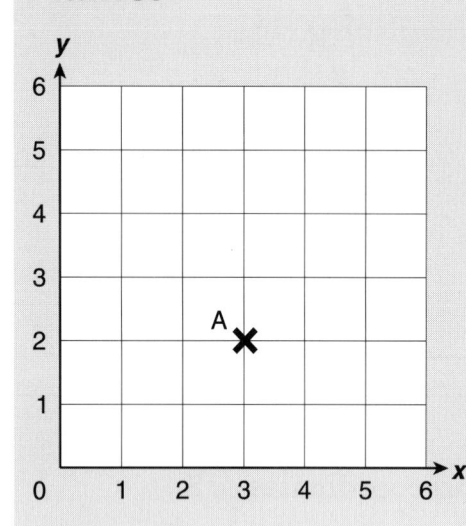

The starting point on the grid is called the **origin**. The coordinates of the origin are **(0,0)**.

The **'across' line** is called the **x axis**.

The **'up' line** is called the **y axis**.

A point on a grid has 2 coordinates: (**x coordinate, y coordinate**).

Example:

A is the point (3,2).
The *x* coordinate of A is 3.
The *y* coordinate of A is 2.

EXERCISE 5

1 Which point has an *x* coordinate of 5?

2 Which point has a *y* coordinate of 1?

3 Which point lies on the *x* axis?

4 Which point lies on the *y* axis?

5 Which point has the same number for its *x* and its *y* coordinates?

6 What are the coordinates of the origin?

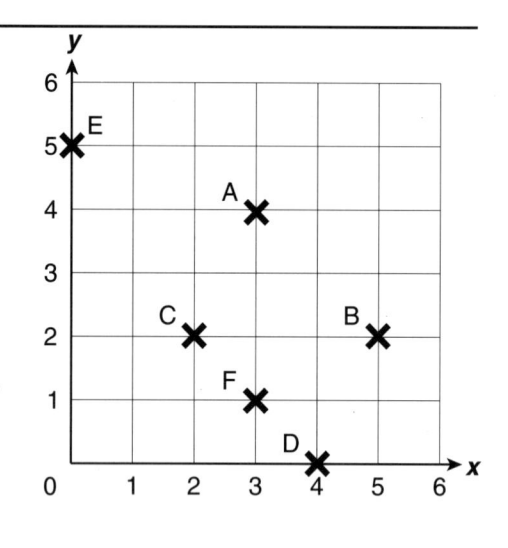

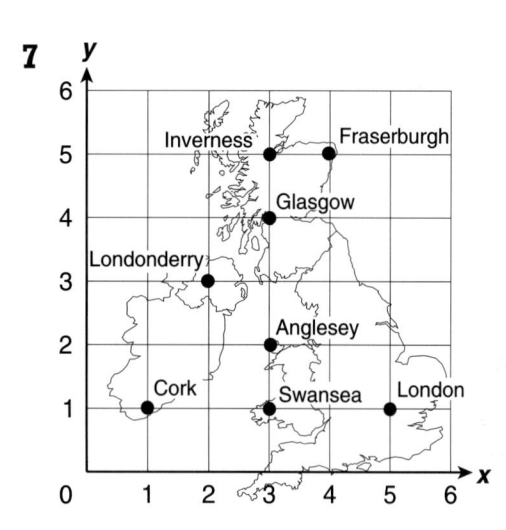

7
   a What is the *x* coordinate of Glasgow?
   b What is the *y* coordinate of London?
   c Which places have an *x* coordinate of 3?
   d Which towns have a *y* coordinate of 1?

CHECK-UP ON COORDINATES

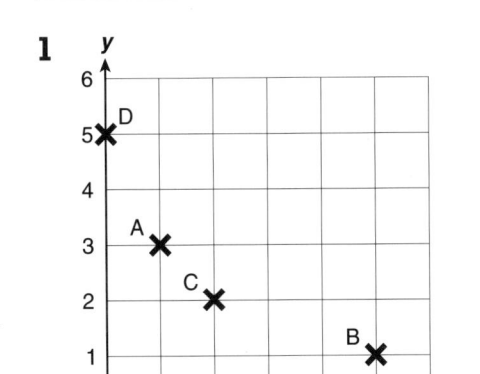

1 Write down the coordinates of the points A, B, C, D and E.

2 Copy this grid onto squared paper. Plot these points on the grid: F(1,2), G(4,2), H(0,3), I(4,4) and J(2,0).

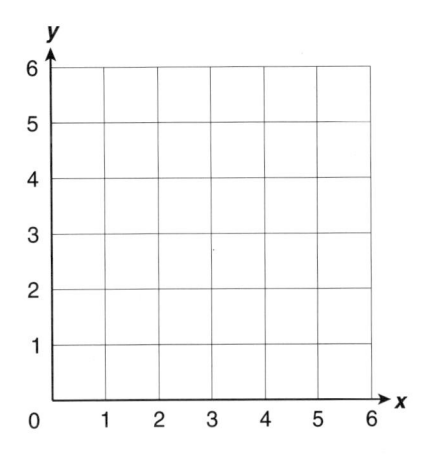

3 Copy this grid onto squared paper.

  a Plot these points: W(2,1), X(1,3) and Y(2,5).
  b Find point Z, so that WXYZ is a **rhombus**.
  c Write down the coordinates of Z.

4 Look at the points on the grid and answer the questions.

  a Which point has an *x* coordinate of 4?
  b What are the coordinates of the origin?
  c Which point has the same number for both its coordinates?
  d Which point lies on the *x* axis?

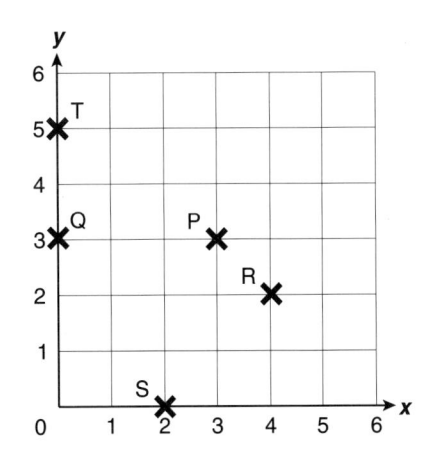

85

10 MEASURES

Length

Remember: length is measured in metres and centimetres.

Meg is a metre tall. By looking at the picture we can see that the basket is about half a metre high, because it is half the size of Meg, and the door is about 2 metres high, as it is twice the size of Meg.

EXERCISE 1

1 Look at these pictures with Meg in them and guess the **height** of:

　a Santa 　　　**b** the tree 　　　**c** the car

2 Use your answers above to guess the height of:

　a the deer 　　　**b** the house 　　　**c** the bus

3 Which **height** label goes with each object?

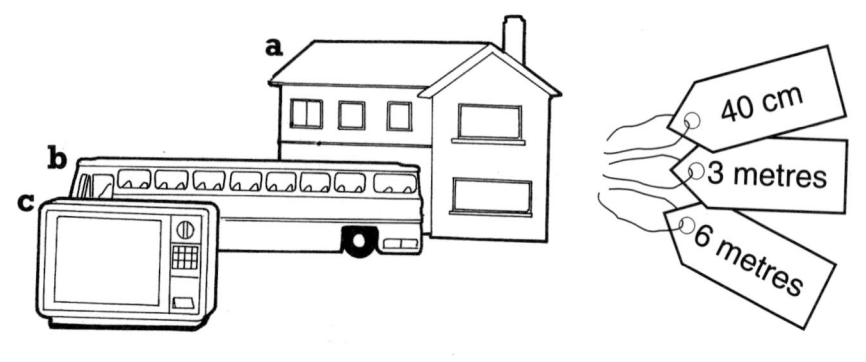

　a　**b**　**c**

Labels: 40 cm, 3 metres, 6 metres

86

10 MEASURES

Metres and Centimetres

Remember: 1 m = 100 cm

metres → ×100 → centimetres

Example:

James is 1.53 m tall.
1.53 × 100 = 153.
So James is 153 cm tall.

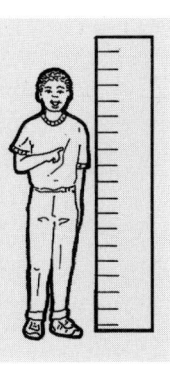

EXERCISE 2

1 Write each of these measurements in centimetres:

   a 3 m   b 5 m   c 12 m   d 45 m   e 98 m
   f 3.50 m   g 4.73 m   h 2.04 m   i 8.6 m   j 9.2 m

2 a Ken's boat is 4.85 m long.
      How many centimetres is this?

   b Each rod is 2.3 m long.
      How many centimetres is this?

3 Write each of these measurements in metres:

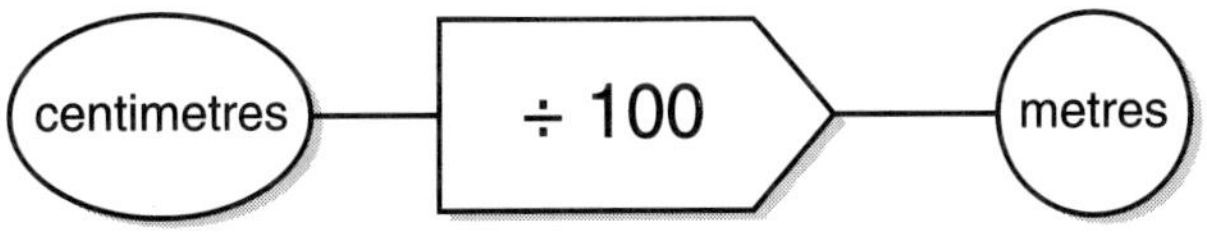

centimetres → ÷ 100 → metres

   a 200 cm   b 600 cm   c 415 cm   d 290 cm
   e 391 cm   f 803 cm   g 96 cm   h 42 cm

4 How long is the bookshelf:

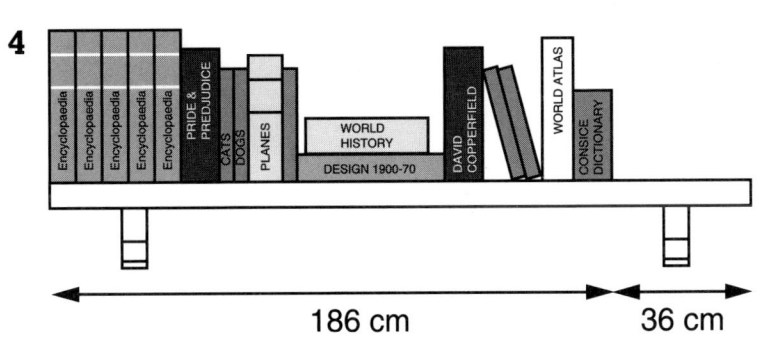

   a in centimetres
   b in metres?

   186 cm   36 cm

5 At the 'Pitch 'n' putt' Lenny hit the ball 15 m.

   a How many centimetres is this?

   Lenny then putts the ball 293 cm into the hole.

   b How many centimetres has he moved the ball altogether?
   c What is this distance in metres?

Do Worksheet 1

87

10 MEASURES

Kilometres and Millimetres

For larger distances **kilometres** are used.

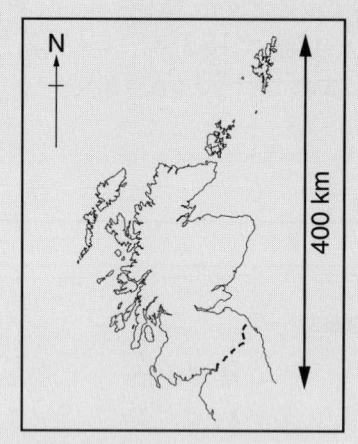

Scotland is about 400 km long.
1 **kilo**metre = **1000** metres

For short distances **millimetres** are used.

A 5 pence piece is about 18 mm wide.
1 metre = **1000 milli**metres

EXERCISE 3

1 What unit of measure would you use to measure these?

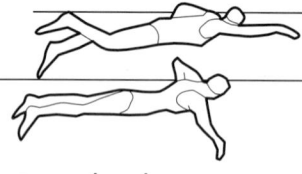

a a swimming race
b a twenty pence coin 
c a dinosaur 
d a seashell 
e a training shoe 
f a flight to Paris 
g a banana 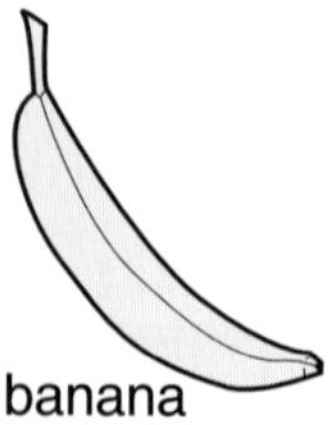
h a length of fence 
i the breadth of Ireland 

2 **a** Multiply by 1000 to turn these kilometres into metres:
   (i) 5 km   (ii) 12 km   (iii) 8.5 km   (iv) 5.42 km
  b Multiply by 1000 to turn these metres into millimetres:
   (i) 6 m   (ii) 23 m   (iii) 6.4 m   (iv) 9.26 m

10 MEASURES

3 a Divide by 1000 to turn these metres into kilometres:
   (i) 4000 m   (ii) 3450 m   (iii) 5292 m
b Divide by 1000 to turn these millimetres into metres:
   (i) 7000 mm   (ii) 3210 mm   (iii) 970 mm   (iv) 840 mm

4 Jeff had driven 3.6 km.
He phoned home.
'I've got 2.5 km to go.'

How long was the whole journey?

5 On exercises the pilot flew 78.4 km on the way out.
He flew the same distance going home.

How far did he fly?

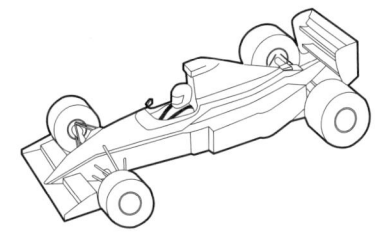

6 Ten times round the circuit and the racer has covered 3.7 km.

a How far is one lap in kilometres? (Hint: divide.)
b How far is it in metres?

7 Margaret had been out for a round of golf.
She played 4 holes before it started raining.
The distances covered for each hole were
241 m, 412 m, 217 m and 357 m.

a How far did she play in metres?
b How far is this in kilometres?

8 Divide each of the following by 10 to change the millimetres to centimetres.

a 30 mm   **b** 40 mm   **c** 45 mm   **d** 230 mm   **e** 465 mm

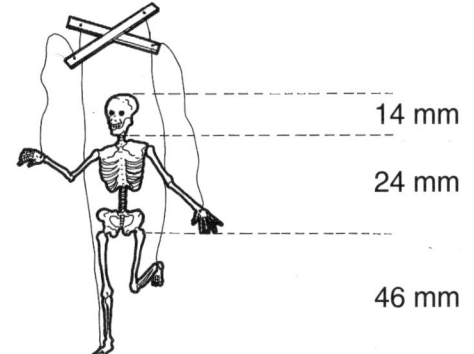

9 The puppet skeleton has a 14 mm long head, a 24 mm long body, and 46 mm long legs.

14 mm
24 mm
46 mm

a How long is the puppet in millimetres?
b How long is this in centimetres?

Perimeter

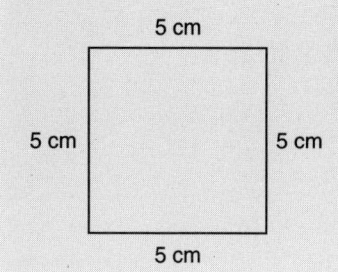

The **perimeter** of a shape is the distance round it.

5 + 5 + 5 + 5 = 20 cm.

EXERCISE 4

1. A company makes tables. They give the perimeter of each table in their adverts.

   Calculate the perimeter of each of these tables.

   a Pentagon

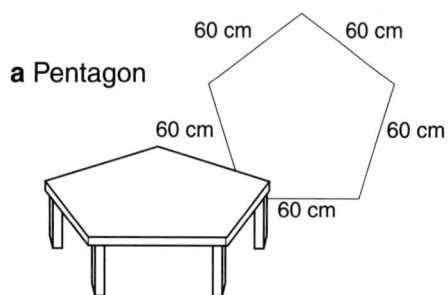

   b Square

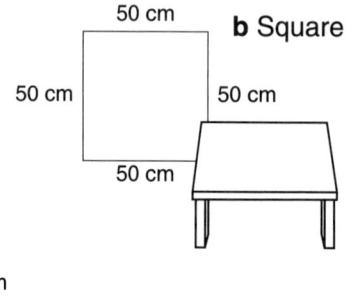

   c Hexagon

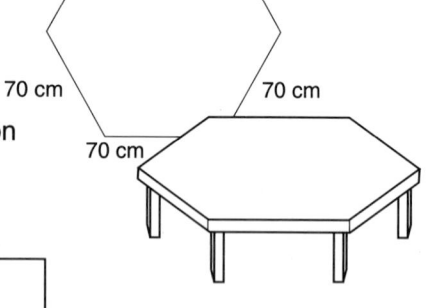

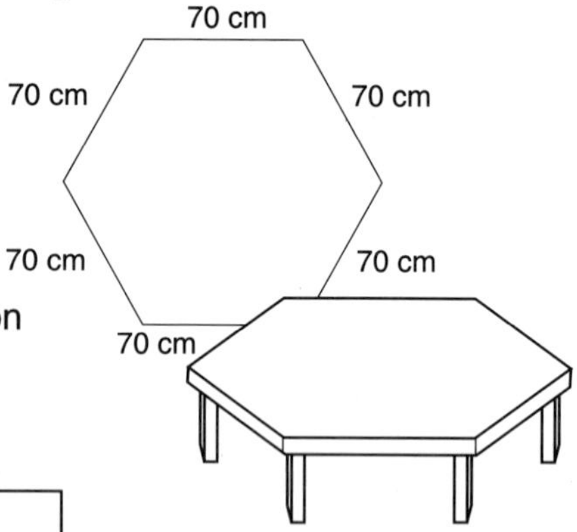

2. **a** 20 m, 8 m, 20 m, 8 m

   b 11 m, 10 m, 11 m, 10 m

   c 8 m, 12 m

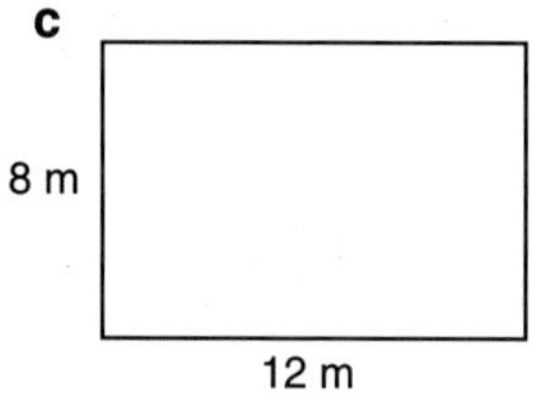

   d 10 m, 20 m

   e 6 m, 3 m, 14 m, 7 m, 20 m, 10 m

   When buying a fence, you need to know the perimeter of the garden.

   Work out the perimeters of these gardens.

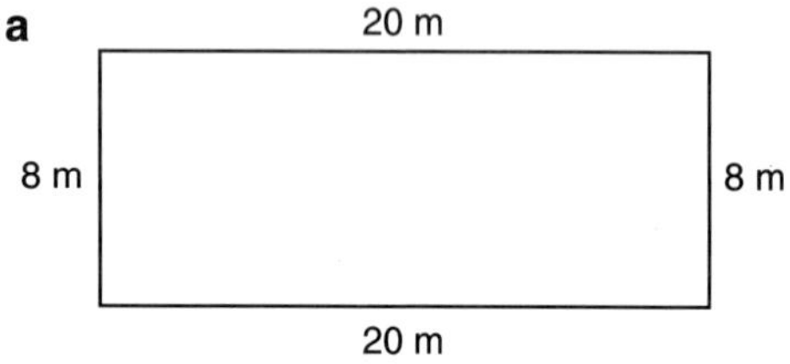

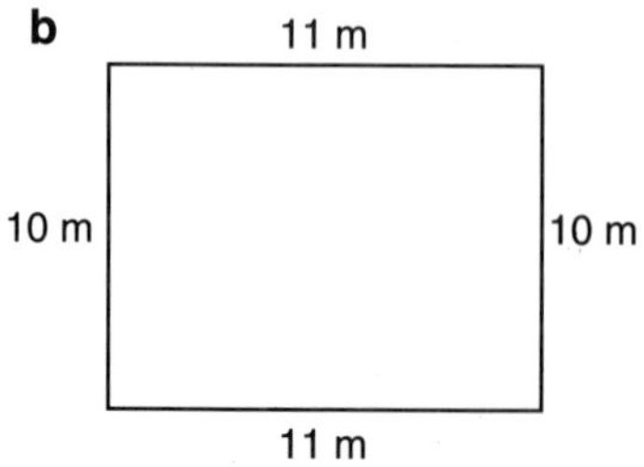

90

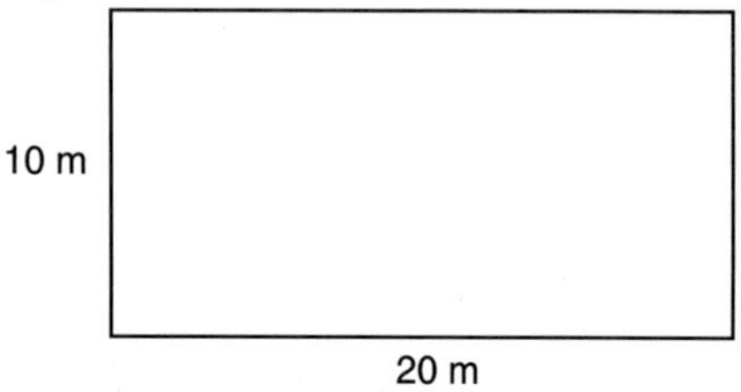

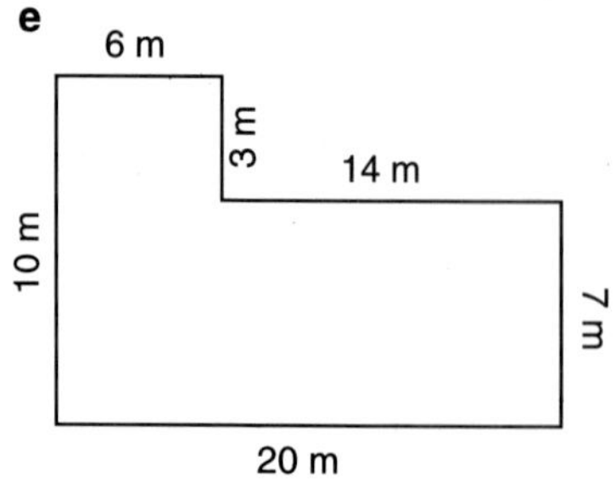

10 MEASURES

Area

We measure area by counting squares.

Window A is 12 squares.
Window B is 15 squares.

So window B has the bigger area.

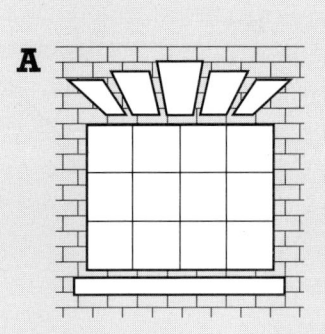

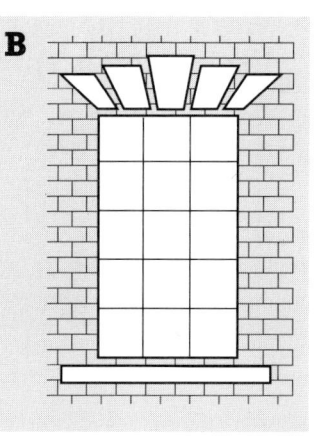

EXERCISE 5

1 Estimate the area of each shape.
  Only count a square **if more than half** of it is filled.

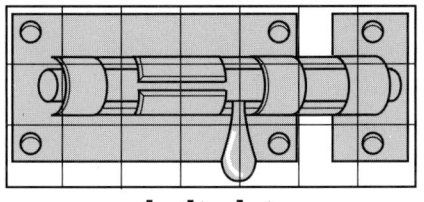

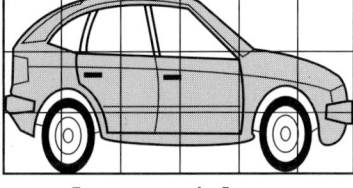

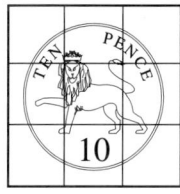

   a bolt plate   **b** car sticker   **c** 10 pence

2 Draw round your shoe on squared paper.

   Estimate the area of leather needed to make a sole for your shoe.

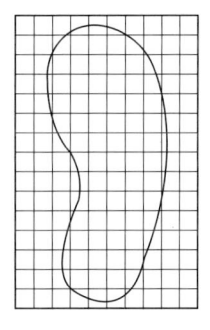

3 **a** Rectangle **b** Square **c** Octagon **d** Hexagon **e** Pentagon

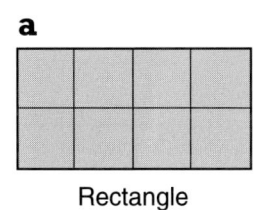

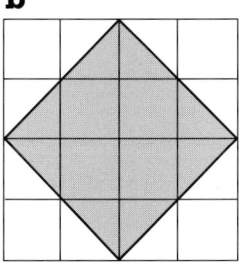

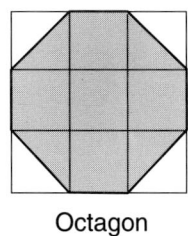

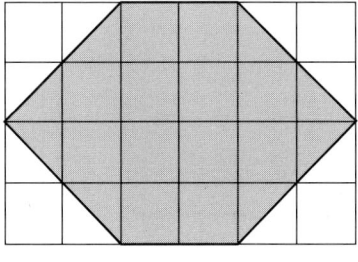

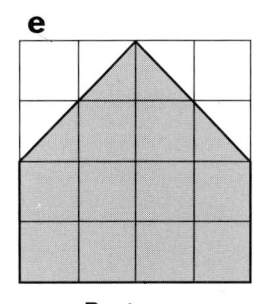

Find the area of each shape exactly.

Each square **represents** 1 square centimetre ($1 cm^2$).

91

10 MEASURES

4 Work out the area of each shape.
Each square **represents** a square centimetre.

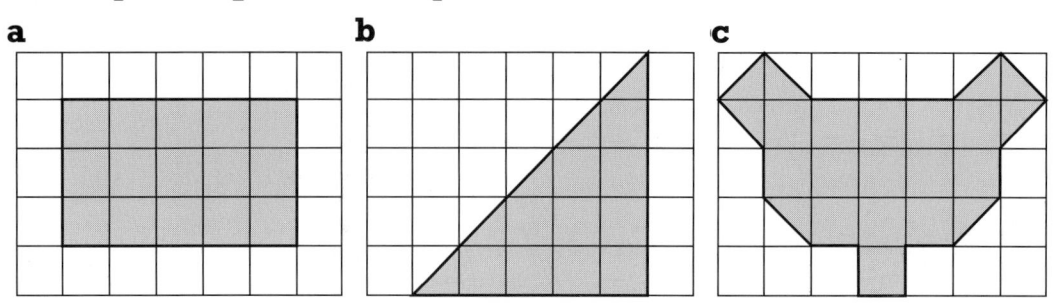

a   b   c

5 Peter's house has four rooms which need carpets.
Work out the area of each floor.
Each square **represents** a square metre.

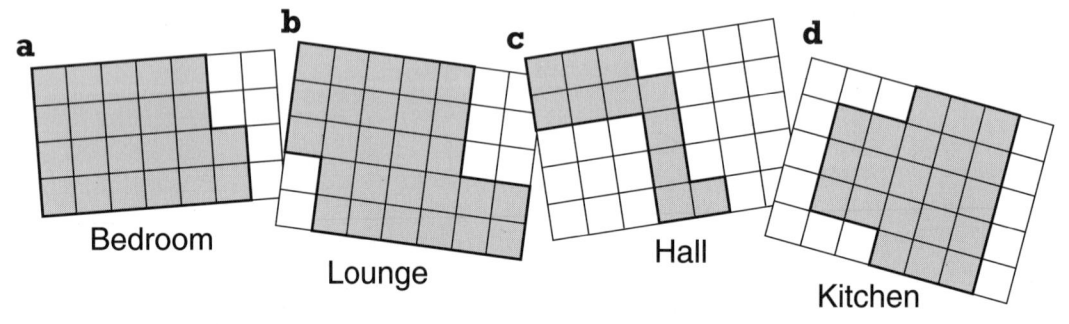

a Bedroom   b Lounge   c Hall   d Kitchen

6 An advert in the local paper costs 20 pence for each square centimetre.
Use a centimetre grid to help you find the cost of each advert.

a **Phone-Lines**
Join our circle of friends.
Phone: 012 345 6789

b **The Pavilion**
Now showing
Snowwhite & the Seven Dwarfs

c **Happy Hols**
Exotic Holidays Abroad.
Phone: 0124 987 9876

d Camera Equipment at reasonable prices.
The Lens Centre

e **The Big Match**
Get your ticket reserved.
Phone: 1234 567 1111

Do Worksheet 2

92

Volume in Cubic Centimetres

We measure volume by counting cubes.

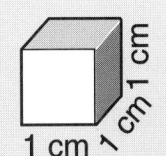

1 cubic centimetre

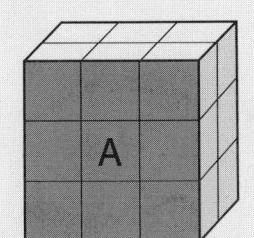

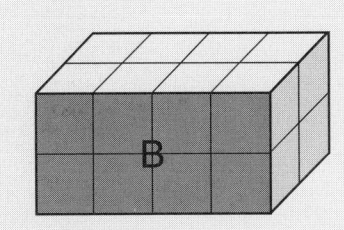

Box A is 18 cubic centimetres.
We write: **18 cm³**.
Box B is **16 cm³**.

Box A has the bigger volume.

EXERCISE 6

1. Work out the volume of each box.

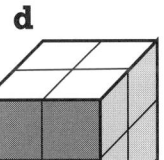

   a   b 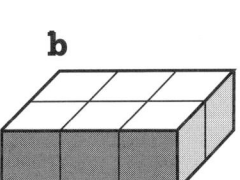   c 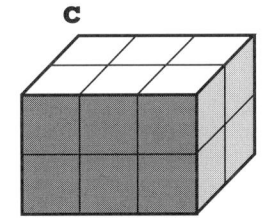   d 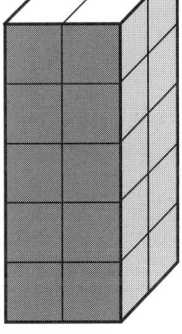   e

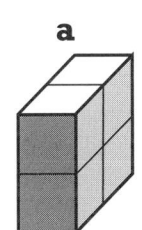

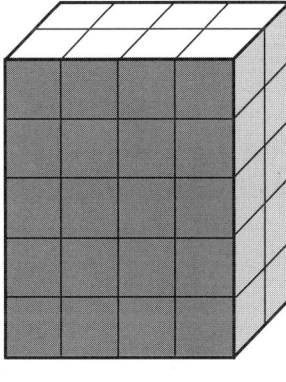

2.
   a. Each cube represents a cubic centimetre. 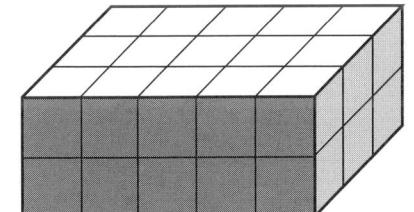 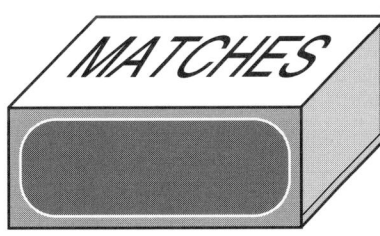

   What is the volume of the matchbox?

   b. Here is a TV remote control beside the box of matches.

   Estimate the volume of the remote control.

   c. The TV set is about 100 times the volume of the remote control. 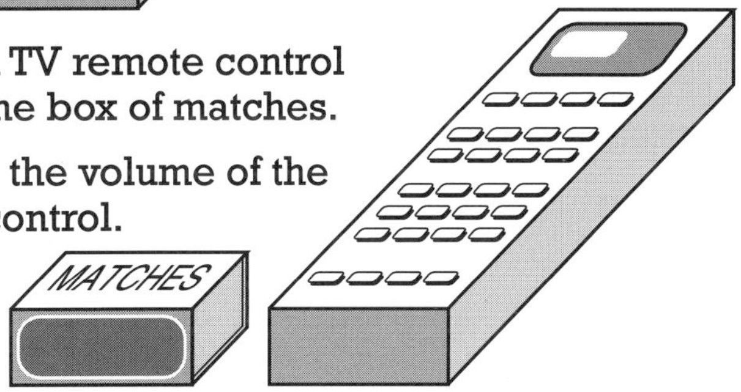  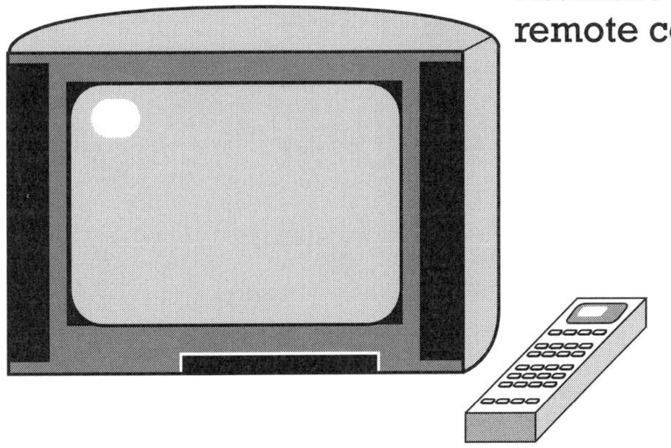

   Estimate the volume of the TV set.

93

10 MEASURES

Volume in Litres

We usually measure larger volumes using **litres**.

1 litre = 1000 cubic centimetres.

1 cubic centimetre is the same as **1 millilitre**.

$1 \text{ cm}^3 = 1 \text{ ml}$

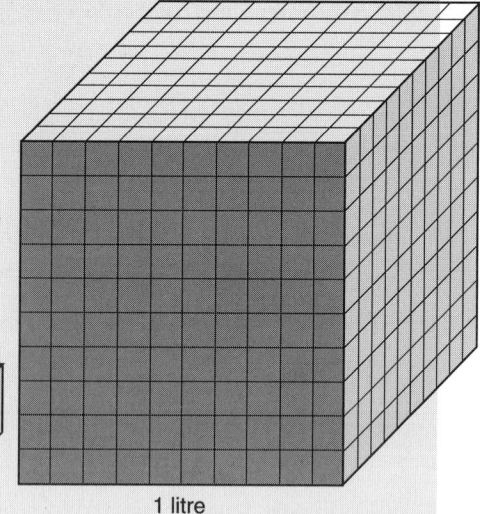

Do Worksheet 3

EXERCISE 7

1 Copy and complete each label.

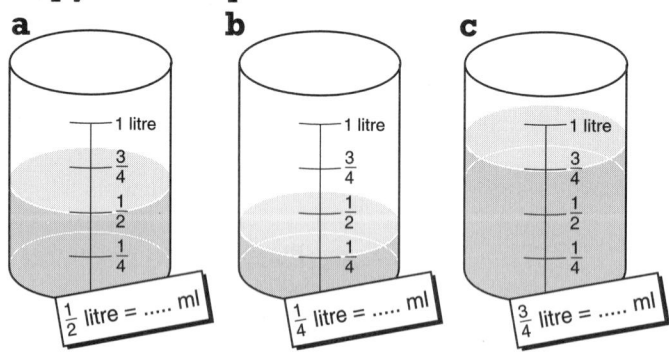

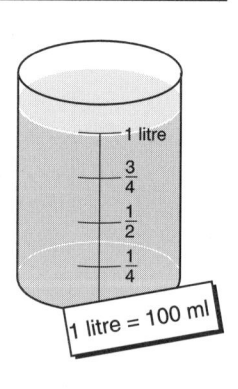

a $\frac{1}{2}$ litre = ... ml

b $\frac{1}{4}$ litre = ... ml

c $\frac{3}{4}$ litre = ... ml

1 litre = 100 ml

2 Multiply by 1000 to turn the following into millilitres:

   a 2 litres   **b** 3 litres   **c** 4.5 litres   **d** 0.25 litre

3 Divide by 1000 to turn the following into litres:

   a 4000 ml   **b** 5000 ml   **c** 2500 ml   **d** 350 ml

4 Petrol can still be measured in the old imperial unit, the **gallon**. A gallon is roughly 4.5 litres.

Multiply by 4.5 to find how many litres each of the following is:

   a 8 gallons   **b** 3 gallons   **c** 10 gallons

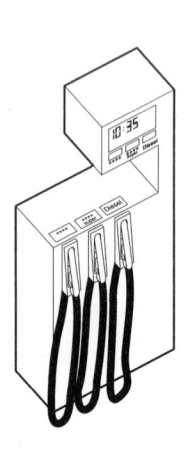

94

10 MEASURES

5 Another old unit still in use is the **pint**.
This is roughly half a litre.

Halve the following to express them in litres.

   a 2 pints   **b** 10 pints   **c** 8 pints

6 Hussein needs 4 litres of paint to do his room.
He buys 10 tins of paint like the one shown.

   a How many millilitres of paint did he buy?
   b Write this in litres.
   c Has he bought enough or too much?

7 Jane's car used 1 litre of petrol to go 10 km.

   How far can she travel on:

   a 2 litres   **b** 3 litres   **c** 10 litres?

8 Husna mixes 750 ml of water with 520 ml of fruit squash.

   a How many millilitres of drink does she make?
   b How many litres of drink is this?

9 Cola comes in bottles which hold 440 ml.
They come in crates of 12 bottles.

   a How many millilitres of cola are in a crate?
   b How many litres is this?

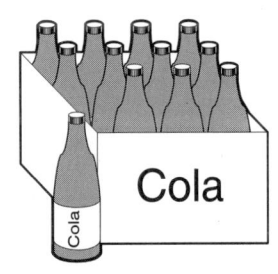

10 15 litres of water are carried in 10 buckets.
Each bucket can carry the same amount.

   a How many litres are in each bucket?
   b How many millilitres is this?

11 Bernard's coffee maker holds 1.5 litres.
It pours 5 equal cups of coffee.

   a How much of a litre is in each cup?
   b How many millilitres are in each cup?

95

10 MEASURES

Weight

We measure weight using scales.

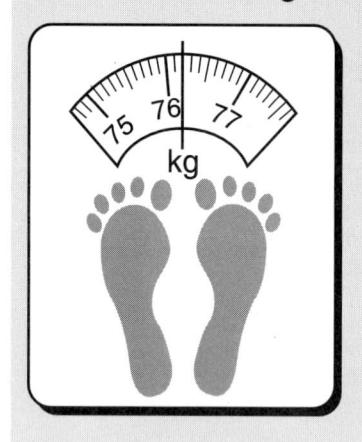

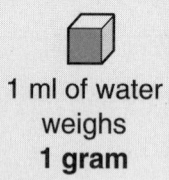

1 ml of water weighs **1 gram**

1 litre of water weighs **1 kilogram**

1000 g = 1 kg

On these scales every mark is worth 100 grams. Here we have 76 kg and 2 marks. We can write this as **76 kg and 200 g** or **76.2 kg**.

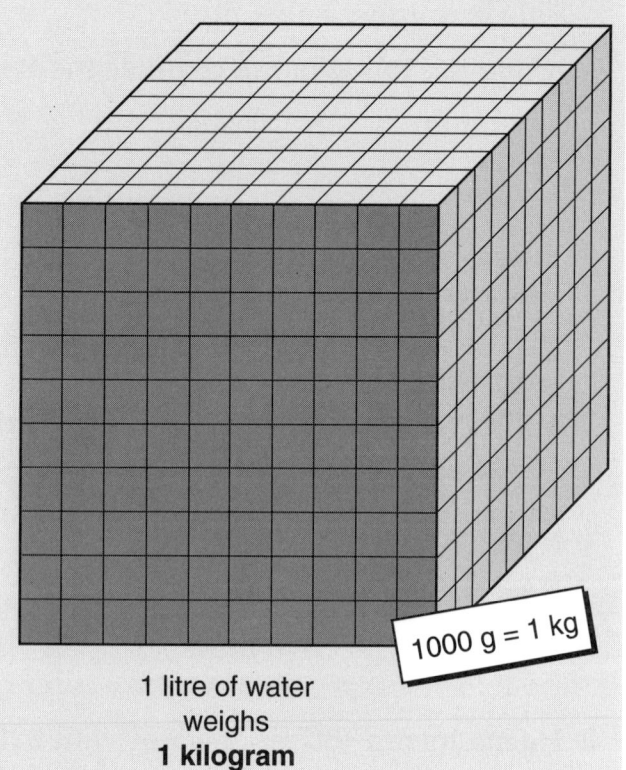

EXERCISE 8

1 Read each of these scales. Write your answer both ways.

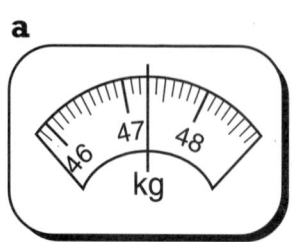

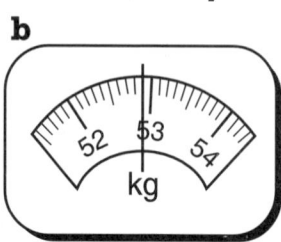

a Mark's weight

b Meena's weight

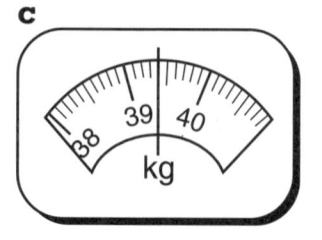

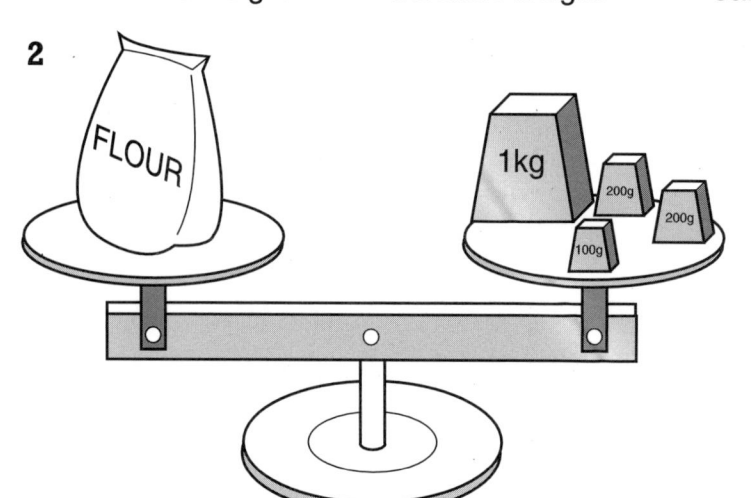

c Jan's weight

2 Sometimes we balance things on scales with loose weights to find out their weight.

What is the weight of the flour:

a in kilograms and grams
b in kilograms?

96

10 MEASURES

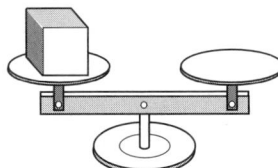

3 What is the weight of the box when it balances with these loose weights?

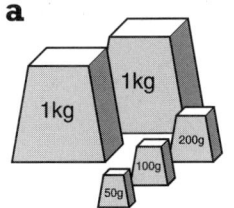

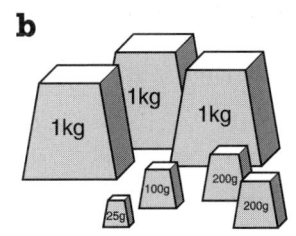

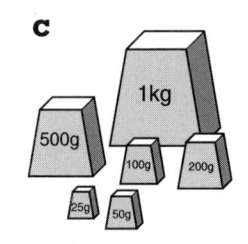

a 1kg, 1kg, 200g, 100g, 50g

b 1kg, 1kg, 1kg, 200g, 200g, 100g, 25g

c 1kg, 500g, 200g, 100g, 50g, 25g

4 Here's Marco's recipe for minestrone soup.

  a What is the total weight of the ingredients in grams?
  b What is this weight in kilograms?
  c How many people does the recipe serve?
  d What is the weight of one serving?

Minestrone soup	
Tomatoes	396 g
Beans	283 g
Mixed veg	340 g
Onion	100 g
Stock	900 g

Serves 6 people

5 Repeat question **4** for these two recipes:

a

Avocado salad	
Shrimps	175 g
Pineapple	175 g
Mayonnaise	100 g
Avocado	700 g

Serves 5 people

b

Rasperry pudding	
Raspberries	700 g
Suger	350 g
Flour	175 g
Milk	300 g

Serves 4 people

6 The table shows the weights of the **average** boy and girl at different ages.

Age (years)	9	10	11	12	13	14
Boy (kg)	26	34	38	40	50	55
Girl (kg)	25	32	36	41	52	56

  a Sam is 12 years old. He weighs 48 kg.
  How much over the average is he for his age?

  b Angela is 13 and weighs 46 kg.
  How much under the average weight is she?

97

10 MEASURES

CHECK-UP ON MEASURES

1 a How many centimetres make a metre?
  b How many millimetres make a metre?

2 Convert these:

  a 2.5 m to centimetres   **b** 3400 mm to metres

3 This model dinosaur is in the museum.

  What is its total length?

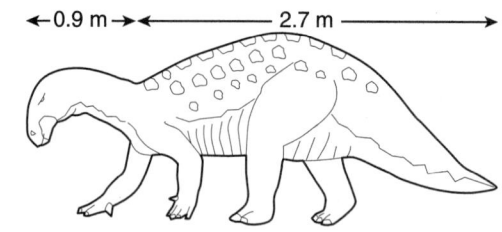

  ←0.9 m→ ←――― 2.7 m ―――→

4 What is the area of each shape?

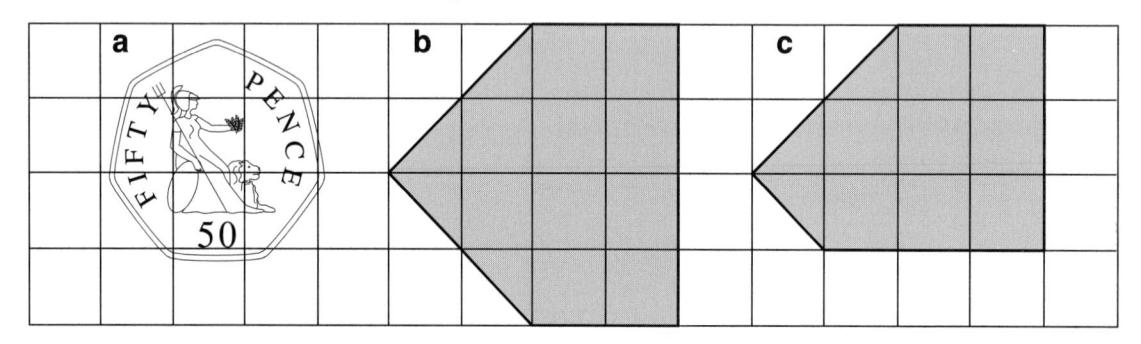

5 a How many millilitres make a litre?
  b Turn the following into litres:
     (i) 5000 ml   (ii) 5250 ml   (iii) 900 ml
  c Turn the following into millilitres:
     (i) 4 litres   (ii) 0.6 litre

6 represents 1 cubic centimetre.

  a What else can you call a cubic centimetre?
  b What is the volume of each box in cubic centimetres?

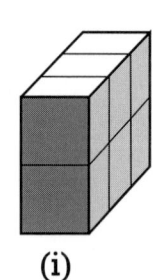

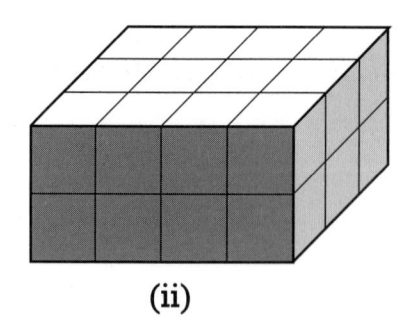

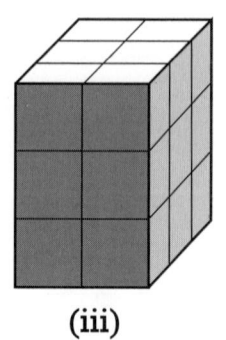

     (i)   (ii)   (iii)

7 a What is the weight of 1 litre of water?
  b How many grams make a kilogram?
  c Change the following weights to grams:
     (i) 3 kg   (ii) 5.5 kg   (iii) 0.8 kg

98

11 TYPES OF TRIANGLES

Recognising Triangles

Triangles have three sides.

Quadrilaterals have four sides.

EXERCISE 1

1 Copy and complete the table.

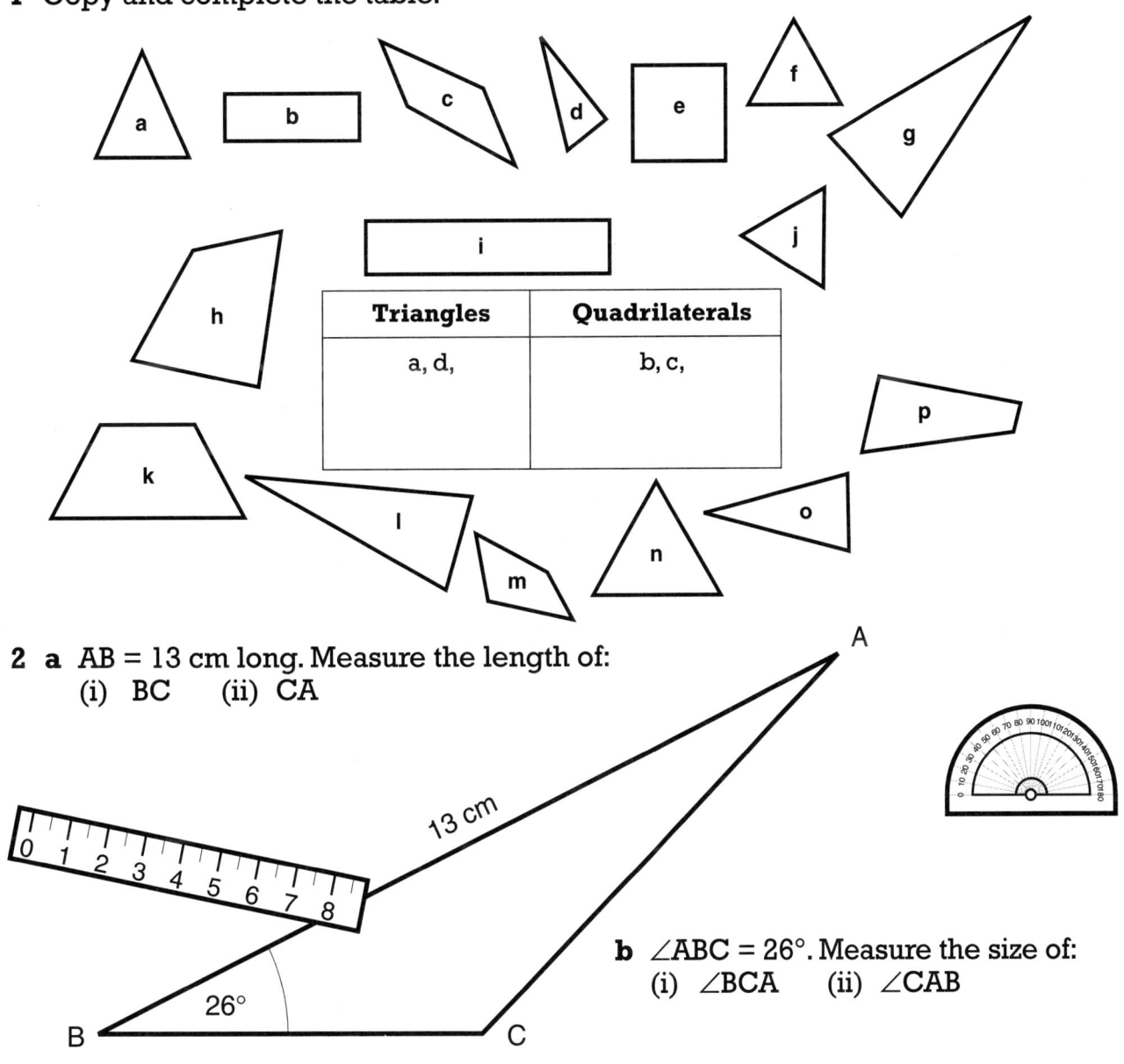

Triangles	Quadrilaterals
a, d,	b, c,

2 a AB = 13 cm long. Measure the length of:
  (i) BC (ii) CA

  b $\angle ABC = 26°$. Measure the size of:
  (i) $\angle BCA$ (ii) $\angle CAB$

99

11 TYPES OF TRIANGLES

3 Which of these solids have triangular faces?

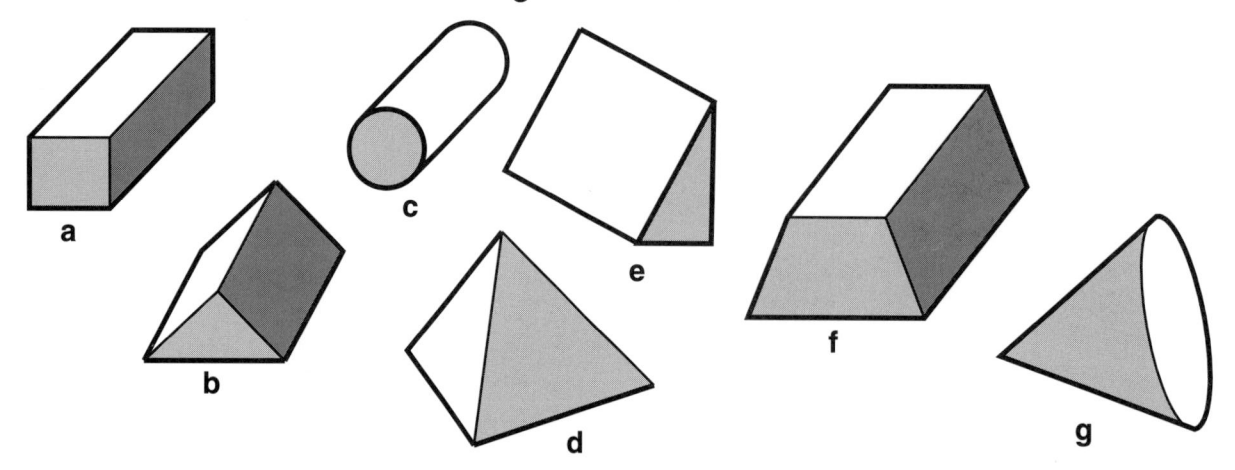

4 This diagram has nine triangles. Copy and complete the list.

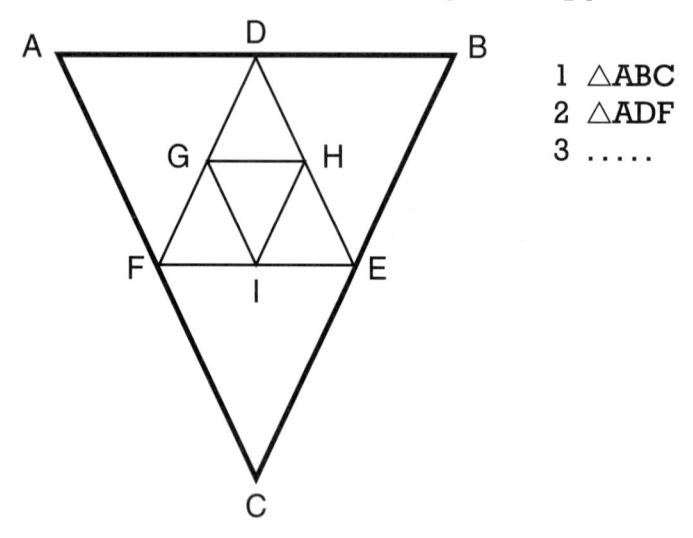

1 △ABC
2 △ADF
3 .....

5 a Cut out a triangle.
 b Use it as a template to make other identical triangles.
 c Make a tiling pattern with your triangles.
 d Try working with different sets of triangles.

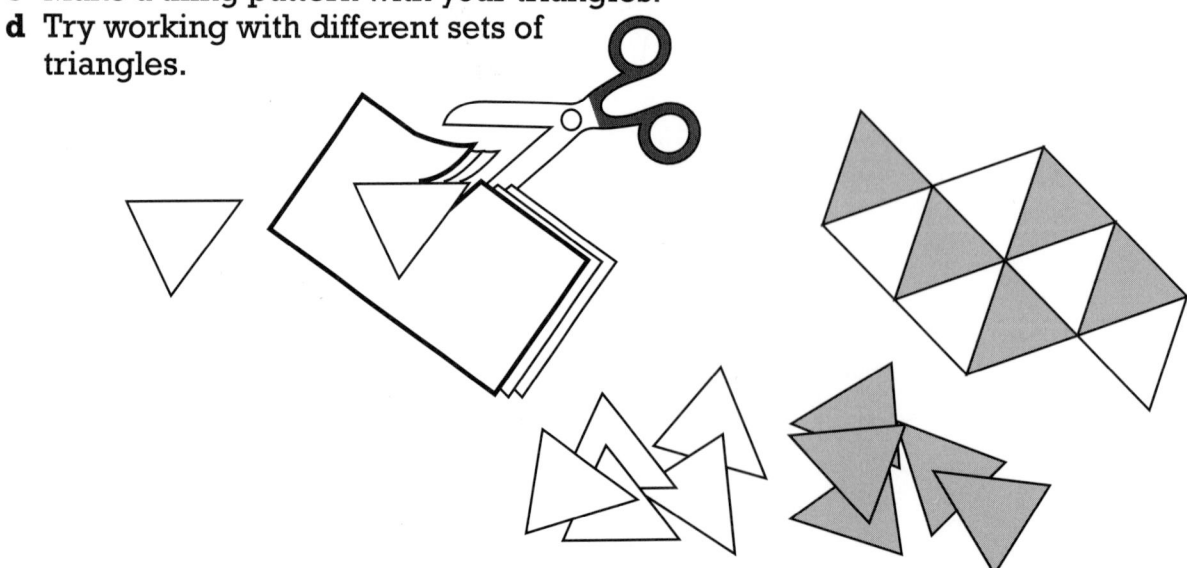

100

11 TYPES OF TRIANGLES

Special Triangles

This picture has a line of symmetry.

An **isosceles** triangle has a line of symmetry.

So an isosceles triangle has two equal sides and two equal angles.

An **equilateral** triangle has three lines of symmetry.

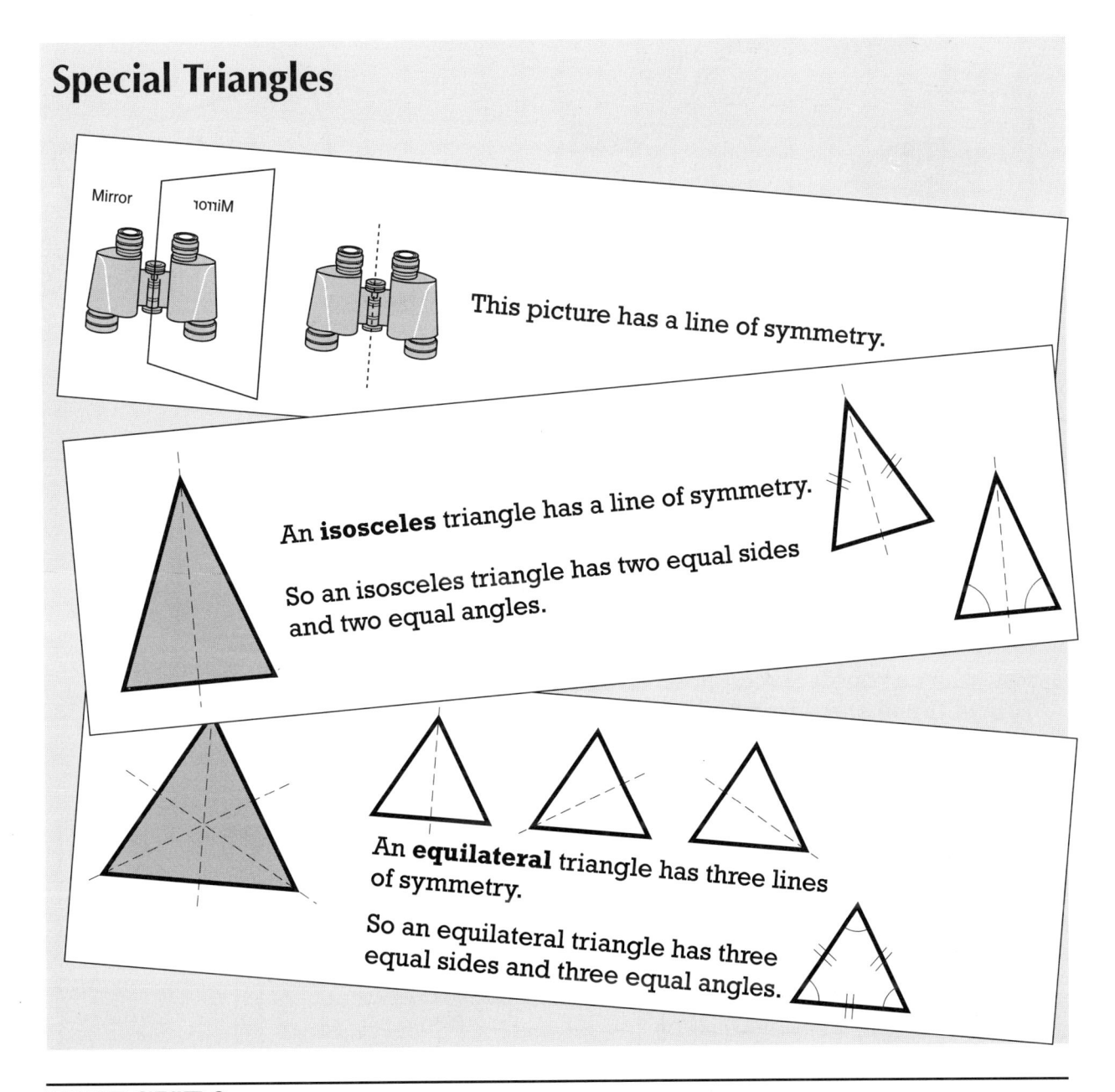

So an equilateral triangle has three equal sides and three equal angles.

EXERCISE 2

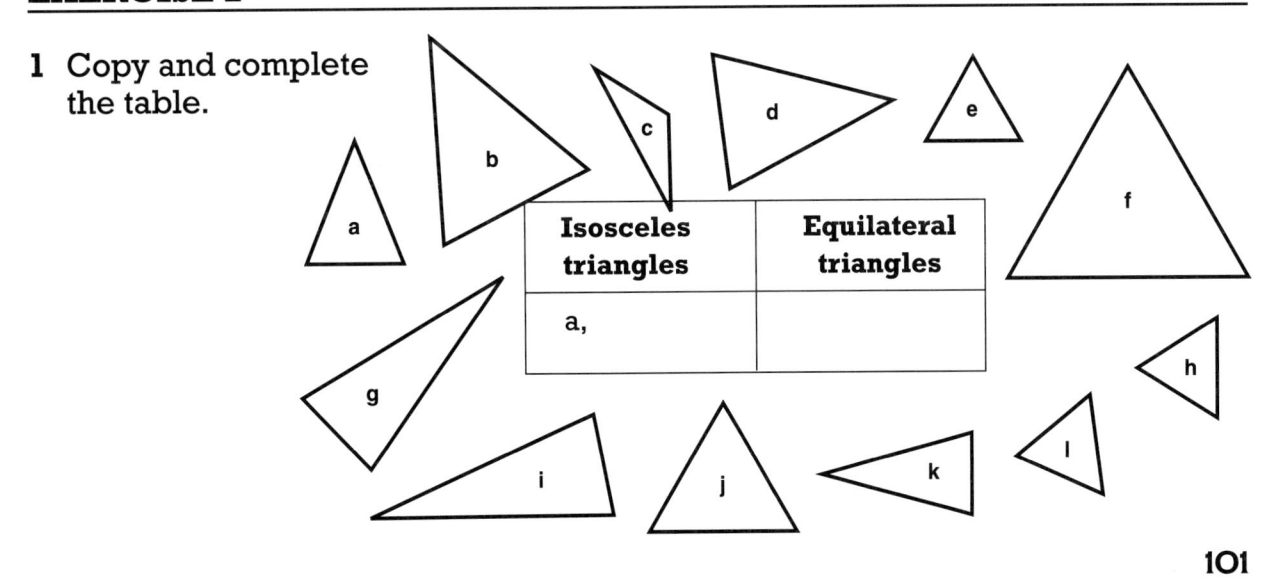

1 Copy and complete the table.

Isosceles triangles	Equilateral triangles
a,	

101

11 TYPES OF TRIANGLES

2 Fold a rectangle in half.  Cut off the folded corner as shown. 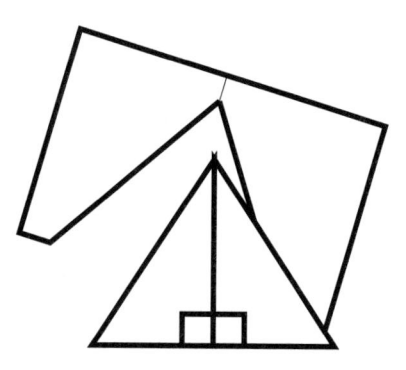 Open out the shape.

You have a triangle with a line of symmetry.
It is an isosceles triangle.
Glue it into your jotter. Mark on it:

a the line of symmetry
b the equal sides
c the equal angles.

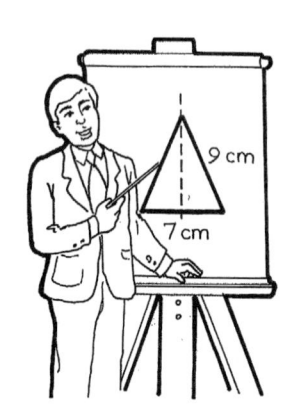

3 Peter has a rough sketch of an isosceles triangle. Follow these steps to make an accurate drawing of the triangle.

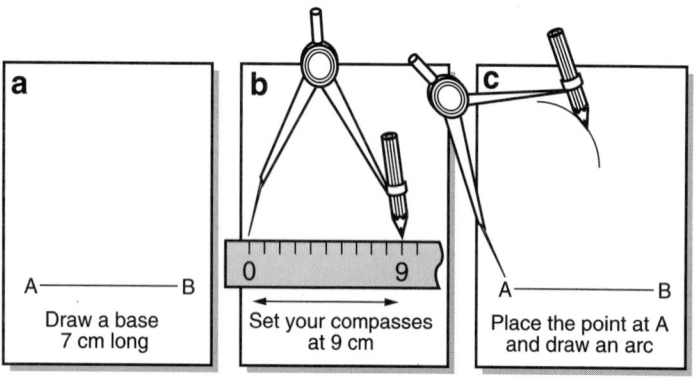

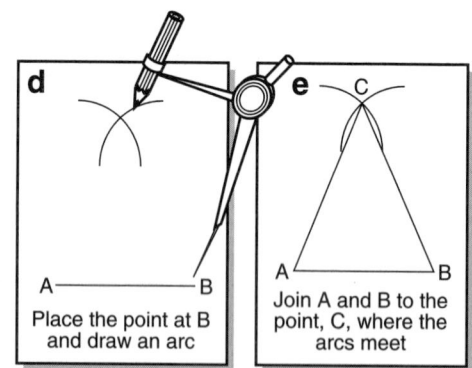

a Draw a base 7 cm long
b Set your compasses at 9 cm
c Place the point at A and draw an arc
d Place the point at B and draw an arc
e Join A and B to the point, C, where the arcs meet

4 Peter has some more rough sketches. Make accurate drawings of them.

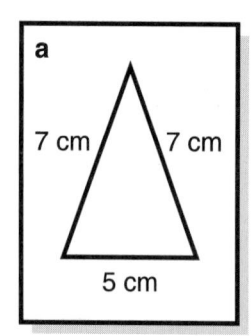

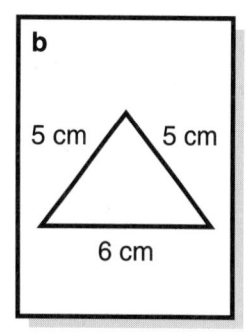

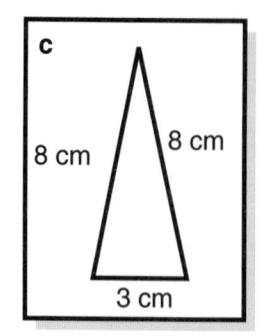

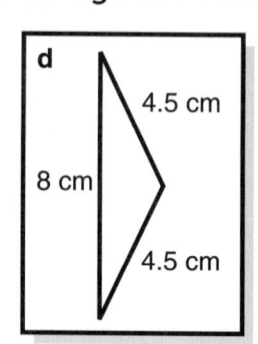

a 7 cm, 7 cm, 5 cm
b 5 cm, 5 cm, 6 cm
c 8 cm, 8 cm, 3 cm
d 4.5 cm, 8 cm, 4.5 cm

In each of your drawings mark:
a the line of symmetry
b the equal angles.

102

11 TYPES OF TRIANGLES

5 Peter now wants an **equilateral** triangle with sides 9 cm. Follow these instructions to draw an accurate equilateral triangle of side 9 cm.

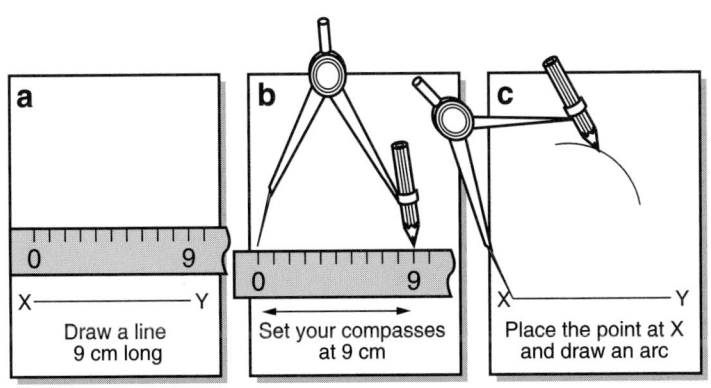

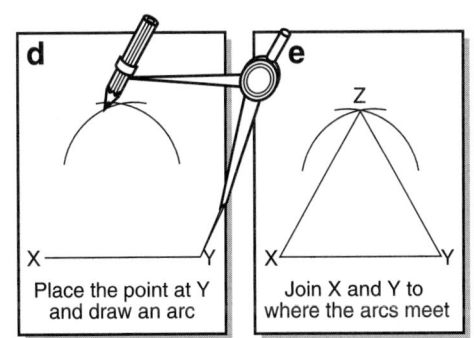

a	b	c	d	e
Draw a line 9 cm long	Set your compasses at 9 cm	Place the point at X and draw an arc	Place the point at Y and draw an arc	Join X and Y to where the arcs meet

6 a Draw **equilateral** triangles whose sides are:
    (i) 5 cm long   (ii) 8 cm long   (iii) 10 cm long.
b Mark the **three lines of symmetry** on each triangle.

7 Equilateral triangles can be used to make solids.

Some adventure games use dice which don't have 6 faces.

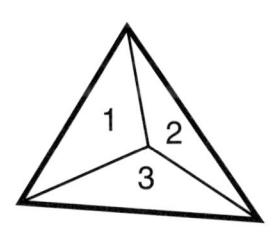

Some have 4 faces: a tetrahedron

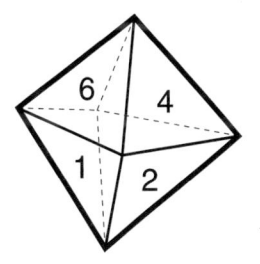

Some have 8 faces: an octahedron

Use the nets on Worksheet 1 to help you make these dice.

Get Worksheet 1

11 TYPES OF TRIANGLES

Another Special Triangle

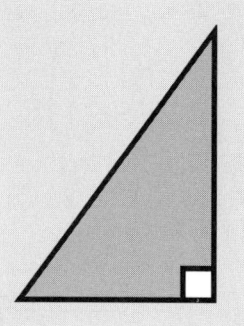

A right-angled triangle has one right angle.

EXERCISE 3

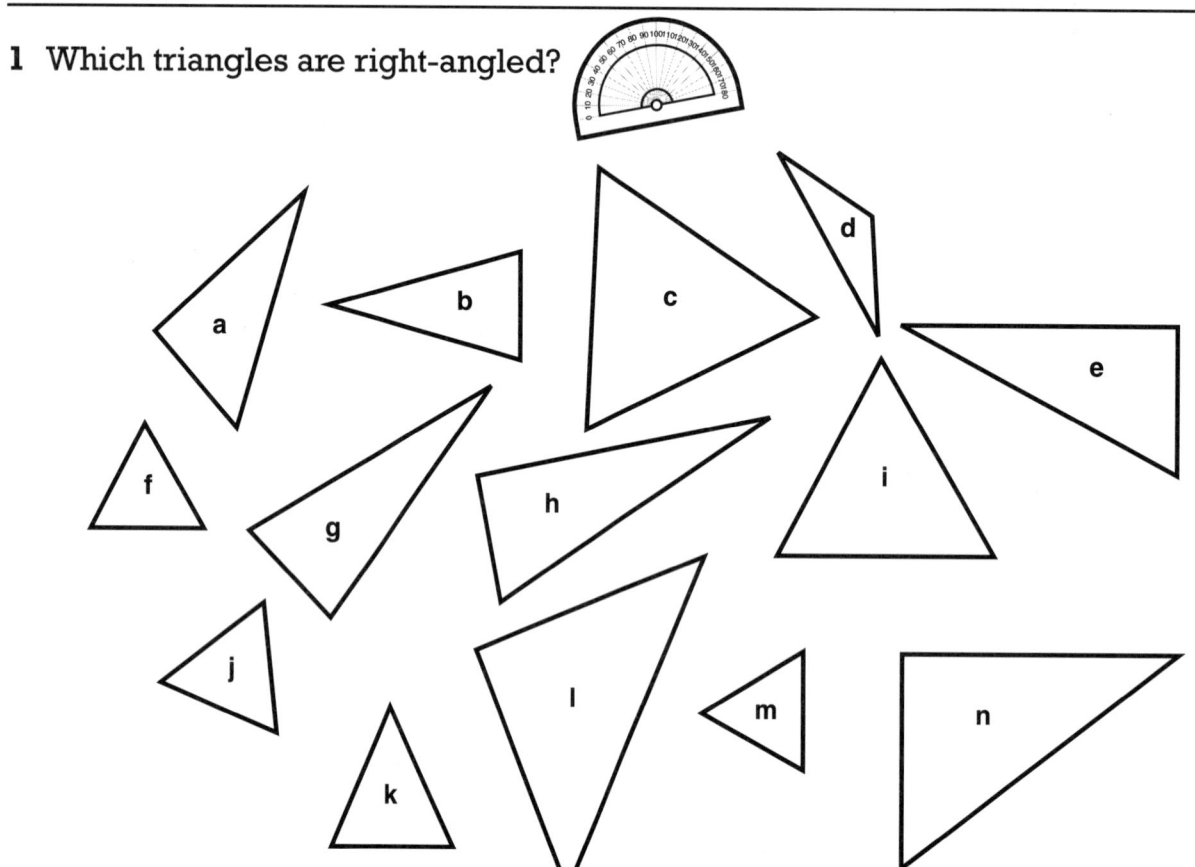

1 Which triangles are right-angled?

2 Find the area of these right-angled triangles. (Count squares and half squares.)

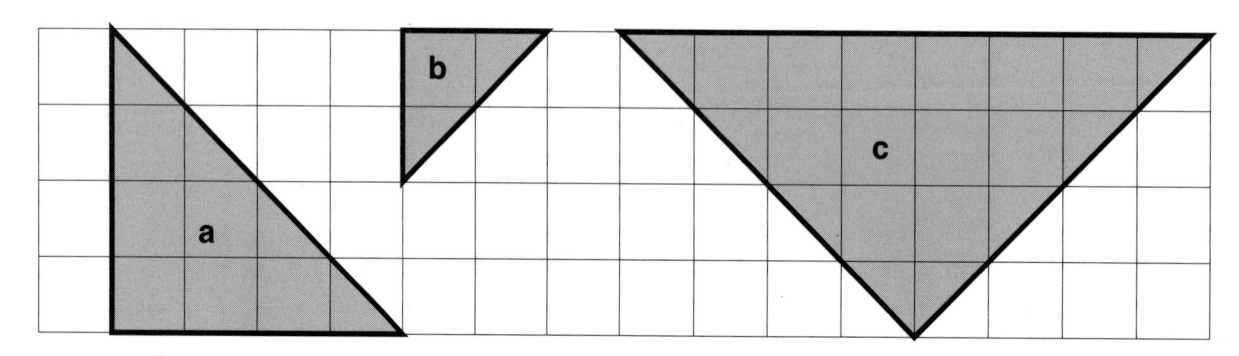

104

11 TYPES OF TRIANGLES

3 Cut out a rectangle like this:

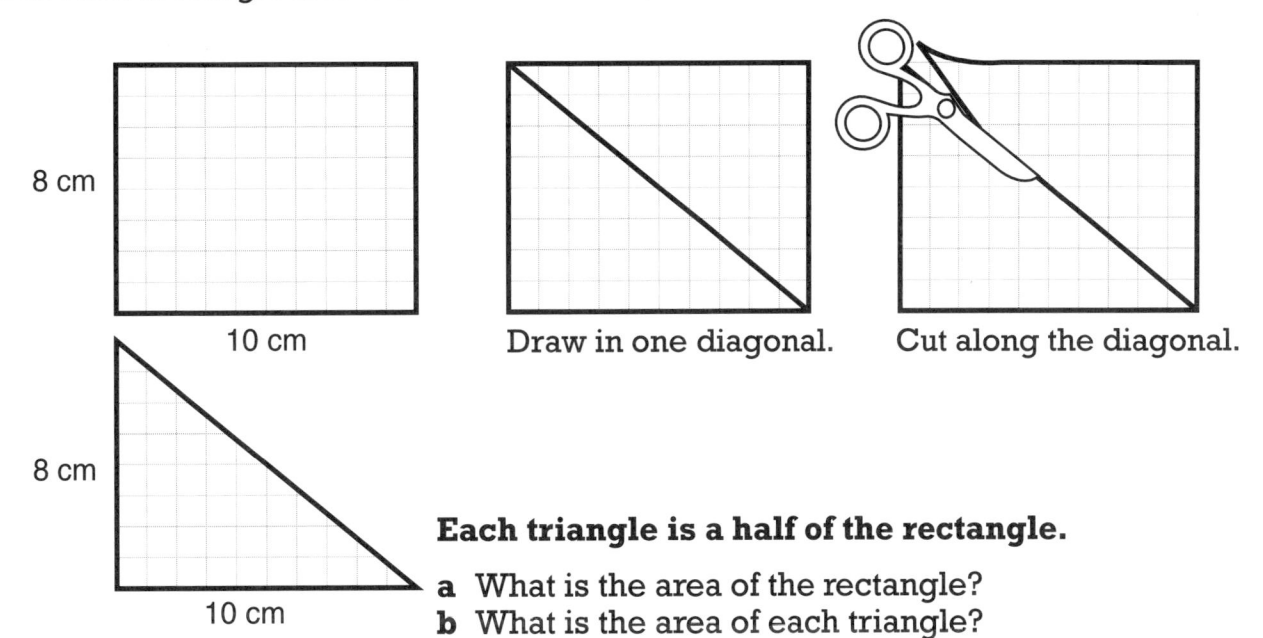

8 cm
10 cm

Draw in one diagonal.

Cut along the diagonal.

8 cm
10 cm

Each triangle is a half of the rectangle.

a What is the area of the rectangle?
b What is the area of each triangle?

4 Find the area of these triangles.

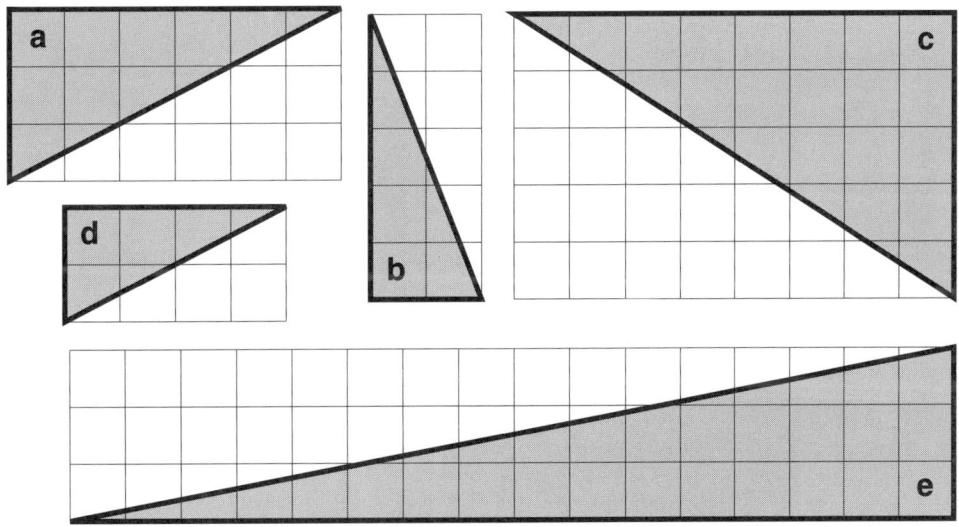

a
b
c
d
e

5 John is making sails for his toy yacht.

a Find the area of each small triangle.
b Find the area of the large triangle.

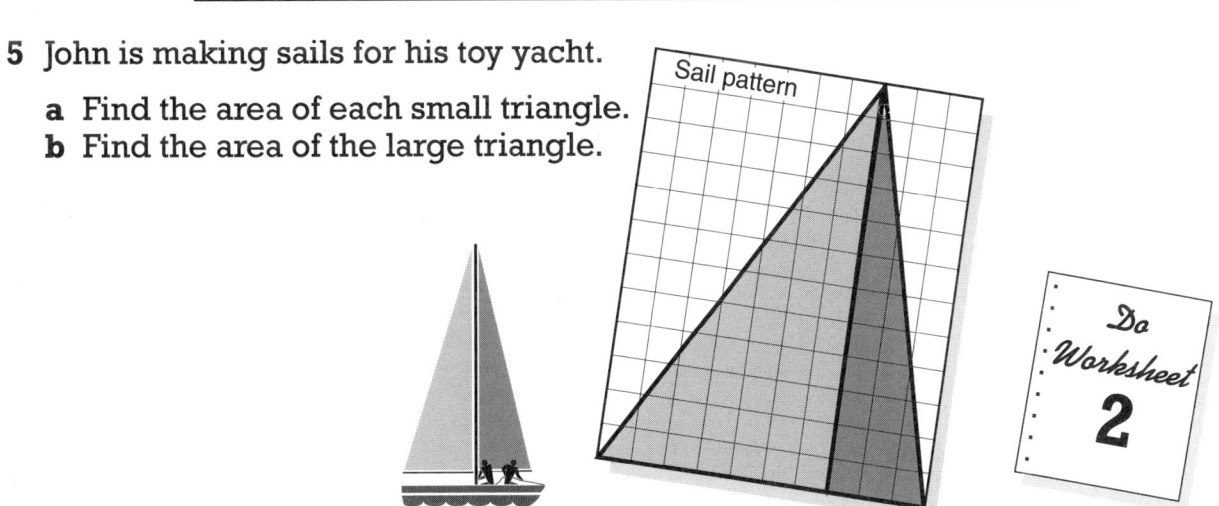

Sail pattern

Do Worksheet 2

105

11 TYPES OF TRIANGLES

EXERCISE 4

1 For both triangles below:

(i) measure each angle in the triangle
(ii) find the sum of the three angles.

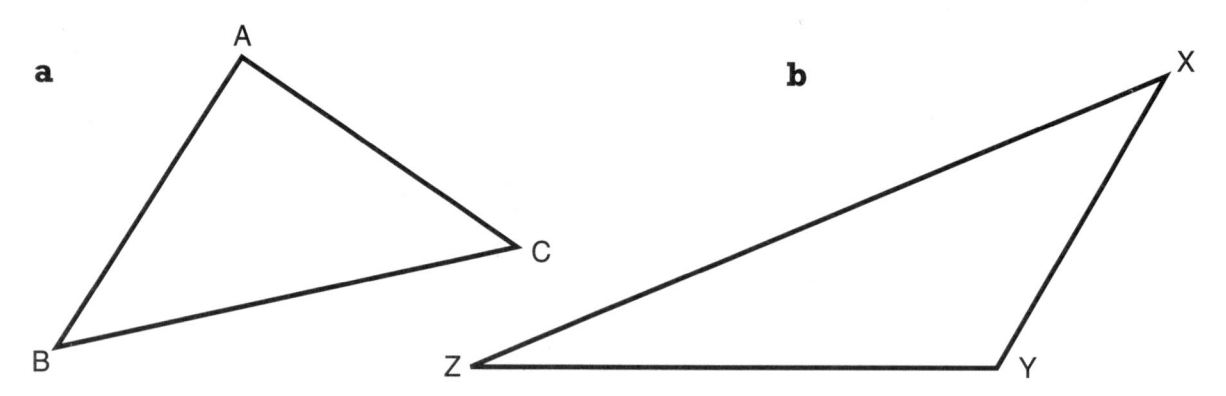

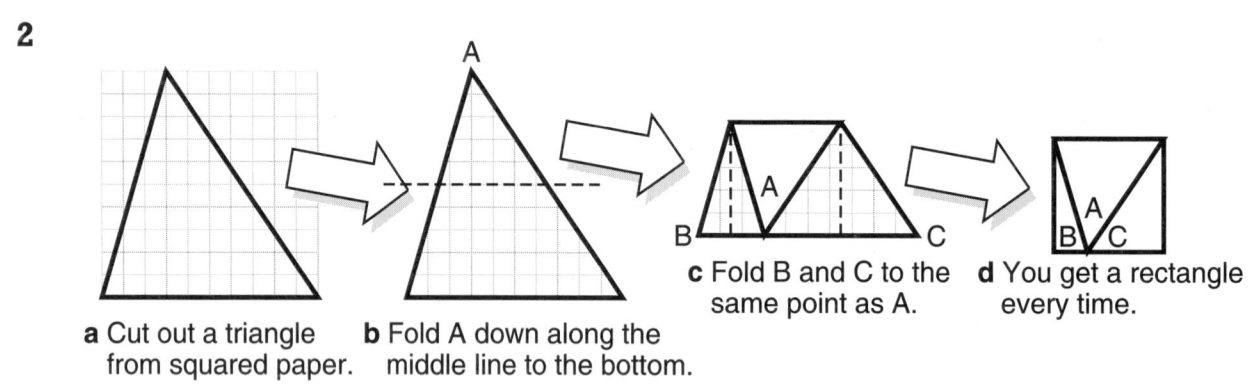

a

b

2

a Cut out a triangle from squared paper.   **b** Fold A down along the middle line to the bottom.   **c** Fold B and C to the same point as A.   **d** You get a rectangle every time.

The three angles of a triangle form a straight line.

3 Draw some triangles of your own.
For each one you draw find the sum of its angles.

The angles of a triangle add up to 180°.

4 (i) Write down the size of the missing angle in each triangle.
(ii) Say what kind of triangle each one is.

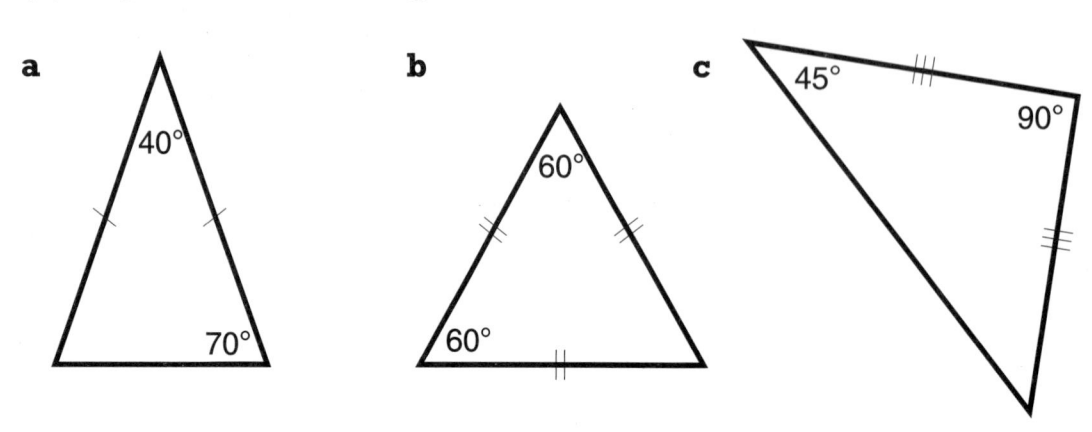

a 40°, 70°

b 60°, 60°

c 45°, 90°

11 TYPES OF TRIANGLES

Perimeter

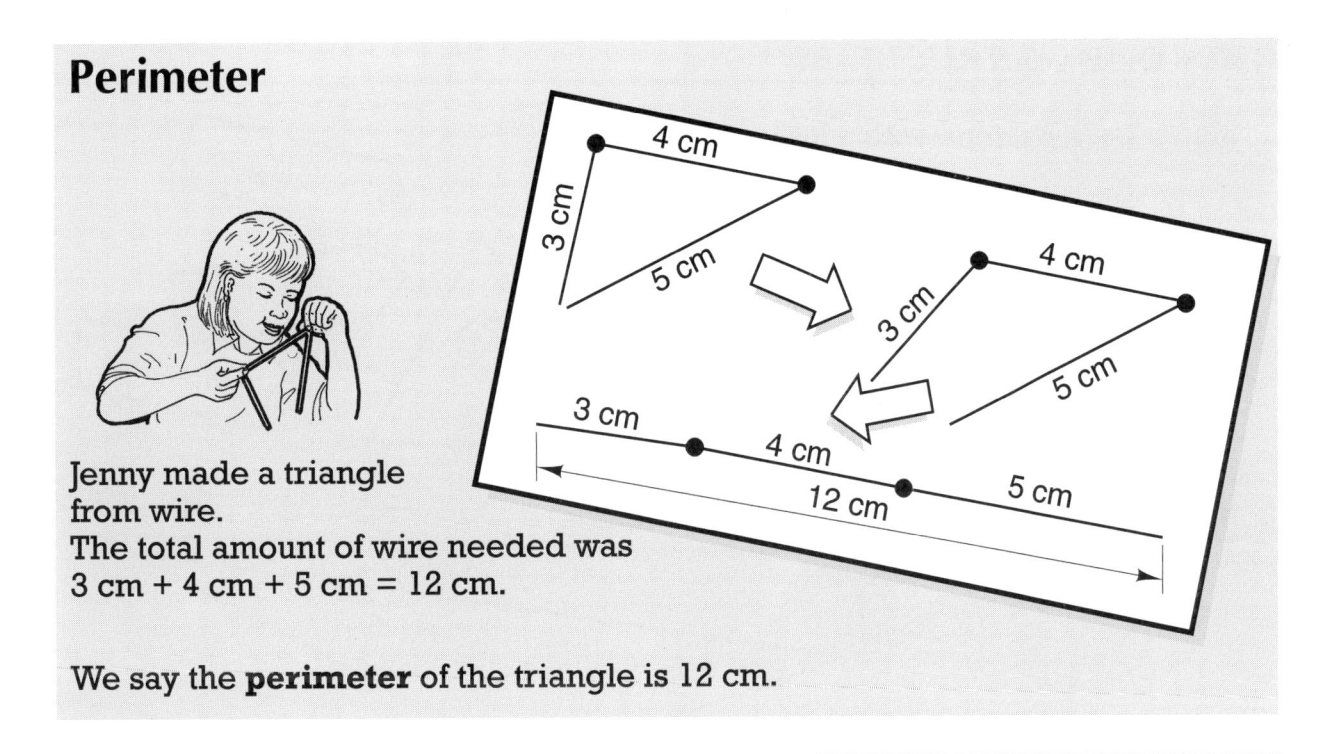

Jenny made a triangle from wire.
The total amount of wire needed was
3 cm + 4 cm + 5 cm = 12 cm.

We say the **perimeter** of the triangle is 12 cm.

EXERCISE 5

1 Write down the perimeter of each triangle.

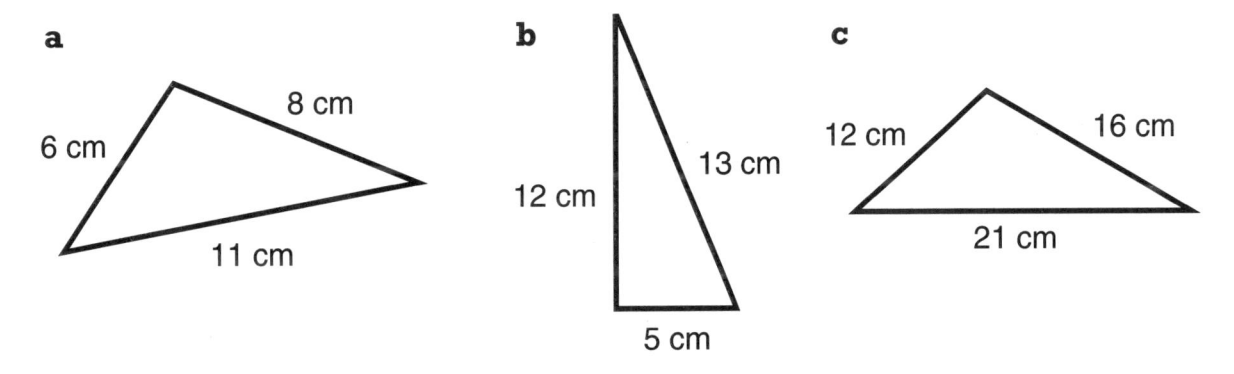

   a 6 cm, 8 cm, 11 cm
   b 12 cm, 13 cm, 5 cm
   c 12 cm, 16 cm, 21 cm

2 Calculate the perimeter in each case.

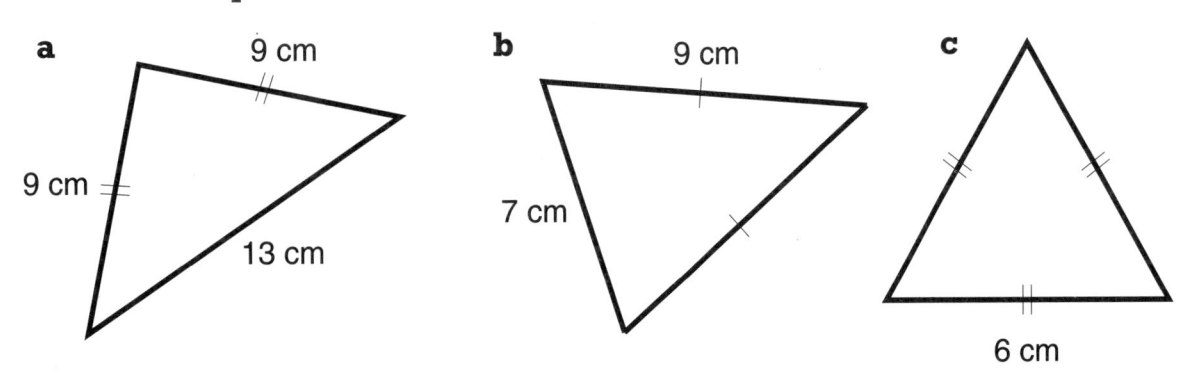

   a 9 cm, 9 cm, 13 cm
   b 9 cm, 9 cm, 7 cm
   c 6 cm (equilateral)

107

CHECK-UP ON TRIANGLES

1 Match each triangle with a label.

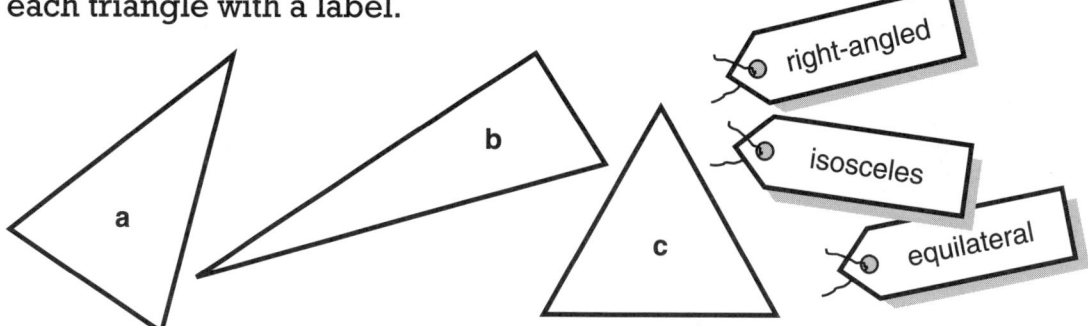

2 Measure the sides and angles of this triangle.

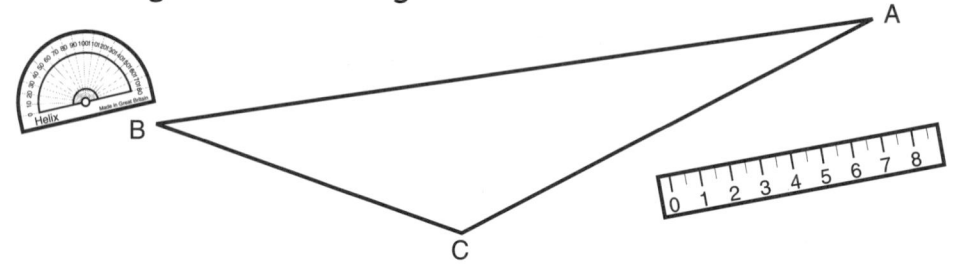

3
  a Draw an isosceles triangle.
  b Mark the sides which are equal.
  c Mark the angles which are equal.
  d Draw in the line of symmetry.

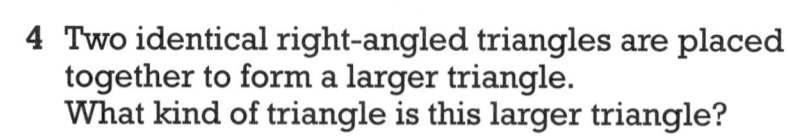

4 Two identical right-angled triangles are placed together to form a larger triangle.
What kind of triangle is this larger triangle?

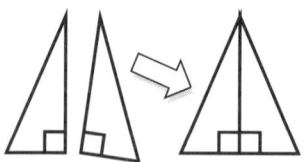

5 Find the area of each triangle.

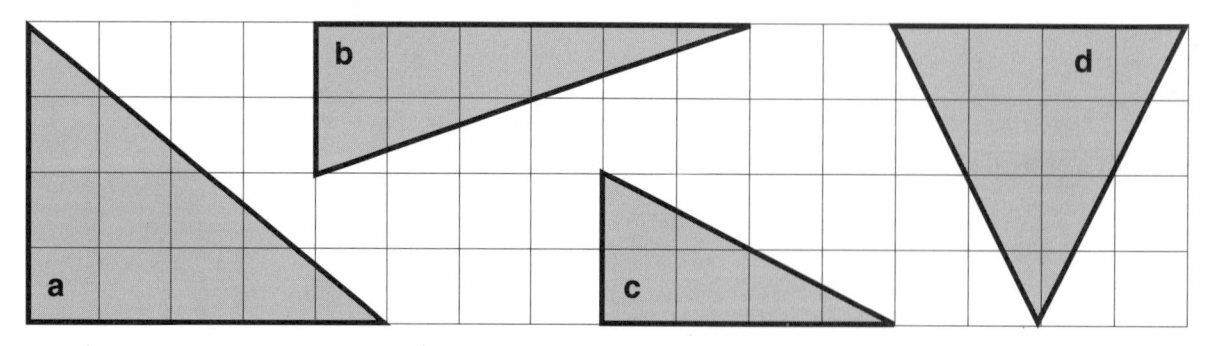

6 Write down the size of the missing angle in each triangle.

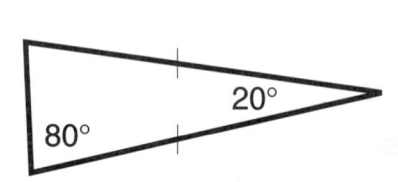

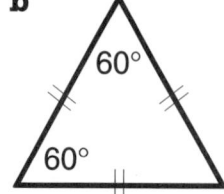

108

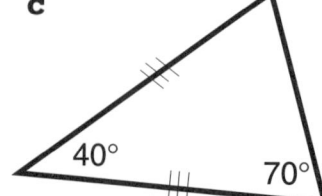

12 PROPORTION

Multiplication

A hot dog at the café costs £1.20.

Twice as many costs twice as much.
2 × £1.20 = £2.40

EXERCISE 1

1 Francine's lunch cost her £3. Jack bought twice as much.

What did it cost him?

2 Sally paid 80 pence for a portion of popcorn. Pat paid for three portions.

How much was that?

3

Cone 60p  | Lolly 45p  | Ice-cream tub 75p

a What will four cones cost?
b How much will three ice-cream tubs cost?
c James bought ten lollies for his friends. How much did it cost him?

4 The ingredients for a pot of soup cost £2.50.

How much will it cost to make:

a two pots of soup
b four pots of soup?

12 PROPORTION

5 An egg weighs 50 grams.
What is the weight of:

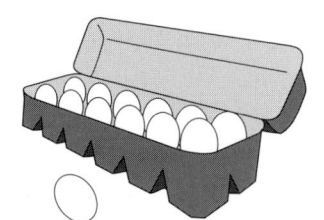

  a 2 eggs
  b 6 eggs
  c a dozen eggs?

6 Haroun's car will go for 16 km on a litre of petrol.
How far will it go on these amounts of petrol?

  a 5 litres
  b 12 litres.

7 Sanjay has made some charts to help him at the tuck shop.
Complete the charts on the worksheet.

  a One bottle costs 40p.

Number of items	Working	Cost
1	1 × 40p	40p
2	2 × 40p	80p
3	3 × 40p	£1.20
4	4 × 40p	
5	5 × 40p	
6	6 × 40p	

  b One packet costs 17p.

Number of items	Working	Cost
1	1 × 17p	17p
2	2 × 17p	34p
3	3 × 17p	
4	4 ×	
5	5 ×	
6		

  c  One ice lolly costs 30p.

  d One sandwich costs 27p.

12 PROPORTION

Find out about One

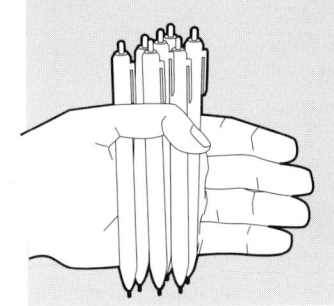

7 pens cost 140 pence.
Find out about one.

$140 \div 7 = 20$.

One pen costs 20 pence.

EXERCISE 2

1 Find out about one in each of the following questions.

a Four golf balls cost 480 pence.
Find the cost of one. ($480 \div 4 = ?$)

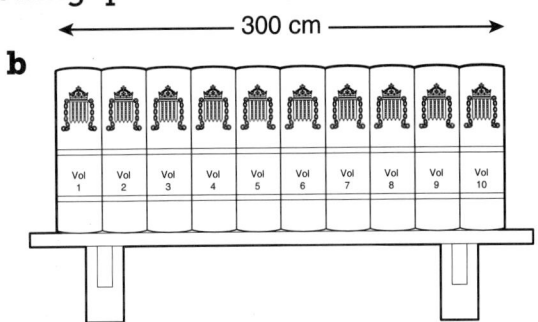

b Ten books are 300 cm wide.
Find the width of one. ($300 \div 10 = ?$)

c Two apples weigh 300 grams.
Find the weight of one.

d Five lettuces cost £2.50.
What is the cost of one?

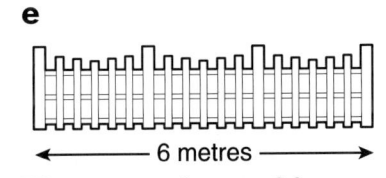

e Three sections of fence have a total length of 6 metres.
What is the length of one?

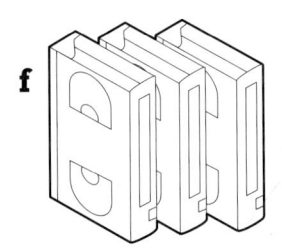

f Three video tapes cost £12.
What is the cost of one video tape?

g A car can go 60 km on 4 litres of petrol.
How far can it go on 1 litre?

h A six minute phone call costs 24 pence.
What does it cost for one minute?

111

12 PROPORTION

Find out about One First

Three cakes cost 60p.
What is the cost of four?

Find out about one first.
60 ÷ 3 = 20
One cake cost 20p.
So four cakes cost 80p.
20 × 4 = 80

EXERCISE 3

1 The teacher is buying equipment for the class.

  a Four pairs of scissors cost £8.
  - (i) What is the cost of one pair?
  - (ii) What is the cost of six pairs?

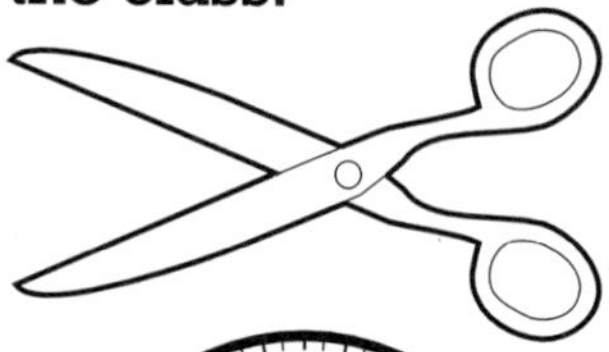

  b Six protractors cost 180p.
  - (i) What is the cost of one?
  - (ii) What is the cost of ten?

  c Five sets of compasses cost £2.00.
  - (i) What is the cost of one?
  - (ii) What is the cost of six?

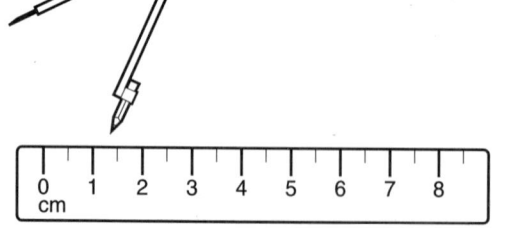

  d Eight rulers cost 72p.
  - (i) What is the cost of one?
  - (ii) What is the cost of five?

  e 20 pencils cost 100p.
  - (i) What is the cost of one?
  - (ii) What is the cost of three?

2 Find the cost of one first for each of these problems.

  a Ten notepads cost 200p. How much will four cost?
  b Five computer discs cost 250p. What is the cost of three discs?
  c Eight folders cost 240p. What is the cost of five folders?

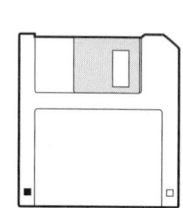

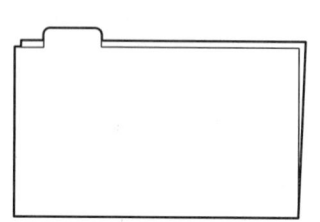

12 PROPORTION

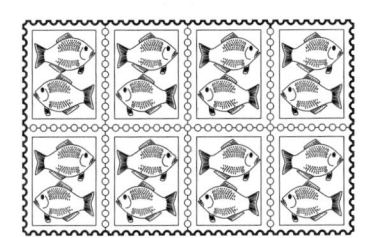

3 Eight stamps weigh 16 grams.
  a What does one weigh?
  b What do six weigh?

4 Two potatoes together weigh 240 grams. Suppose all potatoes weigh the same.
  a What is the weight of one potato?
  b What is the weight of seven potatoes?

5 Three pieces of cake together weigh 330 g. The whole cake was cut into eight pieces. What was the weight of the cake?

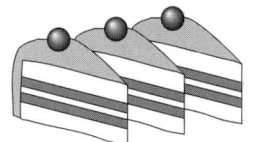

6 Four cars bumper to bumper make a 12 m queue.
  a How long is one car?
  b How long is a queue of three cars?

7 In the computer room, four desks take up 200 cm space.

How much space will three desks take up?

8 Five episodes of a TV programme last a total of 100 minutes.
  a How long is one episode?
  b How long do six episodes last?

9 In two hours Jim flies 300 km.

How far can he fly in three hours?

10 Six oranges give 300 ml of juice.
  a How much juice can we get from one orange?
  b How much juice will we get from seven oranges?

11 Five lemons give 100 ml of juice.

How much juice will we get from six lemons?

Conversions

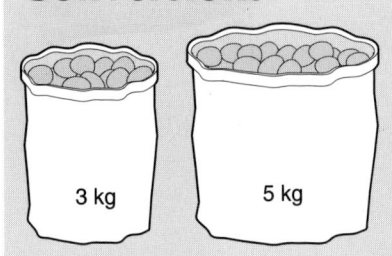

3 kg of potatoes are roughly 6 pounds in weight. How many pounds are 5 kg of potatoes?

First find the number of pounds in 1 kg.
6 ÷ 3 = 2 so 1 kg = 2 pounds.
So 5 kg = 2 × 5 = 10 pounds.

EXERCISE 4

1 There are 8 weeks in 2 months.

  a How many weeks make 1 month?
  b How many weeks make 3 months?

2 Two weeks make 14 days.

  How many days are in these?

  a 1 week
  b 4 weeks
  c 5 weeks
  d 10 weeks

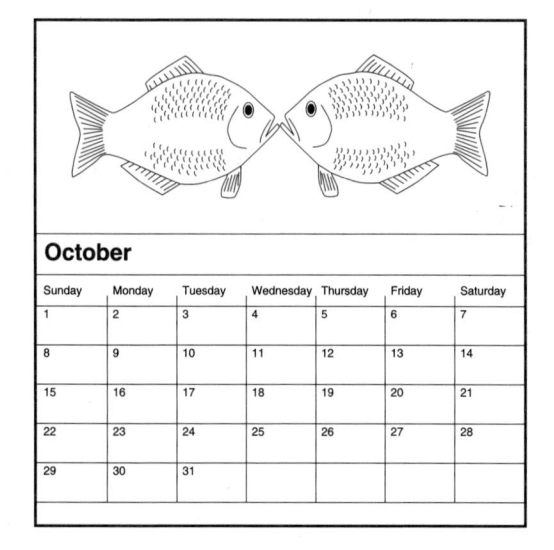

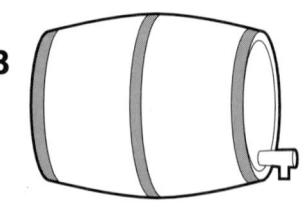

3 5 litres is roughly 10 pints.
The barrel holds 30 pints.

How many litres is this?

4 £4 is worth about $6.

  a How many dollars do we get for £8?
  b How many dollars do we get for £1?
  c How many dollars do we get for £3?

5 The length of a horse race is often measured in **furlongs**.
5 furlongs is roughly 1000 m (1 km).

  a How many metres are there in 1 furlong?
  b How many metres are there in 3 furlongs?

12 PROPORTION

Scale

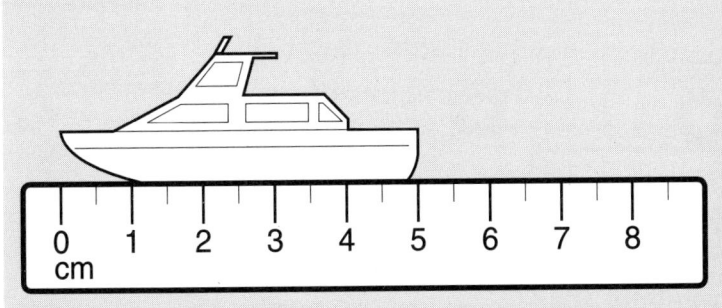

This model is 5 cm long.

The real thing is 300 cm long.

So 5 cm on the model stands for 300 cm.

Find out about 1 cm on the model.

300 ÷ 5 = 60
So 1 cm on the model stands for 60 cm on the real thing.

EXERCISE 5

1. The toy motorbike is 8 cm long. The real thing is 240 cm long.

   What does 1 cm on the model stand for?

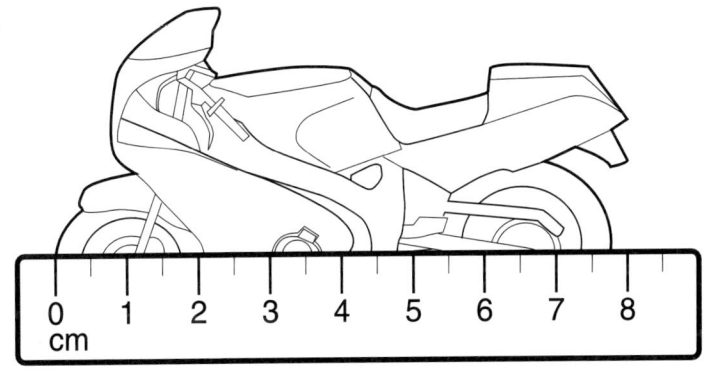

   240 ÷ 8 = ?

2. The model plane is 7 cm long. An actual plane is 910 cm long.

   What does 1 cm on the model stand for?

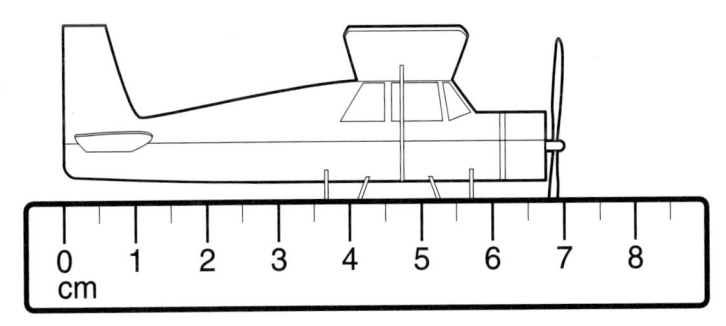

   910 ÷ 7 = ?

3. This house is really 12 m wide. 6 cm stands for 12 metres.

   What does 1 cm stand for?

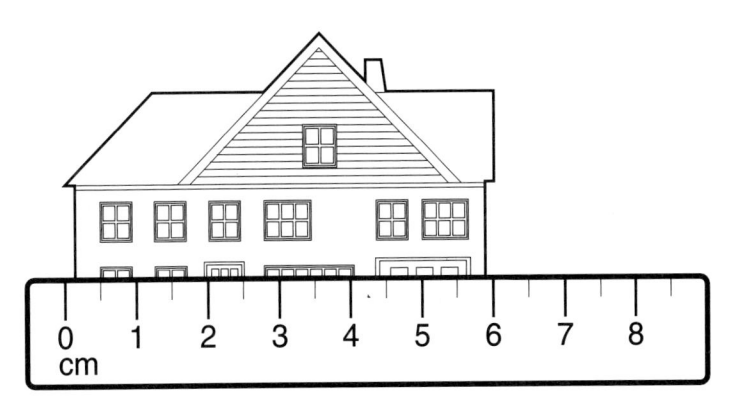

   12 ÷ 6 = ?

4 The model is 8 cm long. The bus is really 800 cm long.

$800 \div 8 = ?$

$100 \times 3 = ?$

a What does 1 cm on the model stand for?
b The panel on the side of the model is 3 cm. How long is the real thing?

5 The picture of the bike is 6 cm long. The real bike is 180 cm long.

a What does 1 cm on the picture stand for?
b A wheel on the picture is 2.5 cm wide.
How wide is the real wheel?
c The picture of the bike is 4 cm high.
How high is the real bike?

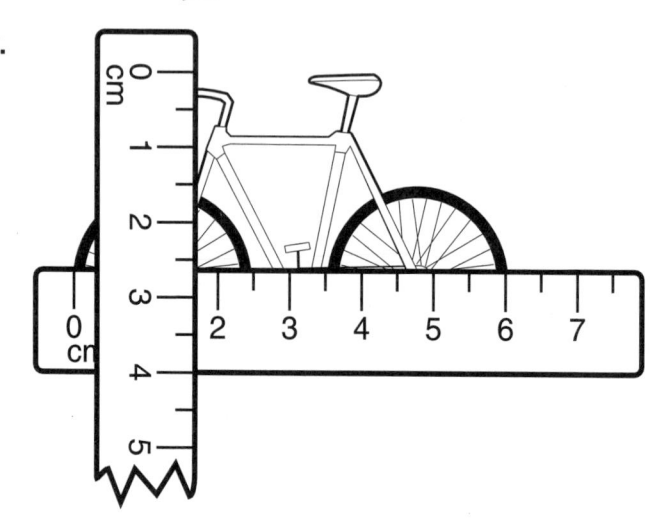

6 A movie studio makes a film of *Tim Thumb*.
They must make props of everyday objects that are **nine times** their actual size.
The bottle's actual size is 20 cm.
They make one $9 \times 20 = 180$ cm high.

a How big should they make the £1 coin? Its normal size is 2.3 cm high.

b How big should these props be?

(i) a football
(actual size 30 cm)

(ii) a phone
(actual size 25 cm)

(iii) a shoe
(actual size 22 cm)

Do Worksheet 2

Do Worksheet 3

CHECK-UP ON PROPORTION

1 A selection of cakes costs 80 pence. How much will it cost for:

  a twice as many cakes
  b three times as many cakes?

2 One ice lolly costs 15 pence. What is the cost of:

  a two lollies
  b four lollies?

3
  a Three tickets for the Hallowe'en Ball cost £6. What is the cost of one ticket?
  b To hire four costumes costs £24. How much is it to hire one costume?

4 Five jars of honey cost 600 pence.

  a What does one jar cost?
  b What do four jars cost?

5 The taxi charges by the mile. A 10 mile journey costs 800 pence. What does a 6 mile journey cost?

6 Using the old imperial system of measures, 5 gallons is the same as 40 pints.

  a How many pints make 1 gallon?
  b How many pints make 3 gallons?

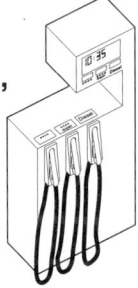

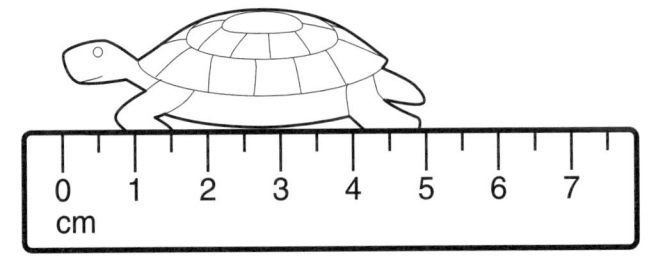

7 The toy tortoise is 5 cm long. The real thing is 30 cm long.

  a What does 1 cm on the toy stand for?
  b The toy head is 1 cm long. How long is the real head?
  c The toy shell is 3.5 cm long. How long is the real shell?

13 THREE DIMENSIONS

Solid Shapes

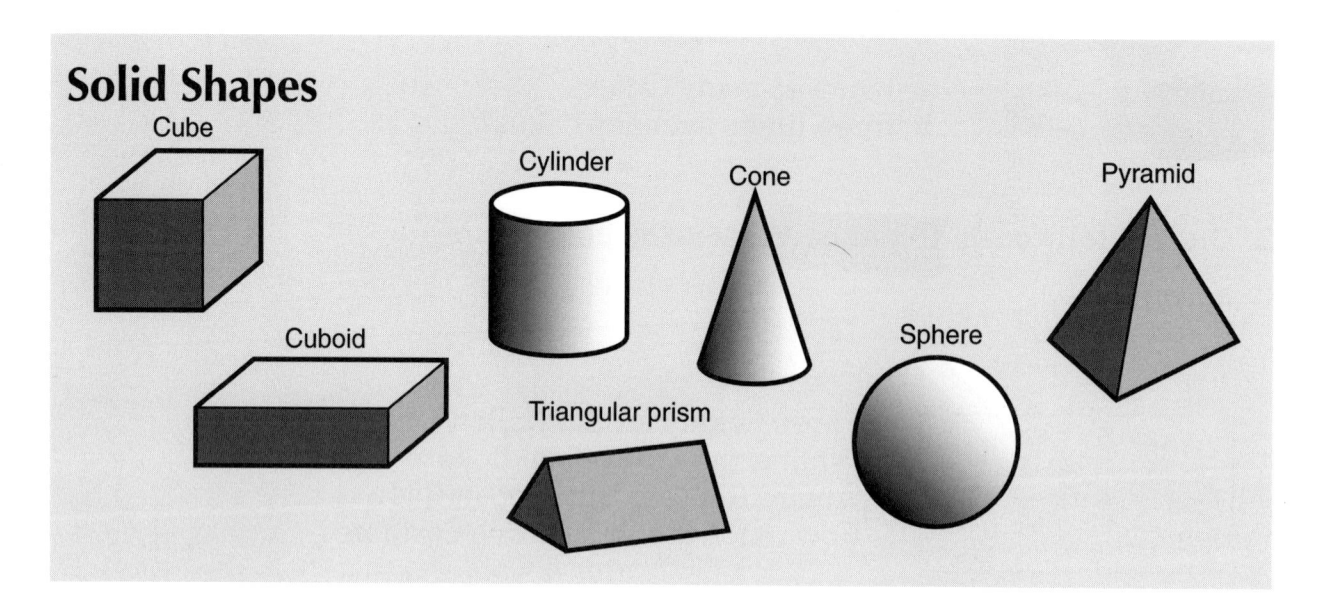

Cube, Cylinder, Cone, Pyramid, Cuboid, Triangular prism, Sphere

EXERCISE 1

1 Name each of these solids.

   a a dice

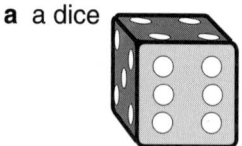

   b a shoebox

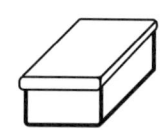

   c a traffic cone

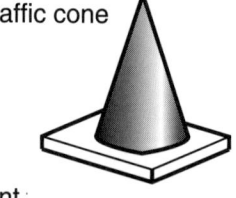

   d an orange

   e a wastepaper bin

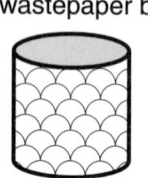

   f a tent

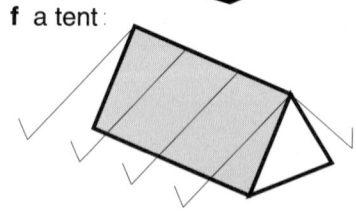

2 The dice has six faces. What is the shape of each face?

3 The shoebox has six faces. What shape is each face?

4 The chocolate box has two types of face. Can you name them?

5 What shape is the base of the cone?

6 What shape is this face?

13 THREE DIMENSIONS

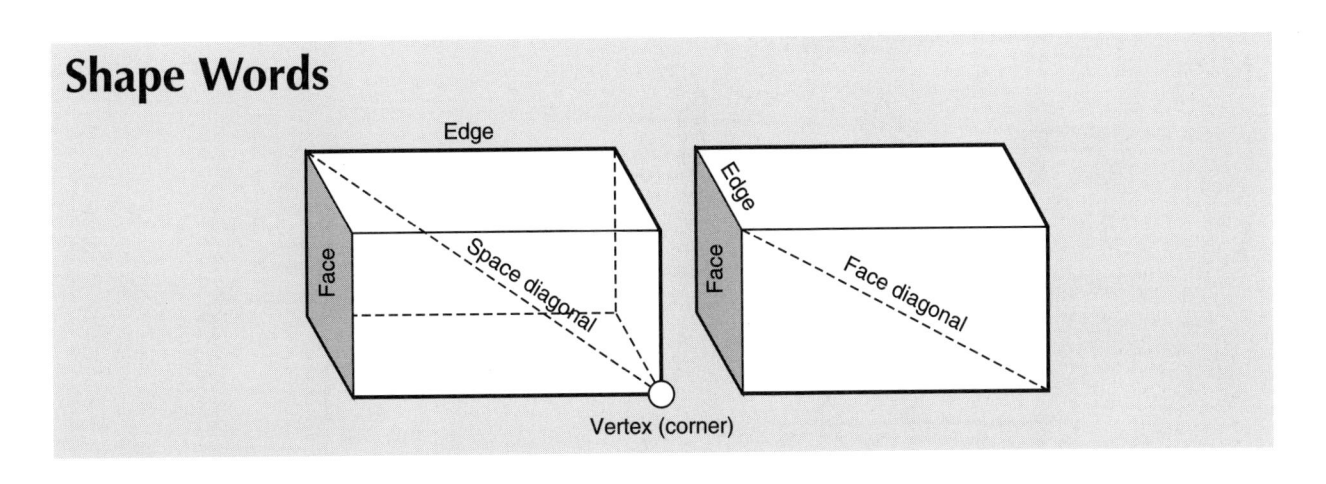

Shape Words

Edge, Face, Space diagonal, Vertex (corner), Face diagonal

EXERCISE 2

Ask your teacher for some 3-D solids to help you.

a Examine these drawings.

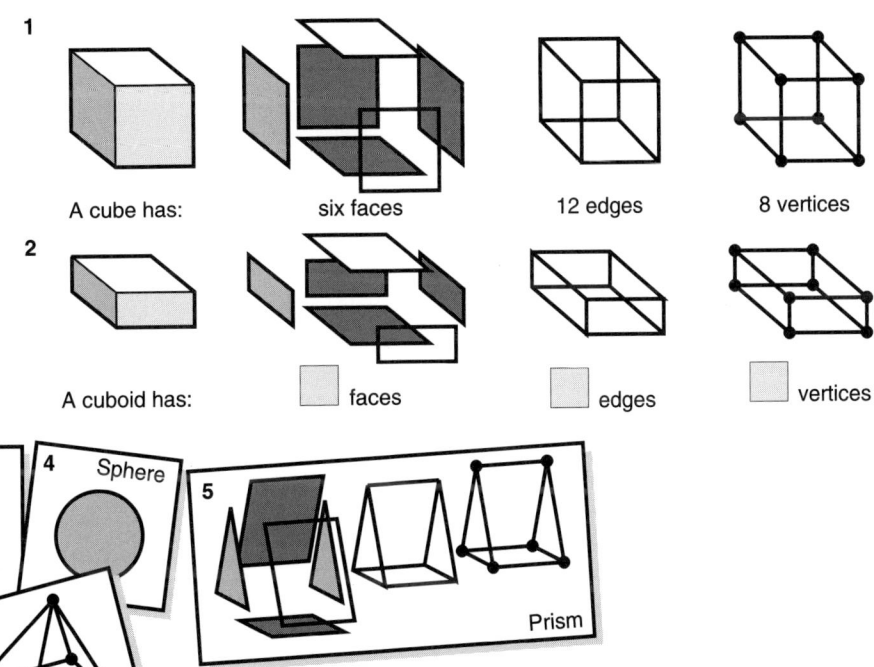

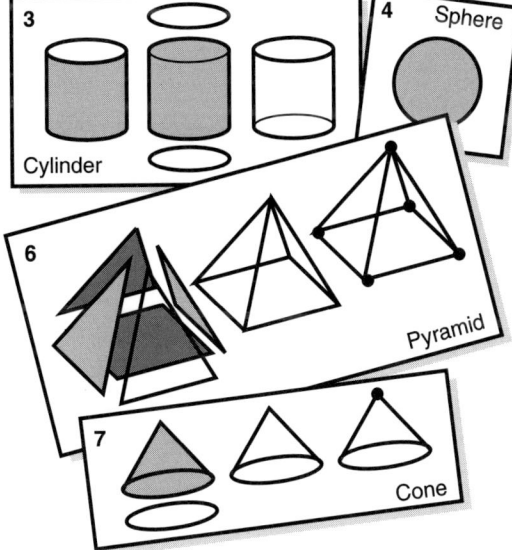

1. A cube has: six faces, 12 edges, 8 vertices

2. A cuboid has: ☐ faces, ☐ edges, ☐ vertices

3. Cylinder
4. Sphere
5. Prism
6. Pyramid
7. Cone

b Copy and complete the table.

Solid	Faces	Edges	Vertices
cube	6	12	8
cuboid			
cylinder			
sphere	1	0	0
prism			
pyramid			
cone			

Do Worksheet 1

119

13 THREE DIMENSIONS

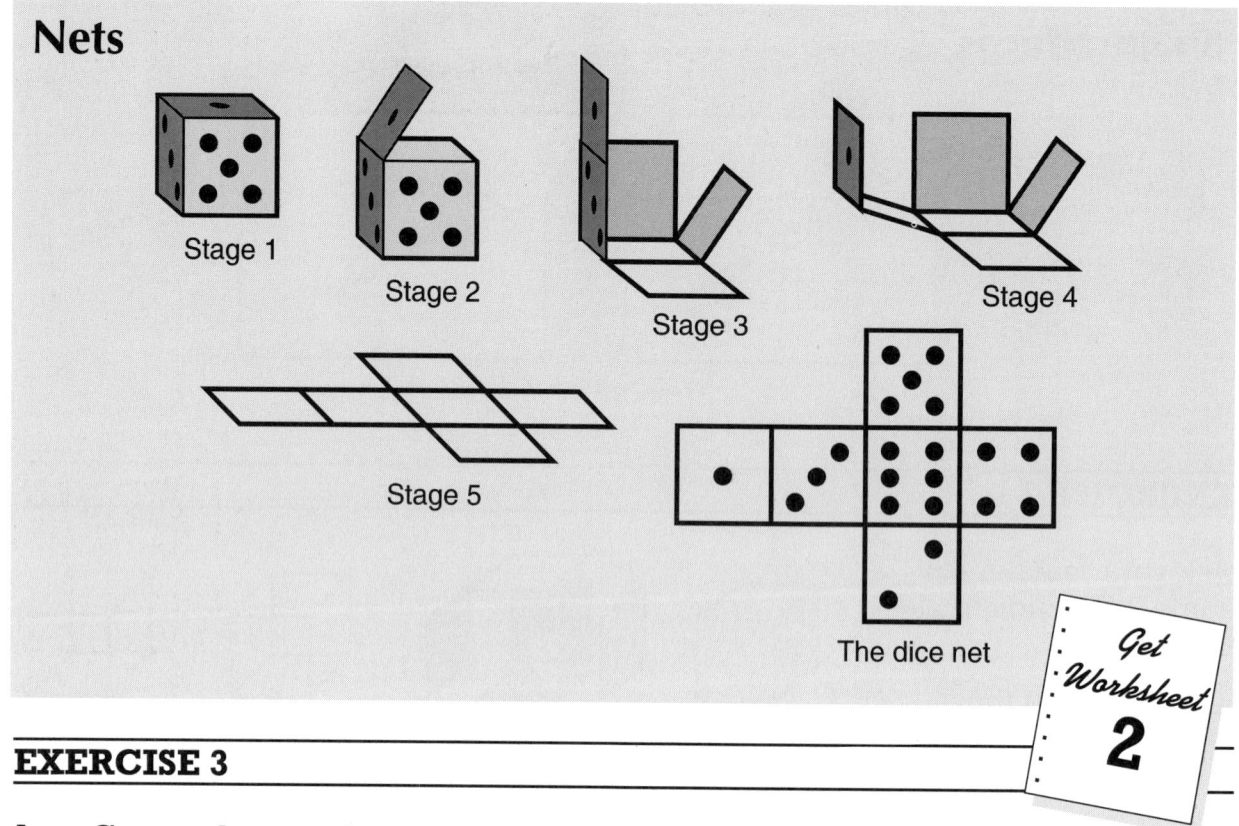

Nets

Stage 1

Stage 2

Stage 3

Stage 4

Stage 5

The dice net

Get Worksheet 2

EXERCISE 3

1 a Cut out the net of the dice on Worksheet 2. Use it to make the dice.
   b Examine the dice. 1 is opposite 6. 2 is opposite 5. 3 is opposite 4.
      What do opposite faces add up to?
   c Copy each of these nets into your jotter.
      Use what you've learned from **a** and **b** to fill in the blank faces.

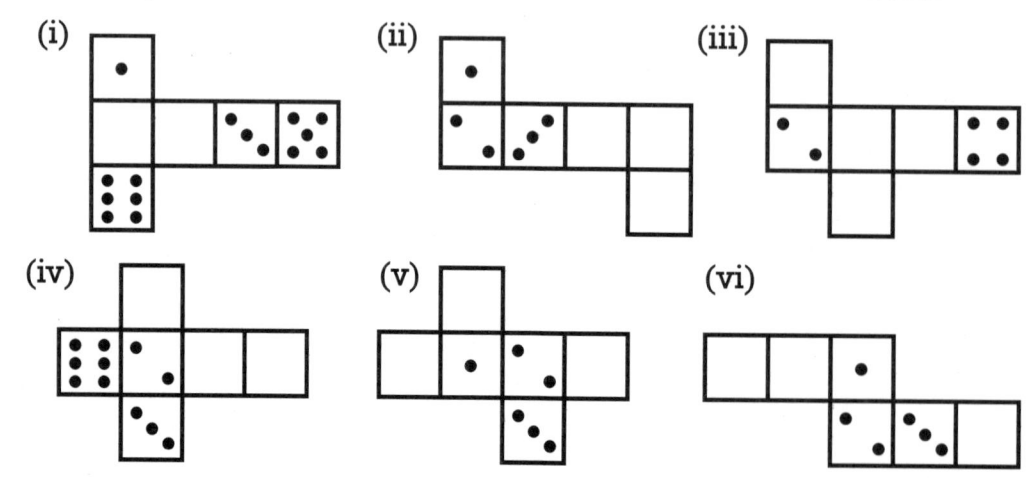

   (i)   (ii)   (iii)

   (iv)   (v)   (vi)

2 Cut out the 'Happy Easter' box on Worksheet 2.

   The flaps are not really part of the net: they hold the shape together so don't cut them off!

   You only have to glue one flap.

   You should be able to open and close the box when it is finished.

13 THREE DIMENSIONS

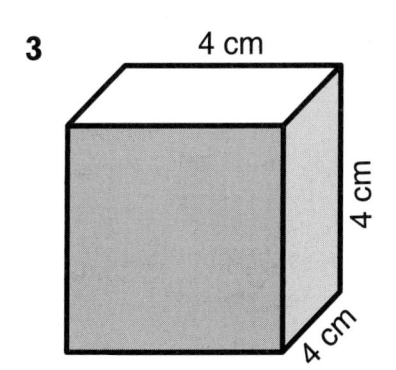

3 Make a net for this cube like the one in the plan.

Each square will have a side of 4 cm.

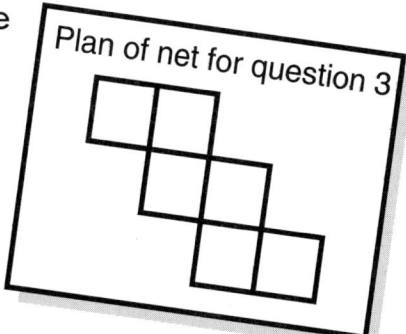

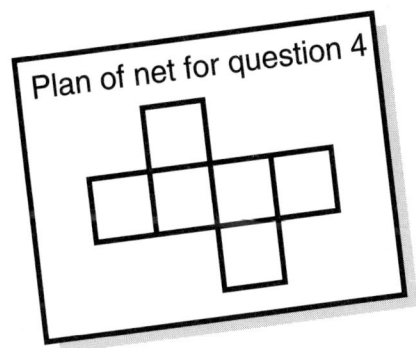

4 Use this plan to make a cube with 2 cm edges.

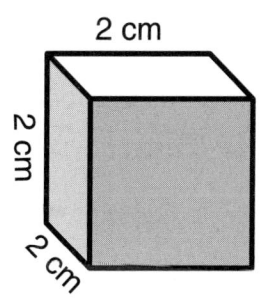

5 Make nets of these two cubes using plans of your own.

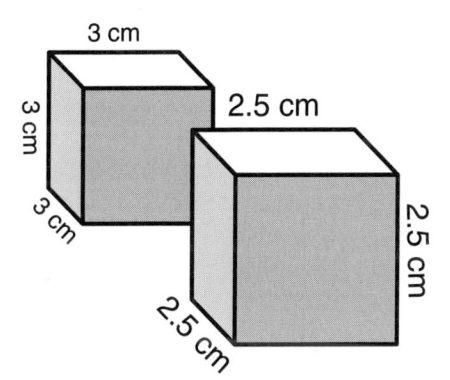

The net of a cuboid

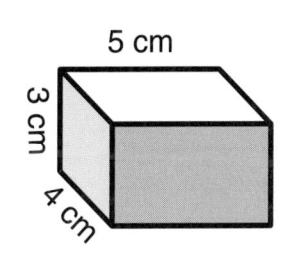

The net has been shaded to let you see the different faces.

EXERCISE 4

1 **a** Cut out the net on Worksheet 3.
   b Fold the net and make the cuboid.

Remember that the flaps are not really part of the net but help to hold it together.

Get Worksheet 3

13 THREE DIMENSIONS

2 Two boxes are shown with their nets.

   a Copy the sketch of each net.
   b Write in as many of the missing sizes as you can.

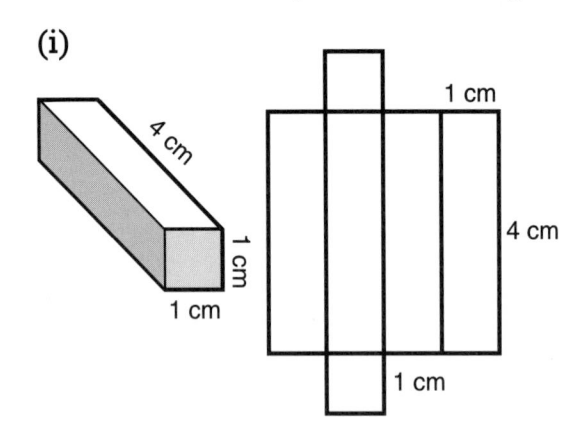

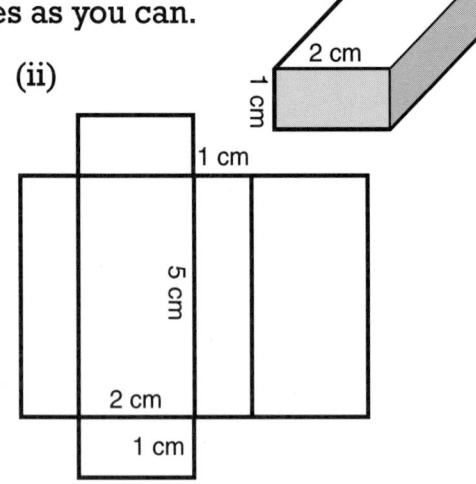

   (i)

   (ii)

3 Two boxes are shown.

   a Make a sketch of each net.
   b Write in as many of the missing sizes as you can.

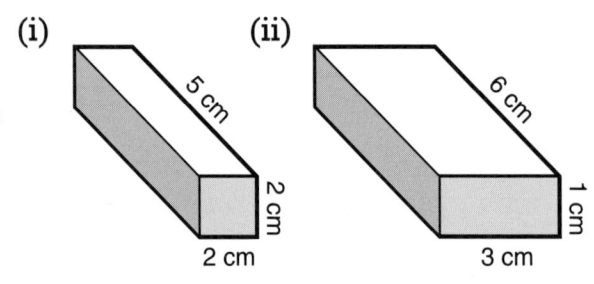

   (i)   (ii)

4 Draw full-size nets of these two cuboids.

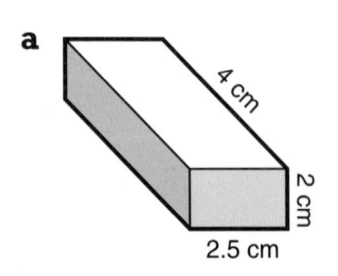

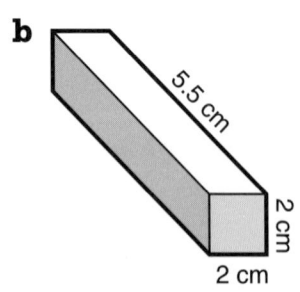

   a   **b**

Get an empty box from home.

Carefully prise it apart at the joins so you can study its net.

If you have two identical boxes you can open up one, leave the other closed and make a wall display.

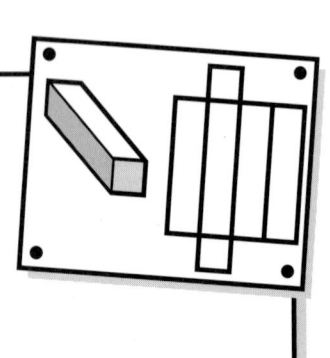

122

13 THREE DIMENSIONS

Skeleton Models

A skeleton model is the framework of a solid.
Here is the skeleton model of a cuboid.
It is made from straws.

To make this model you need:

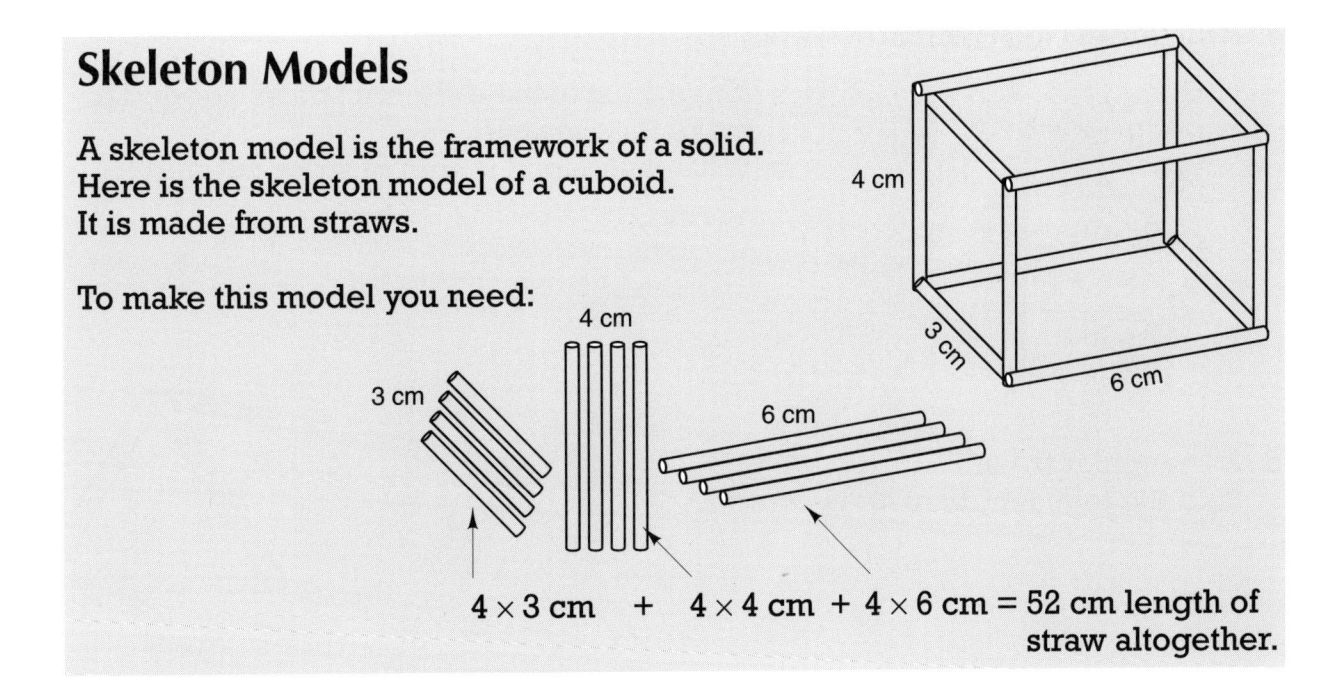

4×3 cm $+ 4 \times 4$ cm $+ 4 \times 6$ cm $= 52$ cm length of straw altogether.

EXERCISE 5

1. 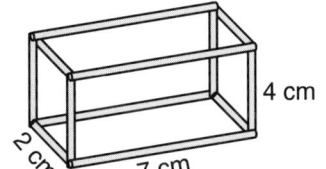
   a. Make a list of all the straws you need to make this skeleton model.
   b. Find the total length of straw needed.

2. Repeat the steps in question 1 for the following skeletons:

   a.

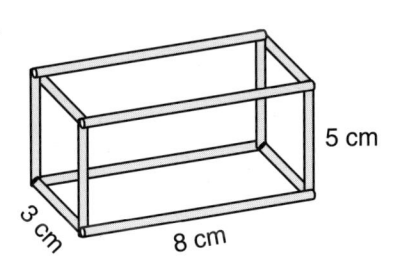

   b.

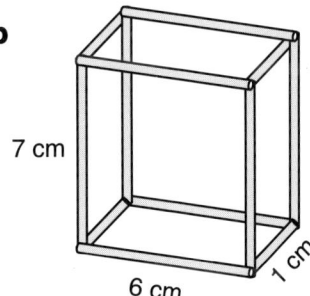

3. Cubes are special. Find the total length of straw needed for each.

   a.

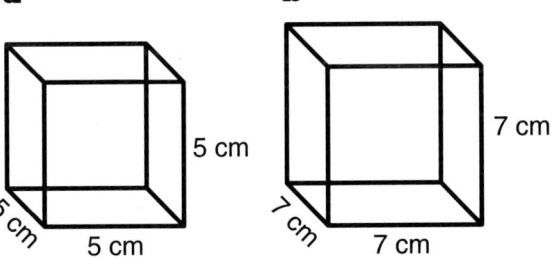

   b.

   c. Is there a quick way of finding the answer for cubes?

123

4 A square-based pyramid.

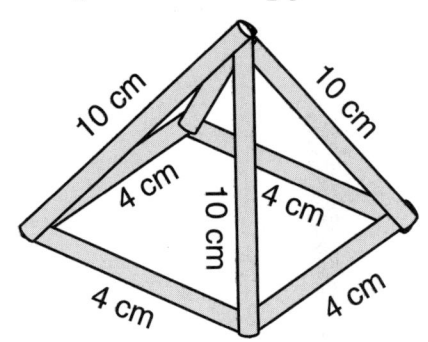

  a Make a list of the different straws needed to make the pyramid.
  b What is the total length of straw needed?

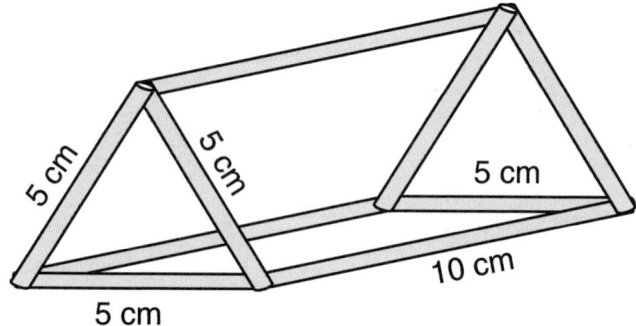

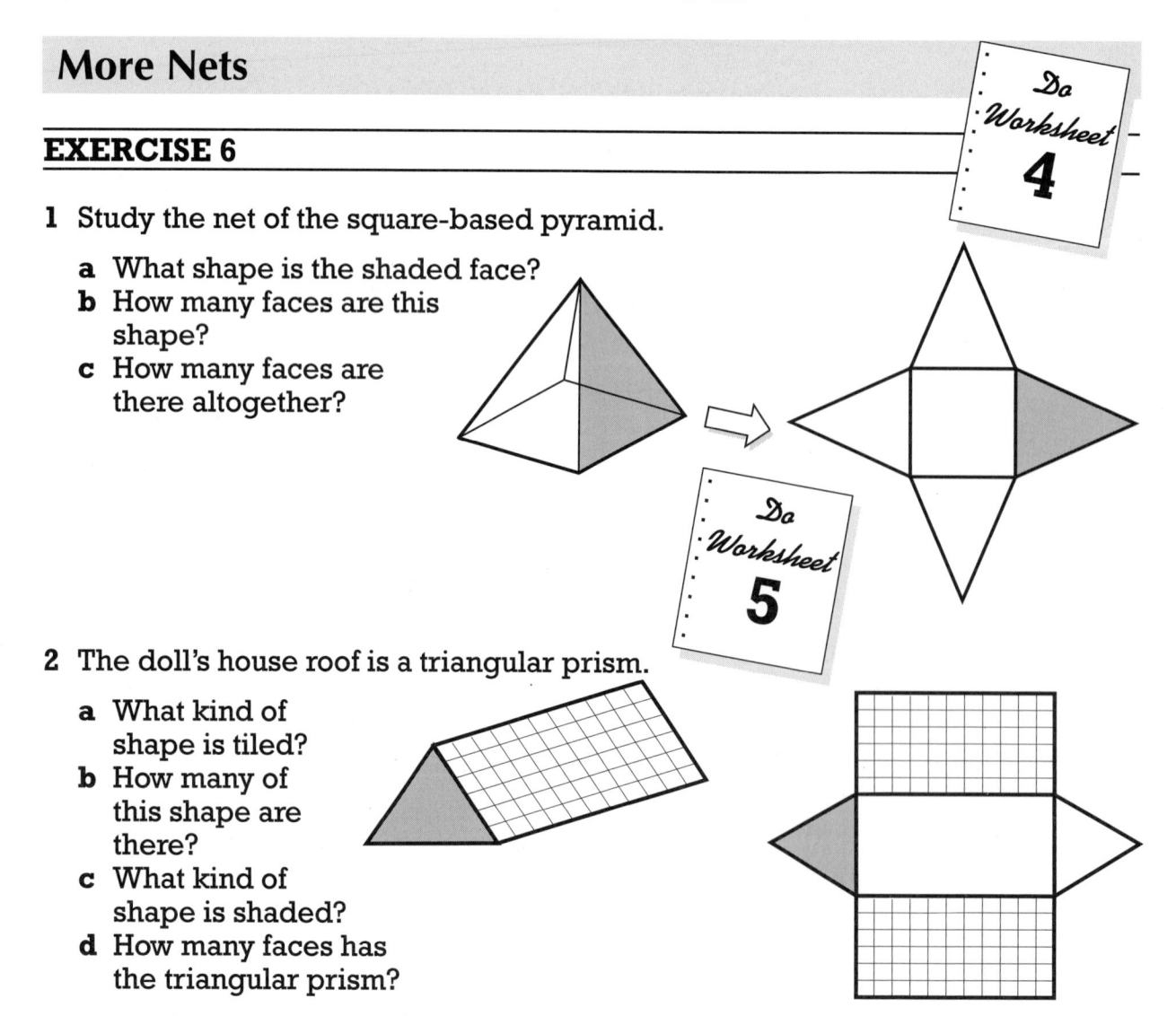

5 A triangular prism.
Find the total length of straw needed.

More Nets

EXERCISE 6

1 Study the net of the square-based pyramid.

  a What shape is the shaded face?
  b How many faces are this shape?
  c How many faces are there altogether?

Do Worksheet 4

Do Worksheet 5

2 The doll's house roof is a triangular prism.

  a What kind of shape is tiled?
  b How many of this shape are there?
  c What kind of shape is shaded?
  d How many faces has the triangular prism?

124

CHECK-UP ON THREE DIMENSIONS

1 a Name each solid.
  b Name the faces indicated with an arrow.

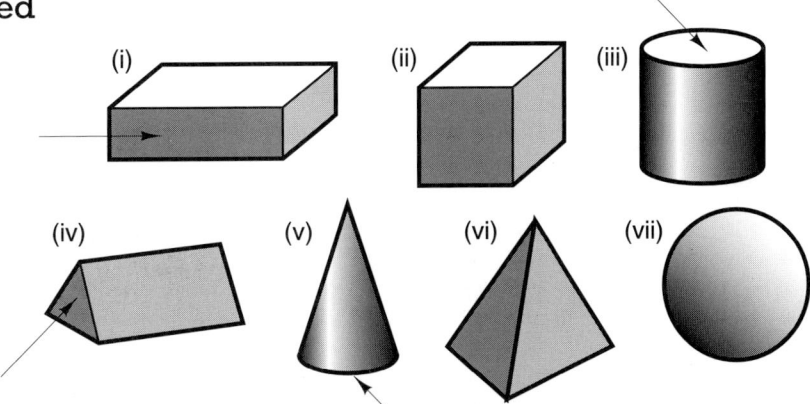

(i) (ii) (iii) (iv) (v) (vi) (vii)

2 For this square-based pyramid how many:

  a faces
  b edges
  c vertices

  can you find?

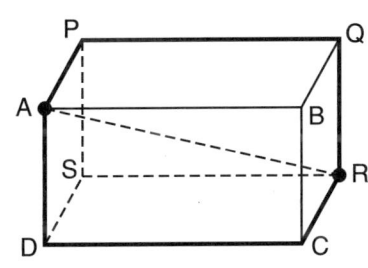

3 AR is a space diagonal of this cuboid. There are **three** others.

Write down the names of the other three space diagonals.

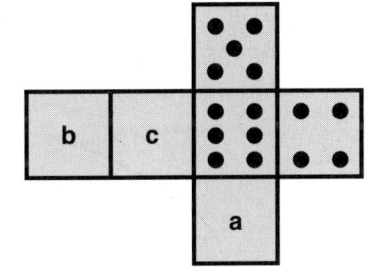

4 This is the net of a cube.
Each side of the cube is 2 cm long.

  (i) Make an exact drawing on squared paper.
  (ii) How many dots should appear in **a**, **b** and **c**?

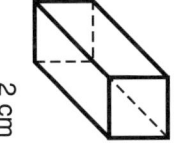

5 Here is a cuboid and its skeleton model.

  a Draw a net of the cuboid.
  b How much straw is needed to make the skeleton?

125

14 TIME

Telling the Time

Remember:

ten to eight
or
seven fifty

eleven fifteen
or
quarter past eleven

EXERCISE 1

1 What time is it on each of these clocks?

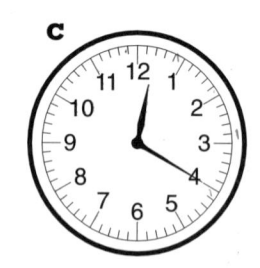

a   b 5:30   c   d 10:35

2

am means **before** noon
so 3.25 am is 25 past 3 *in the morning*

pm means **after** noon
so 8.45 pm is quarter to 9 *at night*.

What do these mean?

a 10.20 pm   b 6.55 am   c 10.55 am   d 12.05 pm

3

10th August 1959 can be written as 10.08.59
02.09.85 stands for 2nd September 1985

a Write in numbers: **23rd February 1997**.
b Write in full what the numbers **17.05.96** stand for.

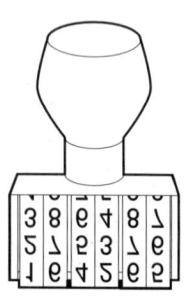

14 TIME

The 24-hour Clock

12-hour clock
We normally use the 12-hour clock in everyday life. Hours go **from 1 to 12** twice each day.

am means *before noon*
pm means *after noon*

24-hour clock
This is used mainly for timetables and digital clocks. Time is given as a 4-digit number.

am becomes **00 00** (*midnight*) to **12 00** (*noon*)
pm becomes **12 00** (*noon*) to **24 00** (*midnight*)
Midnight is given as **00 00** or **24 00**.
13 00 is **1 pm**.

This time scale matches up the 12-hour clock with the 24-hour clock.

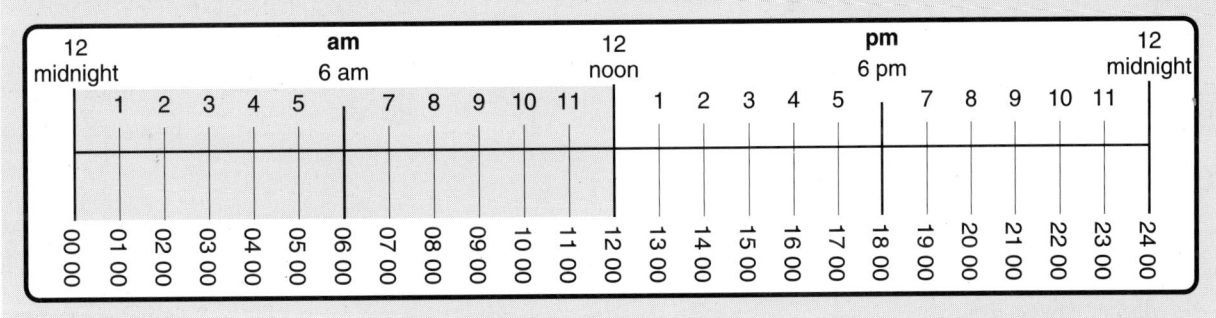

Examples:

before noon
5 am → 05 00
8.45 am → 08 45

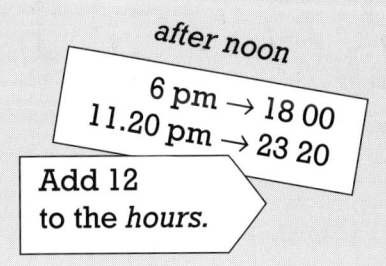

after noon
6 pm → 18 00
11.20 pm → 23 20
Add 12 to the *hours*.

EXERCISE 2

1 Use the time scale above to help you write these 12-hour times as 24-hour times.

    a 7 am   **b** 9 am   **c** 2 pm   **d** 5 pm
    e 7.20 am   **f** 9.55 am   **g** 2.15 pm   **h** 5.30 pm

2 Use the time scale above to help you write these 24-hour times as 12-hour times.

    a 08 00   **b** 10 00   **c** 14 00   **d** 22 00
    e 04 35   **f** 11 40   **g** 13 45   **h** 23 10

Do Worksheet 1

14 TIME

Here is a chart showing parts of Angelo's day.

	Get up	Breakfast	Play football	Lunch	Visit library	Watch TV	Bedtime
12-hour	8 am	8.30 am	11.15 am	12 noon	1.55 pm	8.05 pm	10.35 pm
24-hour	08 00	08 30	11 15	12 00	13 55	20 05	22 35

EXERCISE 3

1 Write each of these times in Claudia's day as a 24-hour time.

    a Get up
       7 am

    b Breakfast
       7.45 am

    c Swimming
       10.05 am

    d Lunch
       1 pm

    e Horse-riding
       2.30 pm

    f Cinema
       6.50 pm

2 Answer these questions about yourself. Give the answers in 24-hour time.

    a At what time did you get up today?
    b What time is it now?
    c At what time did you go to bed last night?
    d At what time does this maths lesson end?
    e (i) What is your favourite television programme?
       (ii) What day or days is it on?
       (iii) At what time does it start?

Ask to play 'Time's Up'.

Do Worksheet 2

How Long?

Pony Trek over Border Hills
10 am till 3 pm
Lunch provided

How many hours are there between 10 am and 3 pm?

Count on the hours from 10 till 3 on the number line.

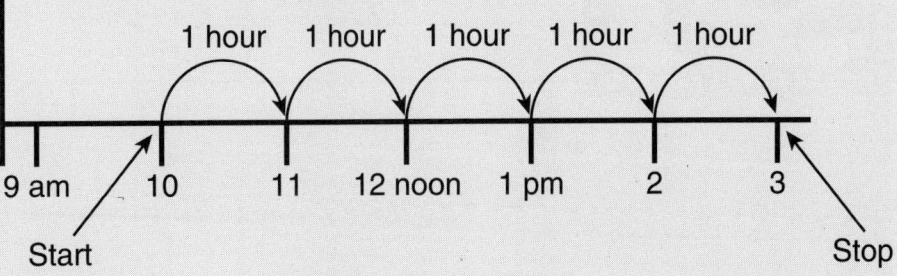

The pony trek lasts **5 hours**.

SITUATIONS VACANT
Office Staff
07 30 to 14 30
Monday to Friday
Experience Essential
Apply: 0463 216790

How long would you work each day?

Count on the hours on the number line.

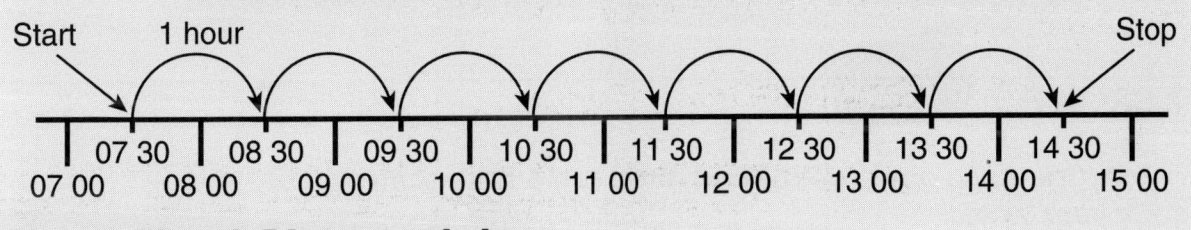

You would work **7 hours** each day.

EXERCISE 4

Get Worksheet 3

You may use the time scales on Worksheet 3 to help you answer the questions.

Work out how many hours there are between these times.

1. 5 am and 8 am
2. 4 pm and 9 pm
3. midnight and 7 am
4. 8 am and noon
5. 9 am and 4 pm
6. 9.30 am and 11.30 am
7. 4.15 pm and 9.15 pm
8. 04 00 and 08 00
9. 11 45 and 17 45
10. 18 15 and 23 15
11. 06 20 and 20 20
12. 22 00 and 04 00 (next day)

14 TIME

The film lasts from 6.30 pm to 9 pm.

How long is that?

Count on the hours first and then the minutes.

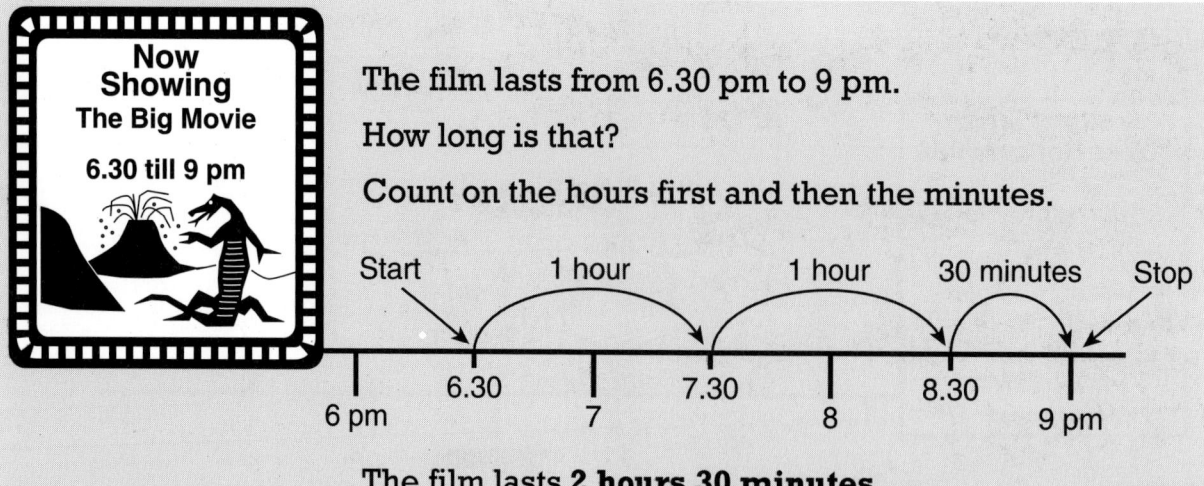

Start — 1 hour — 1 hour — 30 minutes — Stop
6 pm | 6.30 | 7 | 7.30 | 8 | 8.30 | 9 pm

The film lasts **2 hours 30 minutes**.

Try to work it out in your head.

How long is it between 9 am and 11.10 am?

9 to 10 = 1 hour
10 to 11 = 1 hour
11 to 11.10 = 10 minutes

The answer is **2 hours 10 minutes**.

Count on the hours first and then the minutes.

EXERCISE 5

Try to work these out in your head, then use a time scale to help you check your work.

Find out how many hours and minutes there are between these times.

1 4 am and 7.30 am
2 3 pm and 4.15 pm
3 08 00 and 12 30
4 14 20 and 18 30
5 21 45 and 23 50
6 6.40 am and 11.50 am
7 10 20 and 13 45
8 22 30 and 00 00
9 00 30 and 04 50
10 23 00 and 02 30 (next day)

Ask to play 'Interval Dominoes'.

Timetables

EXERCISE 6

1

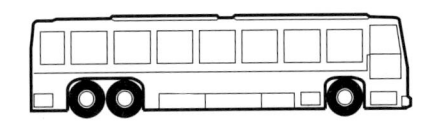

```
Hawick                    12 30
Ashkirk                   12 42
Selkirk                   12 55
Galashiels  arrive        13 15
            depart        13 25
Borders General           13 40
Hospital
```

Here is part of a bus timetable.
It shows the times when people can get on or off the bus at each place.

a When does the bus get to the hospital?
b How long does the bus wait in Galashiels?
c You get to the bus stop in Hawick at 12 15.
   How long will you have to wait for the bus to arrive?
d You are sitting in the bus.
   The time on your watch is 1 pm.
   Between which two towns are you travelling?

2 This is part of a timetable for three trains.
It shows when the trains *arrive* at each station.

	Train 1	Train 2	Train 3
Stirling	11 20	15 20	19 50
Bridge of Allan	11 25	....	19 55
Dunblane	11 33	15 33	....
Perth	12 00	16 05	20 30

a The first train gets to Dunblane at 11 33.
   When does the second train get to Dunblane?
b When does the third train get to Bridge of Allan?
c The first train takes from 11 20 to 12 00 to get from Stirling to Perth.
   (i) How much time does it take?
   (ii) How long does the second train take to do the same journey?
d The third train does not stop at Dunblane.
   The row of dots shows this.
   At which station does the second train *not* stop?
e Suzie is going to the pictures in Perth.
   She gets the 15 20 train from Stirling.
   The film is due to start at 17 30.
   How long will she have to wait in Perth before the film starts?

131

CHECK-UP ON TIME

1. Write these as **24-hour times**.

   a 7.25 am　　　**b** 3.55 pm　　　**c** 12 noon

2. Write these as **12-hour times**.

   a 14 15　　　**b** 02 35

3. How long does the concert last?

   Tonight's Concert
   The Martians
   July 26th
   7.30 to 11.15 pm

4. How long does the flight to Madrid last?

   Flight 702:
   Depart
   　London　　15 35
   Arrive
   　Madrid　　19 00

5. This is part of a bus timetable.

Longtown	17 40
Canonbie	17 55
Rowanburn	18 00
Penton	18 10
Longrow	18 22
Newcastleton	18 30

   a When does the bus get to Penton?
   b How long does the bus take to get from Longrow to Newcastleton?
   c I am waiting at the bus stop in Rowanburn.
   　　My watch says the time is 5.50 pm.
   　　How long will I have to wait for the bus to come?

15 TILING AND SYMMETRY

What is a Tiling?

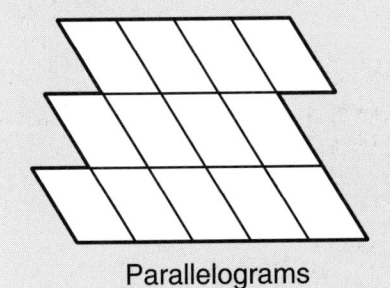

A tiling is a set of shapes that fit together with no gaps or overlaps in a regular pattern.

There may be more than one kind of shape used in a tiling.

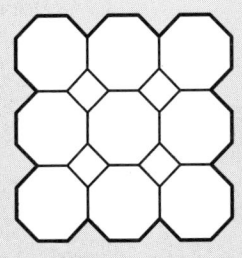

Parallelograms

Octagons and squares

Hexagons

EXERCISE 1

1 Which of these shapes will tile?

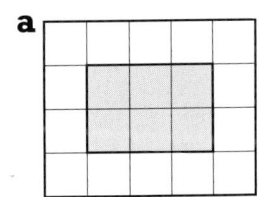

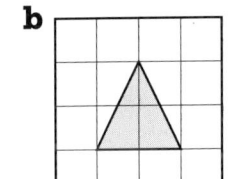

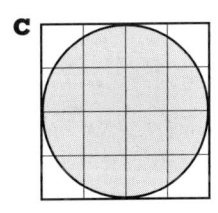

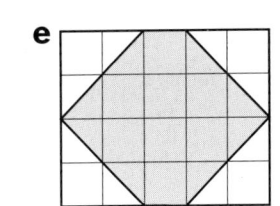

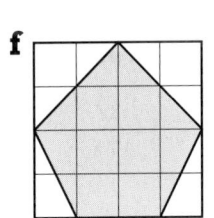

a   b   c

d   e   f

Make tilings of the ones that work on square dotty paper.

2 Some tilings are made with more than one shape:

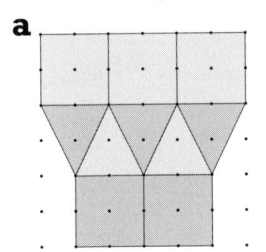

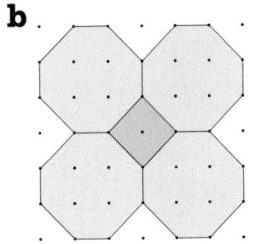

a   Square and triangle

b   Octagon and square

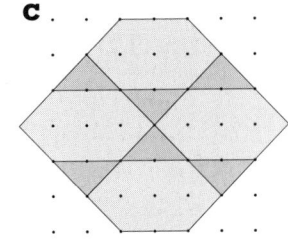

c   Hexagon and triangle

On square dotty paper copy each tiling and extend it.
Colour it in to pick out the different shapes.

133

15 TILING AND SYMMETRY

3 Interesting tiles can be made by changing shapes that tile.

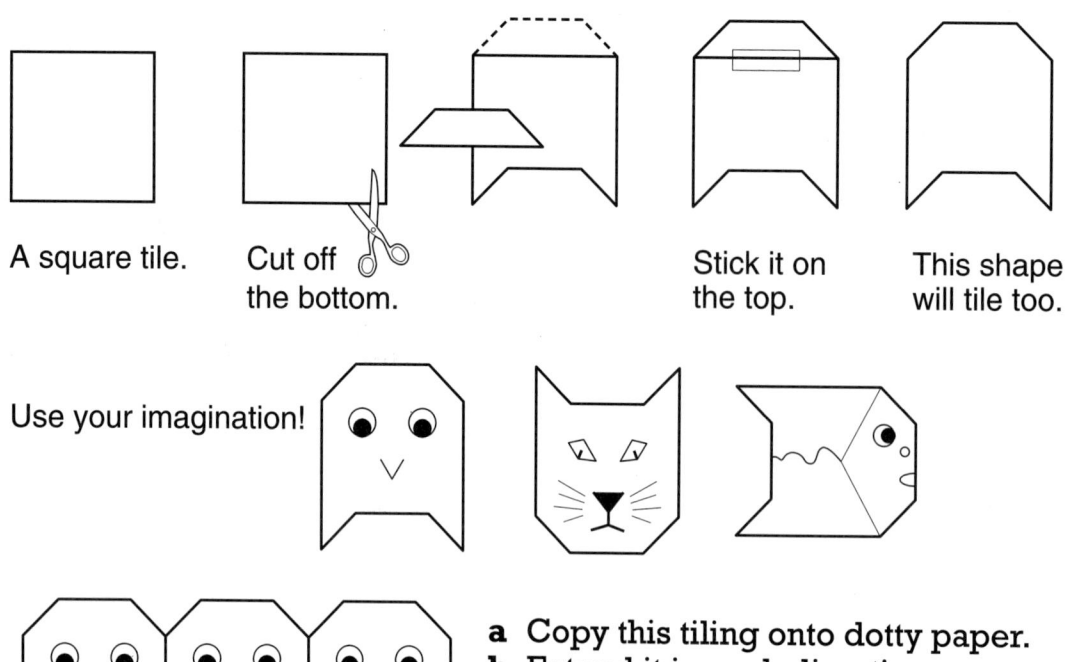

A square tile.   Cut off the bottom.   Stick it on the top.   This shape will tile too.

Use your imagination!

a Copy this tiling onto dotty paper.
b Extend it in each direction.
c Make a cat tiling in the same way.

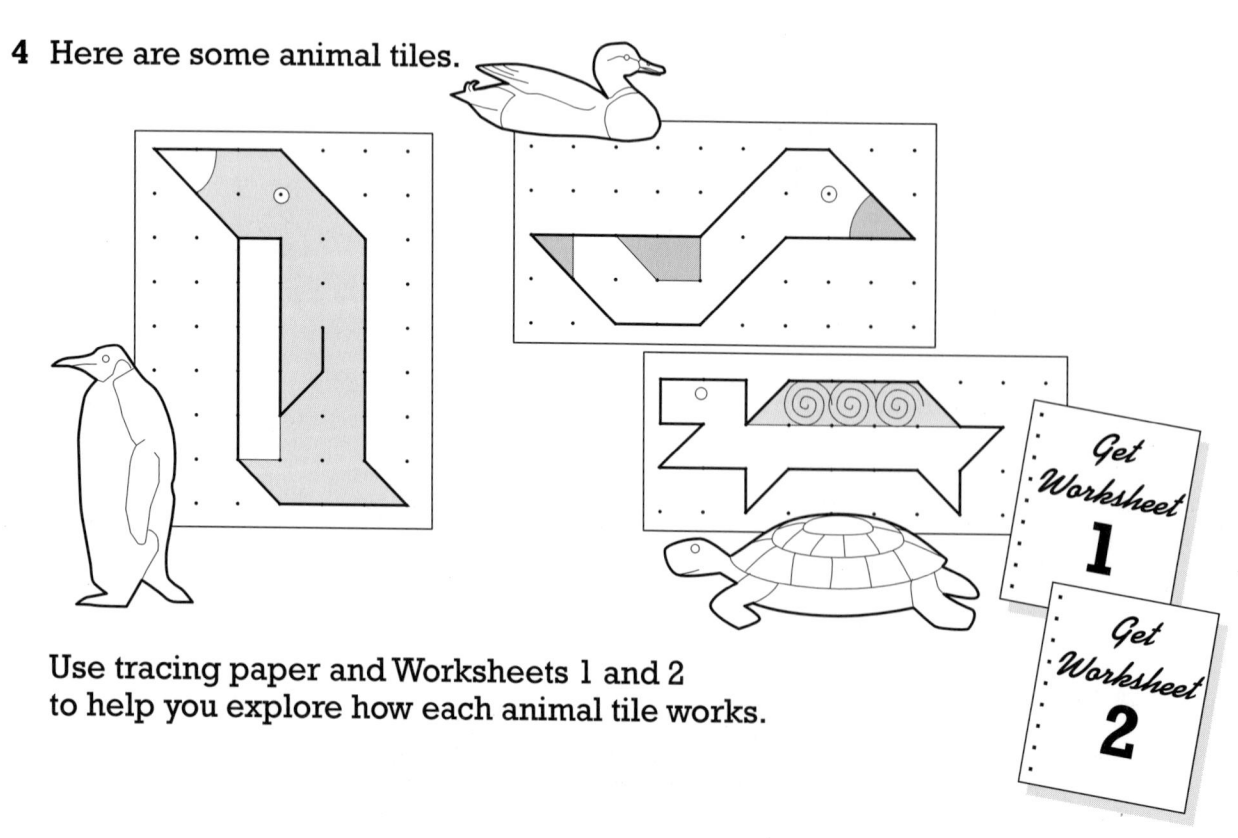

4 Here are some animal tiles.

Use tracing paper and Worksheets 1 and 2 to help you explore how each animal tile works.

Get Worksheet 1

Get Worksheet 2

134

Mirror Symmetry

This picture of a lamp has **line symmetry**.

One side of it is the mirror image of the other.

A line of symmetry is called an **axis of symmetry**.

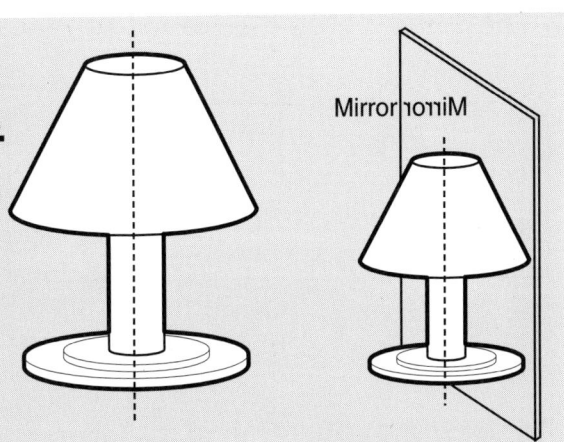

EXERCISE 2

1 Which skeleton is showing line symmetry?

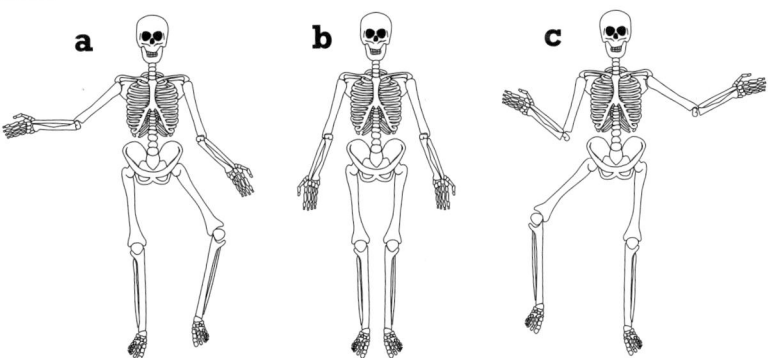

a b c

2 Which objects are showing line symmetry?

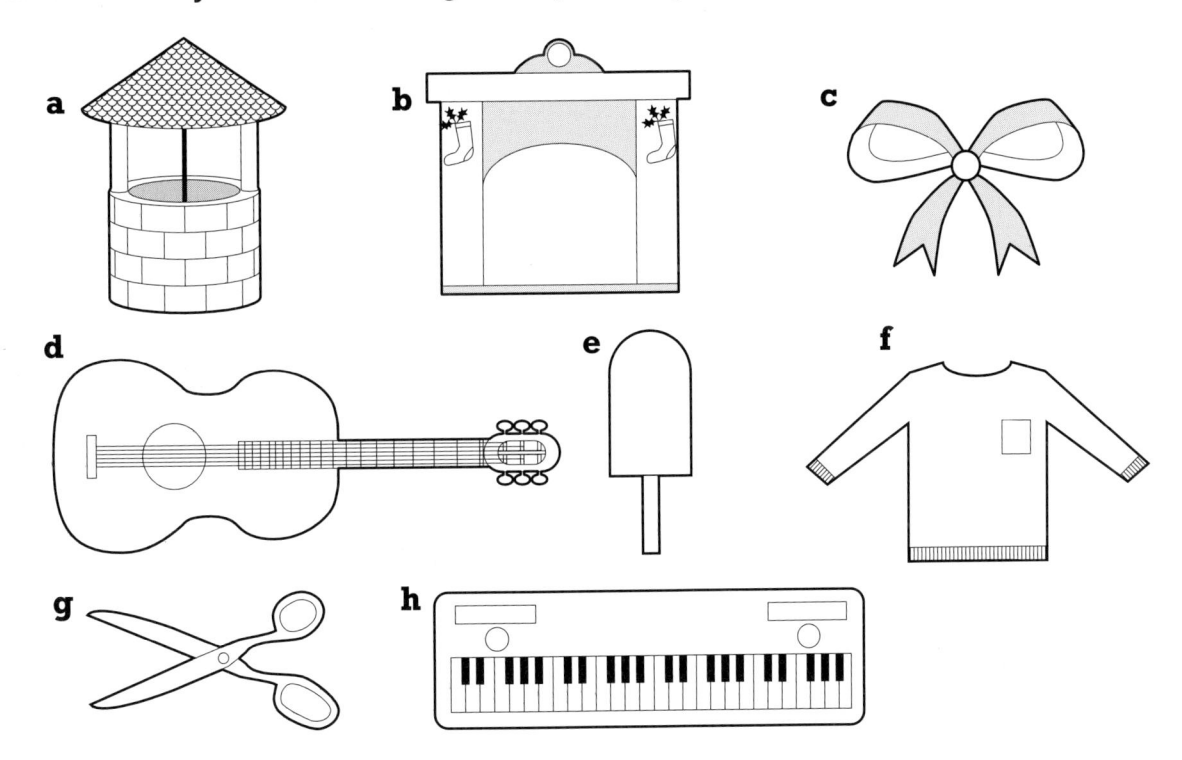

a b c

d e f

g h

15 TILING AND SYMMETRY

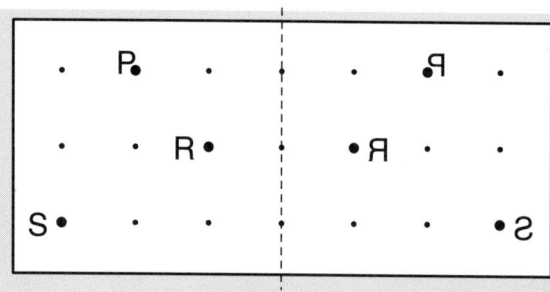

Each point and its reflection are the same distance from the line or axis of symmetry but they appear on opposite sides of it.

Point P is 2 cm away.
Point R is 1 cm away.
Point S is 3 cm away.

To draw the reflection of a shape:
 a reflect its corner points
 b join them up.

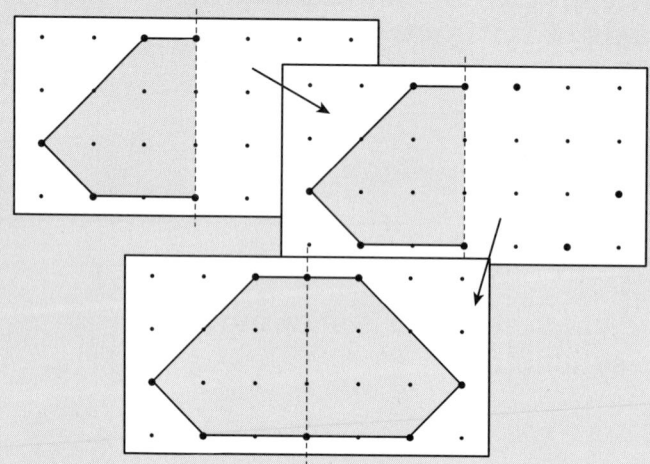

EXERCISE 3

1 Copy these shapes on dotty paper and draw their reflections.

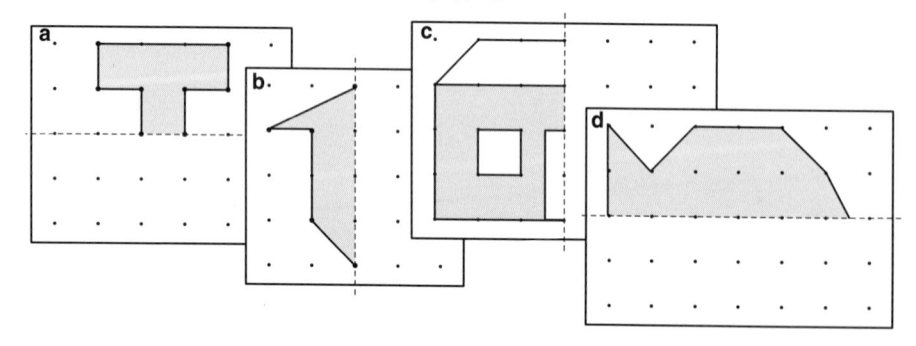

2 When the axis or line of symmetry is sloping, use a mirror to check your answer.

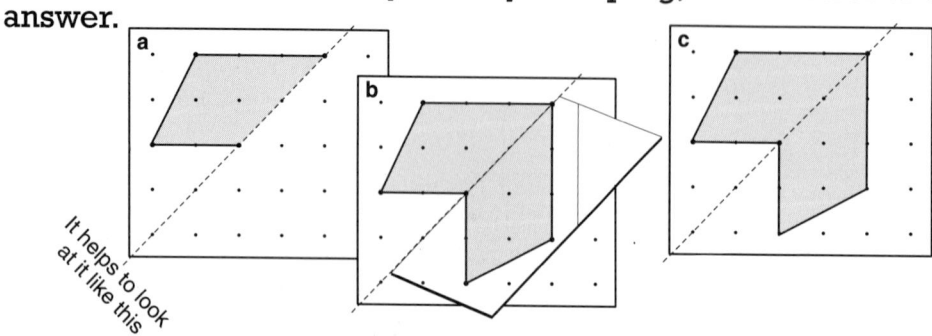

It helps to look at it like this

 a Draw this shape on dotty paper.
 b Use a mirror to check your answer.
 c Draw the shape's reflection.

Do Worksheet 3

15 TILING AND SYMMETRY

More than One Axis

Many shapes have more than one axis of symmetry, that means there is more than one place to put the mirror to reflect the shape accurately.

The plural form of axis is **axes**.

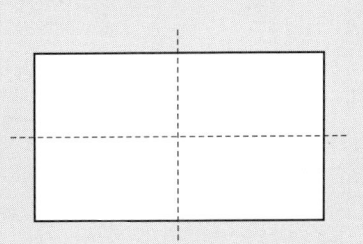

A rectangle has 2 axes.

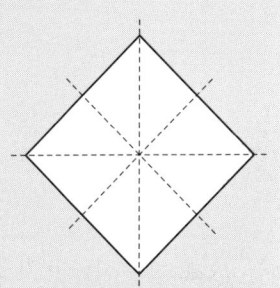

A square has 4 axes.

EXERCISE 4

1 Count the number of axes in each of these:

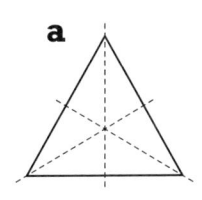

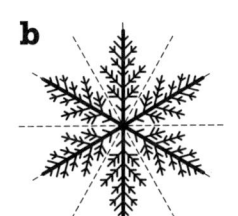

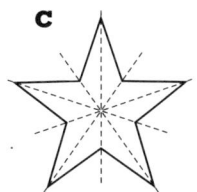

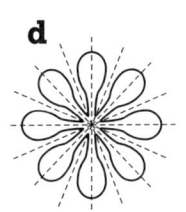

   a   b   c   d

2 Make a shape that has more than one axis of symmetry. Follow these steps.

   Get a sheet of paper.

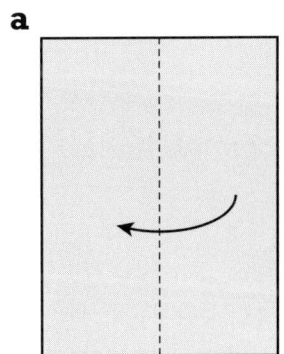

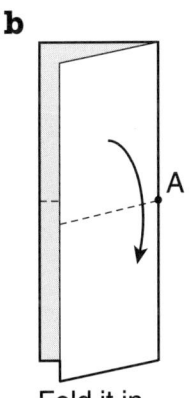

   a Fold it in half.

   b Fold it in half again.

   c The paper should look like this.

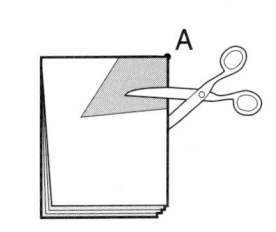

   d Cut a shape out of corner A.

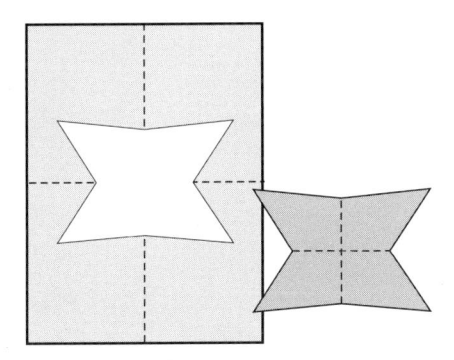

   e Unfold both pieces of paper. You now have two shapes, and each has two axes of symmetry (where the folds appear).

   f Place a mirror on each fold to check that they are lines or **axes** of symmetry.

137

15 TILING AND SYMMETRY

3 Get a **square** sheet of paper.

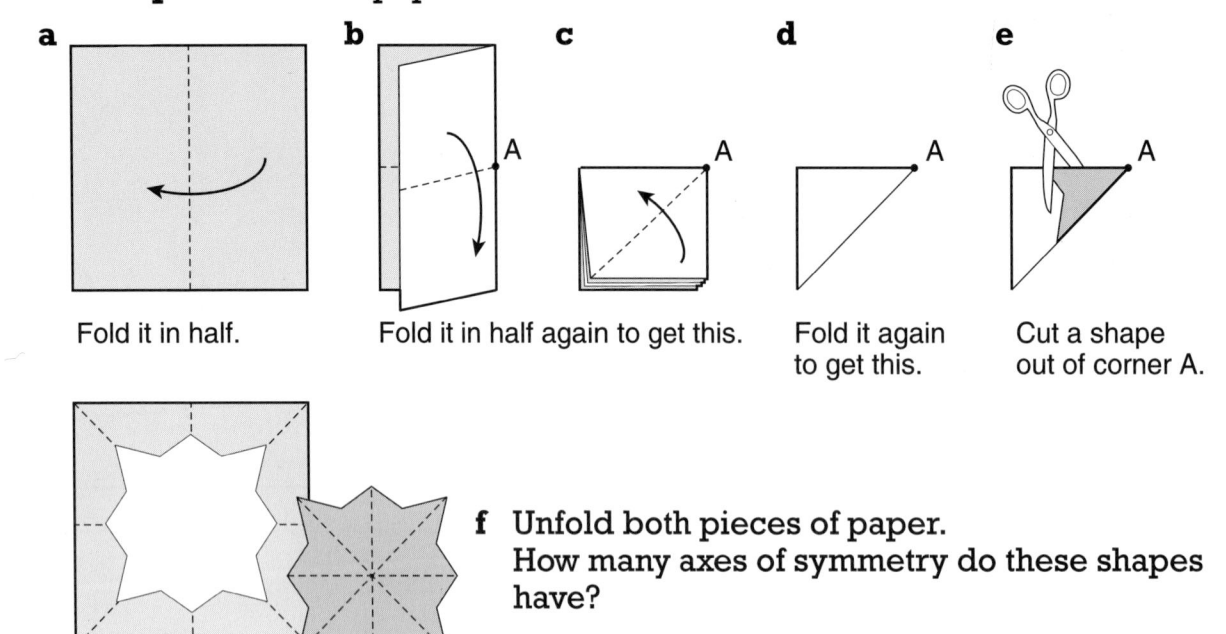

a Fold it in half.

b Fold it in half again to get this.

c

d Fold it again to get this.

e Cut a shape out of corner A.

f Unfold both pieces of paper.
How many axes of symmetry do these shapes have?

(Use a mirror to check.)

4 a Get a **square** sheet of paper.

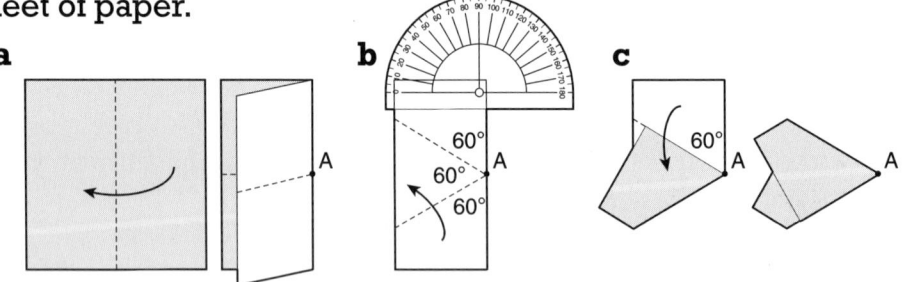

a Fold it in half. Find A.

b Use a protractor to mark off 60° angles at A as shown. Draw the lines.
c Fold along both lines.
d Cut out a shape at A.
e Open out the shape. How many axes of symmetry has it?

5 a Get a **square** sheet of paper.

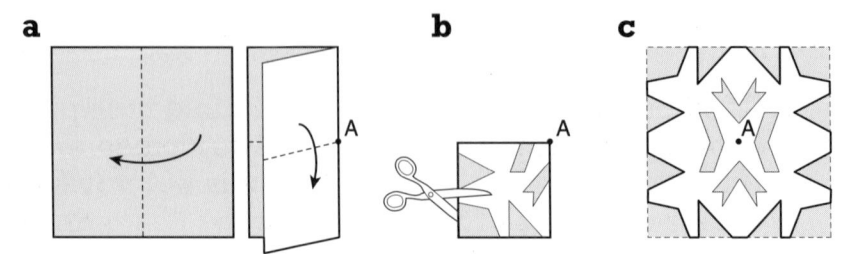

Fold it in half. Fold it again.

b Cut out shapes all round the folded paper. Make sure you don't cut A off!
c Unfold the sheet. How many axes of symmetry does it have?

15 TILING AND SYMMETRY

6 See if you can use what you've learnt to make snowflakes!

7 How many lines or axes of symmetry does each of these shapes have?

a b  c

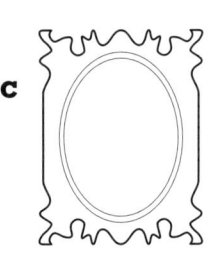

d 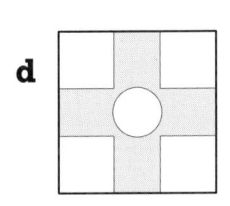 e 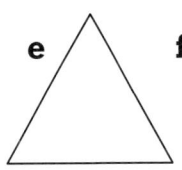 f  g

8 A dice has 6 faces.
   a How many lines of symmetry has each face?
   b Draw each face and show the lines of symmetry.

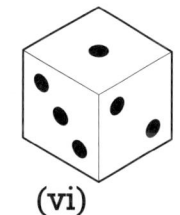

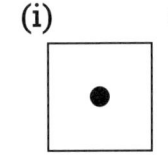

(i) (ii) 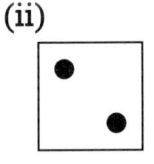 (iii) 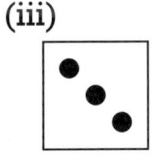 (iv) 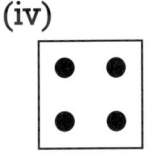 (v) 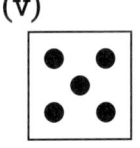 (vi)

   c Each design is based on this grid.
   Draw the grid. Show the axes of symmetry.

9 These two coins have an outline based on a **heptagon**.

   a Find out what a heptagon is.
   b How many axes of symmetry has a heptagon?
   c In the centre of the 20p coin there is a Tudor Rose.
   How many axes of symmetry has the Tudor Rose?

139

15 TILING AND SYMMETRY

CHECK-UP ON TILING AND SYMMETRY

1 a Which of these shapes will tile?

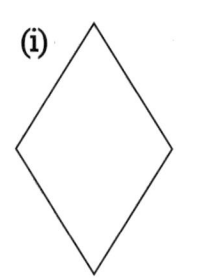

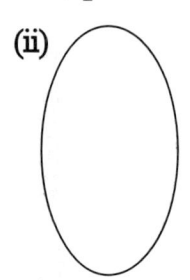

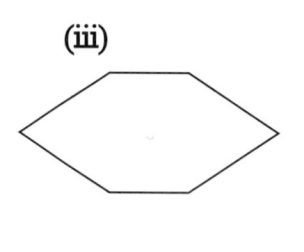

(i) (ii) (iii)

b Show these tilings on dotty paper.

Get Worksheet 4

2 Copy and continue these tilings.

a

b

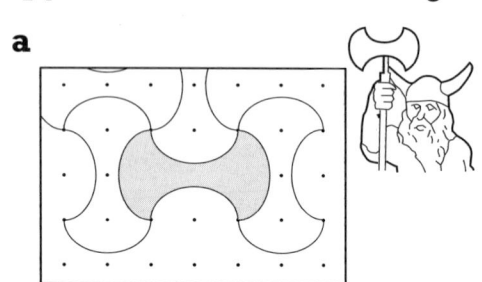

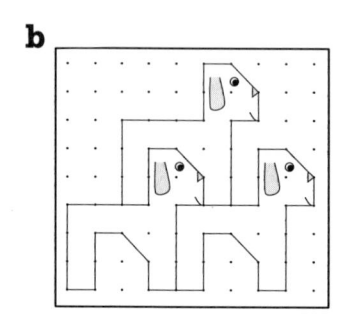

3 Copy these pictures onto dotty paper. Complete the pictures using the dashed line as a line of symmetry.

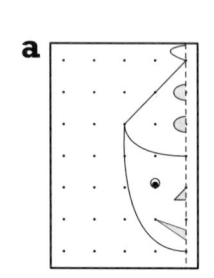

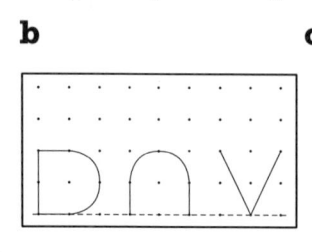

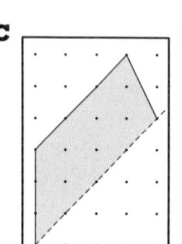

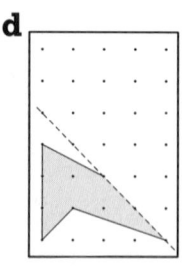

a   **b**   **c**   **d**

4 How many lines of symmetry does each of the following figures have?

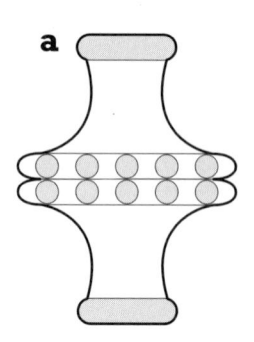

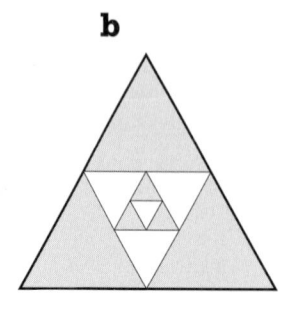

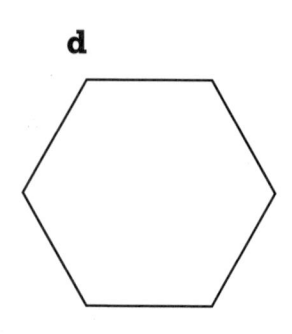

a   **b**   **c**   **d**

140

16 FORMULAE

Multiplication

Tom puts photos in his album.
Each is fixed to the page by four mounts.

The number of mounts needed is **four times** the number of photos.

This is called a formula, a rule for working out one thing when you have information about another.

photos —[× 4]— mounts

EXERCISE 1

1 Use the formula above to figure out the number of mounts needed for:

   a 6 photos   **b** 5 photos   **c** 10 photos   **d** 100 photos

2 *The number of prongs is **three times** the number of plugs.*

Use the formula and find out how many prongs there are for each of these.

   a 4 plugs   **b** 5 plugs   **c** 10 plugs

3 A baker puts a decorative wrap round birthday cakes. Use the formula to work out the length of wrap he needs for a:

   a 20 cm cake   **b** 30 cm cake

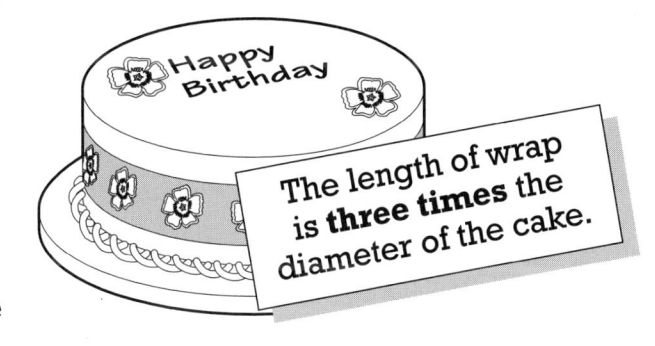

*The length of wrap is **three times** the diameter of the cake.*

4 *The number of rolls of wallpaper is **half** the perimeter of the room.*

Matthew is decorating. He is given a formula to work out the number of rolls of wallpaper he needs. Use the formula to work out how many rolls are needed for rooms with these perimeters.

   a 10 m   **b** 14 m
   c 18 m   **d** 22 m

16 FORMULAE

5 Youssou's scales give his weight in stones.
He wants it in kilograms.

Change the following to kilograms using the formula.

a 10 stones   b 12 stones
c 9 stones   d 18 stones

*The weight in kilograms is **six times** the weight in stones.*

6 The caterers get 5 cups of tea from a litre.

How many cups of tea can they get from these?

a 3 litres   b 10 litres
c 12 litres   d 5 litres

*The number of cups is **five times** the number of litres.*

7 The length of a horse race is often given in furlongs.

How many metres long are the following races?

a 5 furlongs   b 10 furlongs
c 12 furlongs   d 2 furlongs

*The number of metres is **200 times** the number of furlongs.*

8 Sarah makes clothes for model figures. She takes real lengths and divides them by six.

Turn these real lengths into model lengths.

a 120 cm   b 180 cm
c 60 cm   d 240 cm

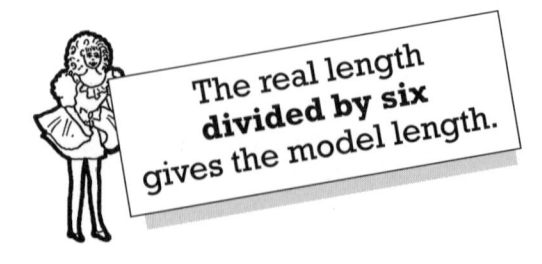

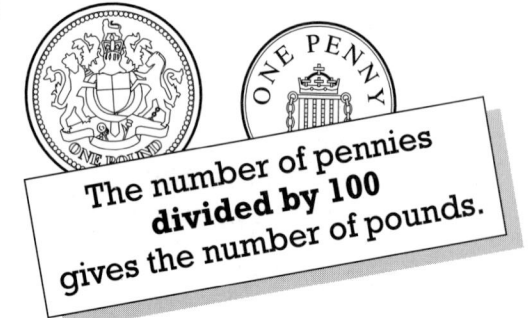

*The real length **divided by six** gives the model length.*

9 Turn these amounts into pounds.

a 300p   b 400p
c 350p   d 674p

*The number of pennies **divided by 100** gives the number of pounds.*

16 FORMULAE

Addition and Subtraction

Some formulae use addition and subtraction. How many teabags do I put in the pot?

The number of teabags is **one more** than the number of people.

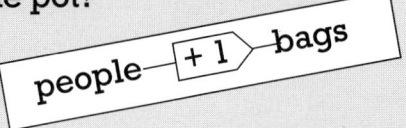

people —[+1]— bags

EXERCISE 2

1 Use the formula to find the number of teabags needed for:

   a 3 people   **b** 2 people   **c** 4 people   **d** 1 person

2 The number of lengths of fence is **one less** than the number of posts.

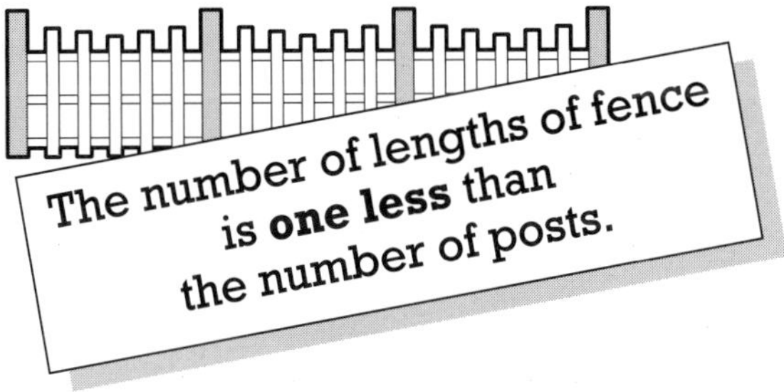

Three lengths of fencing need four posts.

How many lengths of fence do we have when there are:

   a 5 posts   **b** 7 posts
   c 8 posts   **d** 16 posts?

3 To hire a power drill costs £1 an hour plus £5.

Work out the charge for:

   a 4 hours   **b** 6 hours   **c** 10 hours

The cost of hire is **£5 more** than the number of hours.

4 The weight of water is **500 g less** than the reading on the scales.

The weight of water in the pot is 500 g less than the reading on the scales.

What weight of water is in the pot when the reading is:

   a 800 g   **b** 1000 g   **c** 1200 g?

5 The clock in the hall is 12 minutes slow.

What is the actual time when the clock says:

   a 2 o'clock   **b** 5 o'clock   **c** 5 past 6?

The actual time is **12 minutes more** than what the clock says.

16 FORMULAE

Two-step Formulae

Sometimes a formula has two steps.
For example, the time (in minutes) to cook a chicken is worked out from its weight.

The weight **times 20 plus 20** gives the cooking time.

weight —×20— —+20— cooking time

EXERCISE 3

1 Work out the cooking times for chickens of the following weights.

 a 1 kg   b 2 kg   c 1.5 kg

2 The taxi service charges by the given formula.

How much does it cost for journeys of these lengths?

 a 5 miles   b 7 miles
 c 10 miles   d 12 miles

*The number of miles **times 2 plus 5** gives the cost in £.*

3  Harriet booked concert tickets. She was told they were £7 each plus a £3 booking charge.

How much is it to book these tickets?

 a 3 tickets   b 4 tickets   c 10 tickets

*The number of tickets **times 7 plus 3** gives the cost in £.*

4 George joins a golf club. It costs him £70 plus £3 a game.

How much would these cost him?

 a 10 games   b 20 games   c 30 games

*The number of games **times 3 plus 70** gives the total cost.*

5  Angling at the fish farm costs £5 a day plus £2 for each kilogram of fish caught.

How much would these catches cost the angler?

 a 2 kg of fish   b 4 kg of fish   c 6 kg of fish

*The weight of fish **times 2 plus 5** gives the total cost.*

16 FORMULAE

Using a Table

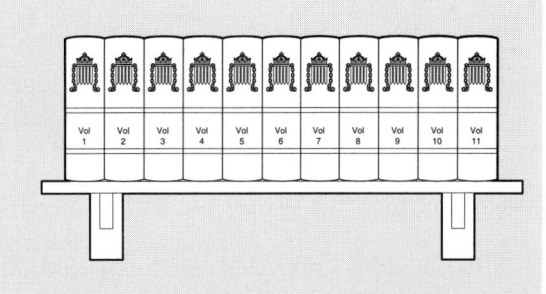

Sometimes a table can be helpful.
A book is 4 cm wide.
How long is a row of books?

The number of books **times 4** gives the length of the row in cm.

Number of books	1	2	3	4	5	6	7	8
Length of row	4	8	12	16	20	24	28	32

EXERCISE 4

Get Worksheet 1

Complete the tables on Worksheet 1 using these formulae.

1 Cost of hiring a bike on holiday.

   Number of days **times 2** gives cost of hire in £.

2 Total cost of buying popcorn for the family.

   Number of packets **times 10** gives total cost in pence.

3 Number of legs is **six times** the number of bees.

4 Number of drawers is **five times** the number of cabinets.

5 Number of nails needed is **seven times** the number of horseshoes.

6 Number of legs is **eight times** the number of spiders.

These formulae require two steps to complete the table.

7 Binta's plant was 20 cm high and grew 5 cm a year.

   Number of years **times 5 plus 20** gives the height of the plant.

145

16 FORMULAE

8 Length of parcel **times 6 plus 30** gives the length of string.

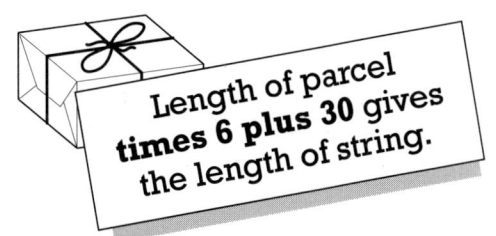

The length of string needed to tie a parcel is six times the length of the parcel plus 30 cm for the bow.

9 The space between two threads on the screw is 2 mm.
This formula works out the total length of the screw.

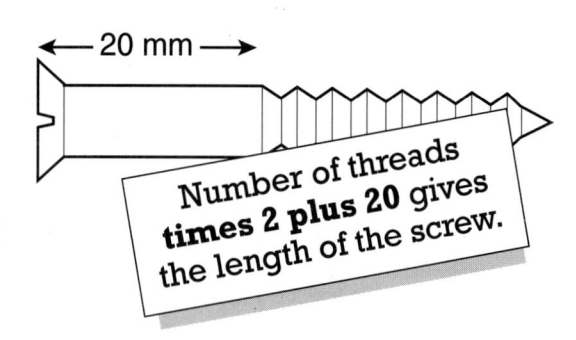

← 20 mm →

Number of threads **times 2 plus 20** gives the length of the screw.

10 Length of call **times 10 plus 15** gives the cost of the call.

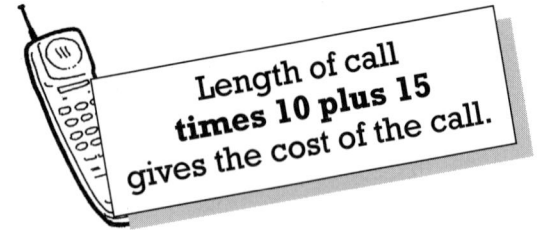

It costs 15p to make a call on the cellular phone plus 10 pence a minute.

Spotting the Formula

When the top row of a table is 1, 2, 3, 4, ... then we can often spot the formula needed to turn the top row into the bottom row.

Example

Top row	1	2	3	4	5	6	7	8	9
Bottom row	3	6	9	12	15	18	21	24	27

Here, the bottom row goes up in **threes** and starts at **3**.
The formula must be:
The bottom row is **three times** the top row.

EXERCISE 5

1 Write down the formula for each of the following tables.

a

Top row	1	2	3	4	5	6	7	8	9
Bottom row	5	10	15	20	25	30	35	40	45

b

Top row	1	2	3	4	5	6	7	8	9
Bottom row	6	12	18	24	30	36	42	48	54

16 FORMULAE

2 Write down the formula for each of the following tables.
The headings should be used.

a

Number of people	1	2	3	4	5	6	7	8	9
Number of eyes	2	4	6	8	10	12	14	16	18

Example: The number of eyes is ☐ **times** the number of people.

b

Number of cats	1	2	3	4	5	6	7	8	9
Number of legs	4	8	12	16	20	24	28	32	36

3 a Write down a formula for this table.
b Use the formula to find the missing entries.

Number of weeks	1	2	3	4	5	6	7	8	9
Number of days	7	14	21	28					

4

Number of gallons	1	2	3	4	5	6	7	8	9
Number of pints	8	16	24	32					

a Work out the formula to turn gallons into pints.
b Use it to complete the table.

Two-step Formulae and Tables

Top row	1	2	3	4	5	6	7	8	9
Bottom row	3	5	7	9	11	13	15	17	19

The bottom row goes up in **twos: times two**.
But the first number is 3, **one more** than two: **add one**.
The formula for this table is:
Top row **times two add one** gives bottom row.

EXERCISE 5B

1 Follow the steps to find a formula for this table.

Top row	1	2	3	4	5	6	7	8	9
Bottom row	5	8	11	14	17	20	23	26	29

    a What size of step does the bottom row **go up** in?
    b Check that 5 is **two more** than the step size.
    c Write down a formula.

2 Find a formula for each of the following tables.

    a

Top row	1	2	3	4	5	6	7	8	9
Bottom row	4	7	10	13	16	19	22	25	28

    b

Top row	1	2	3	4	5	6	7	8	9
Bottom row	6	9	12	15	18	21	24	27	30

3 **a** What is the step size of the bottom row?
    b Check that 5 is **one more** than the step size.
    c Write down a formula for the table.
    d Use it to find the four missing numbers.

Top row	1	2	3	4	5	6	7	8	9
Bottom row	5	9	13	17	21				

4

Top row	1	2	3	4	5	6	7	8	9
Bottom row	3	7	11	15	19				

    a What is the step size of the bottom row?
    b Check that 3 is **one less** than the step size.
    c Write down a formula for the table.
    d Use it to find the four missing numbers.

16 FORMULAE

CHECK-UP ON FORMULAE

1 *Number of notepads **times 12** gives the number of pages.*

A notepad has 12 pages.

How many pages are in these?

a 4 notepads **b** 10 notepads

2 Jill is making patterns with coins. She always needs one more 5p piece than 1p.

How many 1p pieces do we need for these?

a six 5p pieces **b** nine 5p pieces

*Number of 1p pieces is **one less** than the number of 5p pieces.*

3 *Number of cakes **times 20 plus 10** gives the total cost.*

The cake shop charges 20p a cake plus 10p for the box.

What is the bill for these?

a 4 cakes **b** 8 cakes

4 *Number of snowflakes **times six** gives the number of spikes.*

Copy and complete the table. Use the formula to help you.

Number of snowflakes	1	2	3	4	5	6	7	8
Number of spikes								

5

Number of wheels	1	2	3	4	5	6	7	8
Number of spokes	9	18	27	36				

a Write down a formula for getting the number of spokes from the number of wheels.

b Use the formula to find the missing entries.

149

17 PROBABILITY

A Likelihood Line

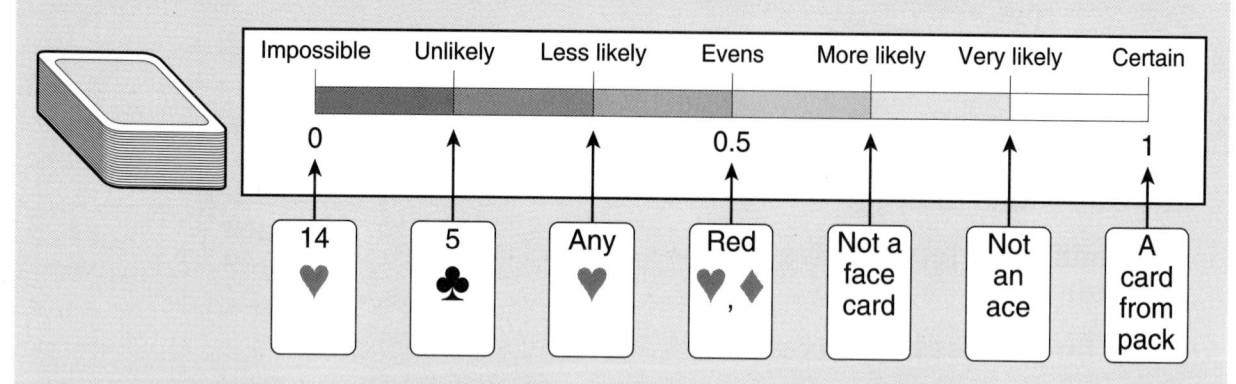

Impossible	Unlikely	Less likely	Evens	More likely	Very likely	Certain
0			0.5			1
14 ♥	5 ♣	Any ♥	Red ♥, ♦	Not a face card	Not an ace	A card from pack

This **likelihood line** shows the chances of picking a certain type of card from a normal pack of playing cards.

EXERCISE 1

1 Match up each event with a letter label on the likelihood line.

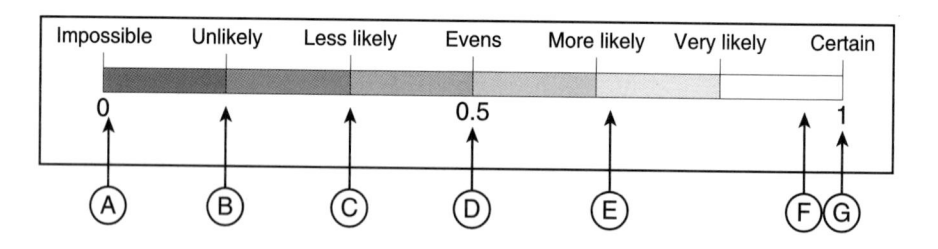

Impossible	Unlikely	Less likely	Evens	More likely	Very likely	Certain
0			0.5			1
Ⓐ	Ⓑ	Ⓒ	Ⓓ	Ⓔ	Ⓕ Ⓖ

Example: A goes with **b**.

a Throw a six.

b Win the jackpot in a prize lottery.

c It will snow in January

d Tuesday follows Monday this week.

e Get 'heads'.

f Pick a club.

g Score less than 5.

150

2 a Ray rolls a dice.

Which result is more likely?
(i) Ray lands on grey.
(ii) Ray lands on white.

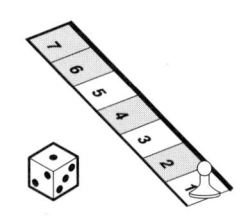

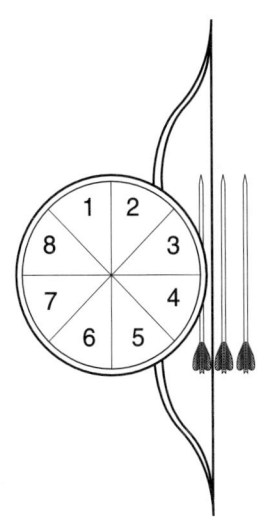

b Salma fires an arrow at this target.

Which outcome is more likely?
(i) It lands on 3 or a higher number.
(ii) It lands on a number that is less than 3.

c These coins are put in a bag. One falls out.

Which is it more likely to be?
(i) A silver coin.
(ii) A copper coin.

3 Which of the following are fair ways to start a game?

a Toss a coin: 'heads' and Ian starts; 'tails' and Sam starts.
b Roll a dice: 'six' and Ian starts; 'not six' and Sam starts.
c Pick a card: the person who chooses the highest number card starts.
d Spin this spinner:

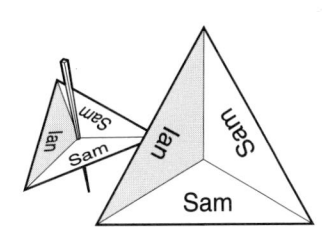

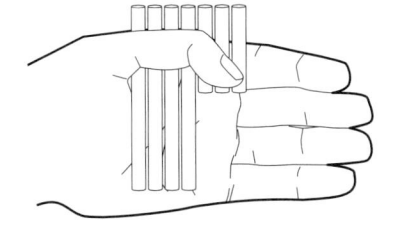

e Pick a straw from these: 'short straw', Ian starts; 'long straw', Sam starts.

Best Outcome

Roll a dice. Here are all the possible outcomes or results.

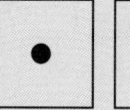

You win if you throw an odd number.

So there are three ways of winning:

And there are three ways of losing:

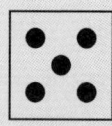

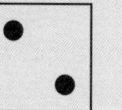

EXERCISE 2

1. Raj picks an unseen card from these five cards. Raj wins if he picks an ace.

   a List the winning cards.
   b List the losing cards.
   c Which outcome is more likely, winning or losing?

   d Which of the following sets would Raj most like to pick an ace from?
   (i)   (ii)   (iii)

2. Stuart wins if he can pick a white ball from the bag without looking.

   a How many ways of winning are there?
   b How many ways of losing are there?
   c Which is more likely, winning or losing?

   d Which of these three bags offers the best chance of winning?
   (i)   (ii)   (iii)

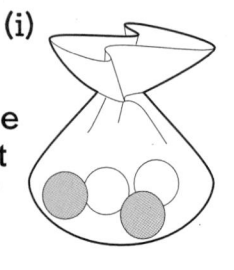

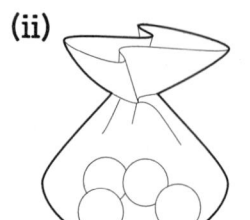

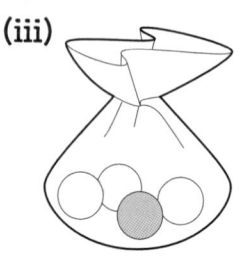

152

3

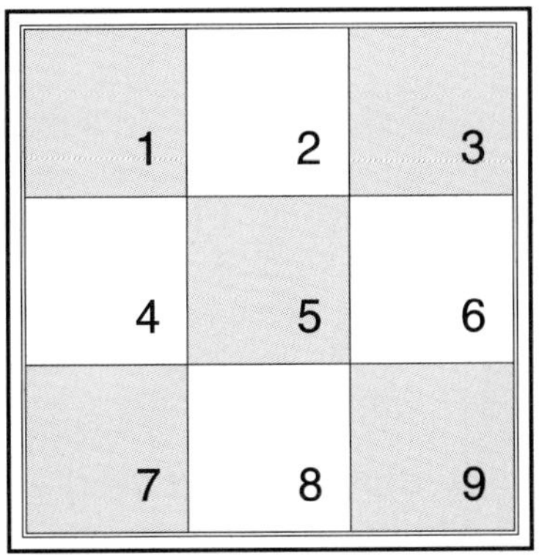

1	2	3
4	5	6
7	8	9

a Make a list of the numbers in the grey squares.
b List the numbers in the white squares.
c Richard is throwing darts at the board.

  (i) Which colour is he more likely to land on?
  (ii) Why?

4 Here are some playing cards.
They are mixed up and turned face down.
You must choose a suit and then turn over a card.
If you pick correctly you win.
Which suit gives you the best chance of winning?

5   (i)   (ii)    (iii)

Which set of cards gives you the best chance of getting:

a a jack
b a red card
c a black jack?

6 Both these hands offer the same chance of picking a jack.
Can you say why?

Exercise 3 will help if you can't say why.

153

Calculating Chance

You will need a calculator.

Four out of **eight** cards are jacks.

$$\frac{4}{8} = 4 \div 8 = 0.5$$

We say the chance of getting a jack is 0.5.

Two out of **four** cards are jacks.

$$\frac{2}{4} = 2 \div 4 = 0.5$$

We say the chance of getting a jack is 0.5.

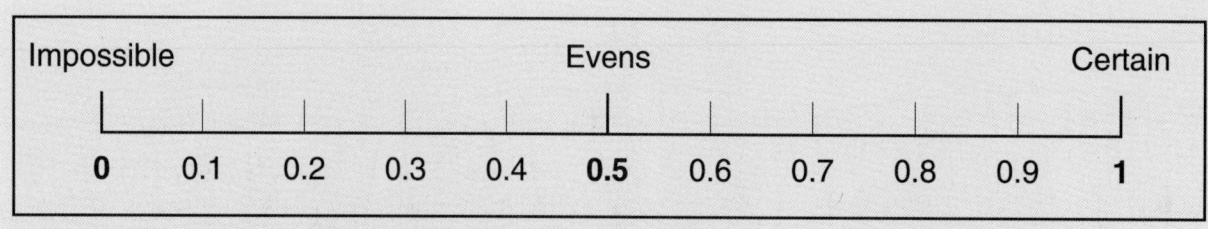

Impossible					Evens					Certain
0	0.1	0.2	0.3	0.4	0.5	0.6	0.7	0.8	0.9	1

We can place the chance on the likelihood line.

EXERCISE 3

1. Rachael rolls the dice. She needs a six.
   a How many numbers are on the dice?
   b How many sixes are on the dice?

   The chance of getting a six = $\frac{1}{6}$

2. a How many cards are here?
   b How many jacks are there?
   c Copy and complete the working out.

   ☐ out of ☐ are jacks.

   So $\frac{\square}{\square}$ = ☐ ÷ ☐ = 0.2

   The chance of getting a jack is 0.2. Find this number on the likelihood line.

17 PROBABILITY

3  One card is picked at random from this set.
  a List the possible choices.
  b How many of the choices result in picking the ace of clubs?
  c Write down the chance of getting the ace of clubs:
  (i) as a fraction   (ii) as a decimal.

4 An arrow hits this target, landing on a number.
  a How many different scores are possible?
  b What is the chance that the score is 7?
   Write the chance as a:
   (i) fraction   (ii) decimal.
  c How many scores are more than 6?
  d What is the chance of scoring more than 6?

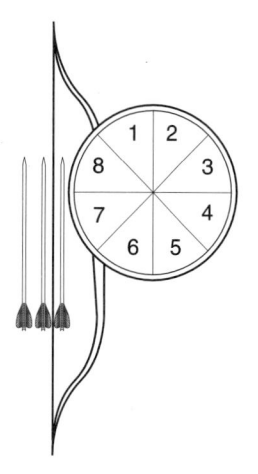

5 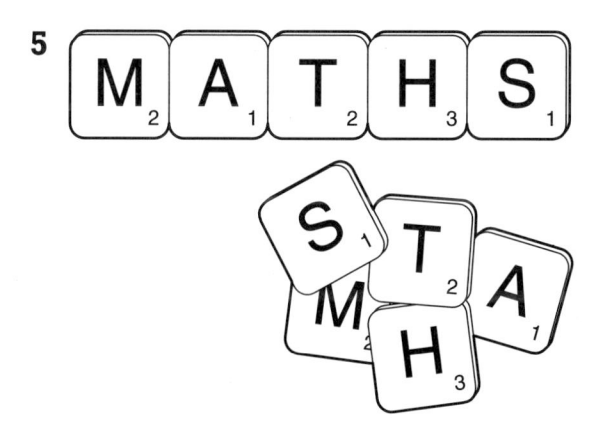 Bimal has made the word 'MATHS' with the Scrabble tiles. He picks up one of the letters from his word.
  a What is the chance that it is an S?
  b M is worth 2 points. How many of the letters in 'MATHS' are worth 2?
  c What is the chance that a letter picked at random from 'MATHS' is worth 2 points?
   Write your answer as a decimal.

6 
  a How many tiles are here?
  b How many tiles show an A?
  c What is the chance of picking an A?
  d What is the chance of picking a:
   (i) T   (ii) G?
  e What is the chance of picking a letter worth:
   (i) 1   (ii) 2   (iii) 3?

Do Worksheet 1

155

17 PROBABILITY

CHECK-UP ON PROBABILITY

1 Pick the more likely event from each of these pairs.

a

b

c

(i) Roll a 1 or 2.
(ii) Roll a 3, 4, 5 or 6.

(i) Pick a red card.
(ii) Pick an ace.

(i) Pick out a 10p coin.
(ii) Pick out a £1 coin.

2 Which of the following are fair?

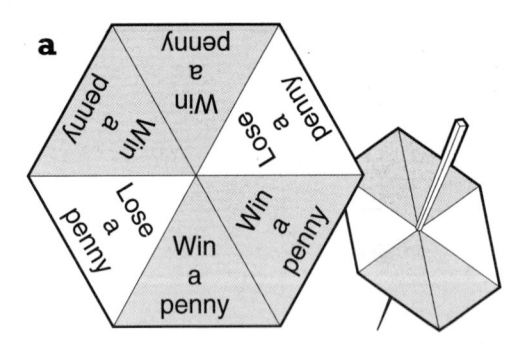

a

b

c

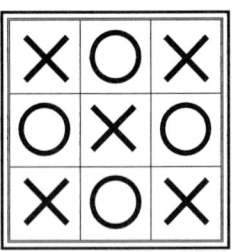

Land on X and lose a penny. Land on O and win a penny.

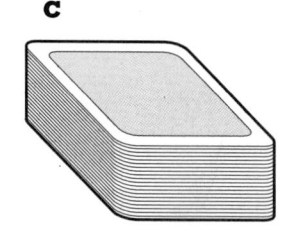

Pick a red card and win a penny. Pick a black card and lose a penny.

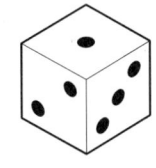

3 You win if the dice score is less than 5.
   a List the winning throws.
   b Are you more likely to win or lose?

4
   a M O T O R I N G   How many letter tiles are shown here?
   b What is the chance of picking:
      (i) O   (ii) R?
   c What is the chance of picking a letter worth:
      (i) 1   (ii) 2   (iii) 3?